"This Means Everlasting Life"

"This

means everlasting life—,

their taking in knowledge

of you, the only true God,

and of the one whom you

sent forth, Jesus Christ."

—John 17:3, NW.

PUBLISHERS

WATCHTOWER BIBLE AND TRACT SOCIETY, INC.
INTERNATIONAL BIBLE STUDENTS ASSOCIATION
Brooklyn, New York, U. S. A.

3,800,000 Edition

Dedicated to the unsectarian education of all people of good-will in the requirements for everlasting life in the righteous new world now at hand.

Abbreviations of Bible versions quoted or cited in this book

AAT — An American Translation, by J. M. P. Smith and E. J. Goodspeed

ASV — American Standard Version, by the American Committee of Revision

Dar. — The 'Holy Scriptures', a New Translation by J. N. Darby

Douay — Translation of the Latin Vulgate made at Douay and Rheims

Lees. — The twenty-four Books of the Holy Scriptures, translated by I. Leeser

LXX — The Septuagint Version of the Hebrew Scriptures, translation published by S. Bagster and Sons Limited

Moff. — A New Translation of The Bible, by James Moffatt

NW — New World Translation of the Christian Greek Scriptures

Roth. — The Emphasised Bible, a New Translation by J. B. Rotherham

Yg. — The Holy Bible, translated by Robert Young

Any quotation not followed by any specific abbreviation should be understood to be made from the Authorized or King James Version.

CONTENTS

"THIS MEANS EVERLASTING LIFE"

CHAPTER I

LIFE was at stake—the life of mankind in a righteous new world! By next afternoon the question must be decided in favor of their enjoying that precious privilege eternally. The feast this night in Jerusalem gave promise that it would be. This was a memorial night, the anniversary of the 14th of Nisan more than fifteen centuries previous when with one irresistible push death invaded the home of every Egyptian family. It was not by any bacteriological warfare, nor by any dreaded atomic or hydrogen bombs dropping from Egypt's clear skies that such widespread destruction of human lives was caused. No! But the destroying angel of the God of the oppressed Hebrews sped through that land of the Nile and, with unerring aim, struck every first-born one of man and beast with sudden midnight death. Miraculously the homes of the Hebrews in the district of Goshen at the Nile's delta were passed over. Heeding the warning of their God by his prophet Moses, the Hebrews had killed the passover lamb, sprinkled its blood on the two doorposts and lintels of their houses, retired indoors and eaten the lamb roasted, along with unleavened bread and bitter

---

1. What question was immediately to be decided? Why favorably?

7

herbs. This meant life for all their first-born ones, and the following morning they prepared to march out of Egypt a free people.

² In celebration of this a group of men, all Hebrews, were met together in an upper room somewhere in Jerusalem this anniversary night of Nisan 14 of A.D. 33. There in obedience to God's law through Moses they ate the passover lamb with unleavened bread and wine-cups of blessing.

³ As we now observe the men, there are twelve of them. One of the original number has gone out, but not to return and rejoin them. His name is Judas Iscariot, and he has hurried down from the upper room on a treacherous mission that speedily leads to the death of the leader of those men the coming afternoon—yes, and to his own suicide by hanging!

⁴ The men remaining continue reclining on their couches about the low passover table. The leader among them is addressing them in a long talk of warning and comfort. He finishes with the words: "I have said these things to you that by means of me you may have peace. In the world you will have tribulation, but cheer up! I have conquered the world." The speaker knew he was destined to die that fourteenth day of Nisan like the unblemished passover lamb slaughtered that same day long ago in Egypt. He knew his death would be

---

2, 3. What special group of men celebrated Passover A.D. 33? Where?
4. What had their Leader conquered? How? With good cheer to whom?

in vindication of the universal sovereignty of the God whom haughty Pharaoh of Egypt had defied to Moses' face. He knew this world was against the rightful sovereignty of God over this earth. Refusal to compromise with this world would spell death for him. Till this moment of his speaking he

had never compromised with this world but had fearlessly proclaimed through all the land the kingdom of the Most High God. By dying uncompromisingly in support of God's kingdom he would conquer the world. By God's wonder-working power he would live again to celebrate his conquest. The world would bring great tribulations to his followers left behind on earth, but by virtue of him his followers could enjoy peace of heart and mind. They had reason to cheer up. As he had conquered the world on the question of God's universal sovereignty, so he would help them also to conquer it and gain an everlasting reward.

[5] Let us hear what he says further, for it has to do with our eternal life. He now raises his eyes to heaven. In a conversational yet prayerful way he says: "Father, the hour has come; glorify your son, that your son may glorify you, according as you have given him authority over all flesh, that, as regards the whole number which you have given him, he may give them everlasting life." By these words we know it is the Son of the heavenly Father that is speaking. God has given him authority over all humanity, "all flesh." Why? Because this Son of God from heaven has become flesh and has made an agreement with God to die for mankind, just as that passover lamb of old died for the deliverance of the Hebrews from death and from Egypt's tyranny. By dying and sacrificing his own assumed humanity he could buy life for "all flesh", that is, for the whole number of people that his heavenly Father would give to him, drawing them in belief and obedience to the Son of God.

[6] What a stirring theme the Son of God strikes upon when he says "everlasting life"! That is what every lover of peace, happiness and good friendship wants. What is required of us to gain it? We are of flesh, and God has given his Son authority over all flesh, including us. So we must listen to the Son of God as he prays on and tells us: "This means everlasting life, their taking in knowledge of you, the only true God, and of the one whom

---

5. Why has his Father given him "authority over all flesh"?
6. What does he say is required of us to gain everlasting life?

you sent forth, Jesus Christ." All the other knowledge in the world is nothing compared with the knowledge taken in of the two most important Persons in the universe, the only true God and the one he sent into the world, Jesus Christ. Our gaining knowledge of Them and believing it means everlasting life for us in the righteous new world now near. How could we accept the gift of everlasting life from God through Jesus Christ unless we knew about it and about how to win it? Such life-giving knowledge is most important for us to get. By these pages we are on our way to get it. We must continue taking in such knowledge.

⁷ Jesus Christ does not address his heavenly Father as a mystifying "triune" God, but as "the only true God"; and he speaks of himself as the inferior one, the Son whom the Father sent forth from heaven. Stressing his own inferiority to God his Father, Jesus said just previously that same night to his faithful followers there: "A slave is not greater than his master, nor is one that is sent forth greater than the one that sent him."* The Son is the Chief Servant of the only real God and is subject to him in carrying out the divine purpose of bringing everlasting life to dying mankind. On earth the Son honored God and recommended him to mankind. That is why we hear him say: "I have glorified you on the earth, having finished the work you have given me to do. So now you, Father, glorify me alongside yourself

---

* Quoted from John 13:16, *New World Translation*.

7. What report did he make to his Father, and with what request?

with the glory which I had alongside you before the world was." In making this report to his heavenly Father of successfully finishing the work meant for him on earth, the Son discloses that he had had life before becoming a man. This could only have been heavenly life as a spirit Son, and he had it already before the earth was made and man was created on it. The life up there was a glorious one, and the Son prays his heavenly Father to glorify him with his prehuman glory, with heavenly glory. The Son shows his willingness to sacrifice his human life forever with such glory in view. His Father must glorify him by a resurrection from the dead to life in heaven in personal association with the only true God.

[8] In carrying out the work given him to do, what did the Son do? Hear his report to his Father and Head: "I have made your name manifest to the men you gave me out of the world. They were yours, and you gave them to me, and they have observed your word. They have now come to know that all the things you gave me are from you; because the sayings that you gave me I have given to them, and they have received them and have certainly come to know that I came out as your representative, and they have believed that you sent me forth." Here a remarkable fact is reported. Jesus testifies that his Father has a name and that he made that name manifest to his followers. This was comparable to the mission of Moses

---

8. What remarkable fact does he report, making him like Moses?

who made known God's name to the oppressed Hebrews down in Egypt. In his writings (Exodus 3:14 and 6:2, 3) Moses tells us of this: "And God said unto Moses, I AM THAT I AM: and he said, Thus shalt thou say unto the children of Israel, I AM hath sent me unto you." "And God spake unto Moses, and said unto him, I am the LORD: and I appeared unto Abraham, unto Isaac, and unto Jacob, by the name of God Almighty, but by my name JEHOVAH was I not known to them."

⁹ Realizing the importance of knowing the name and what it means, Jesus manifested it to his followers. As the Son of God sent from heaven God's representative knew the divine name better than Moses did. Before setting out on his public work of proclaiming the kingdom of God he was subjected to three special tests while alone forty days in the wilderness. He met the first test with these words to the tempter: "It is written, 'Man must live, not on bread alone, but on every utterance coming forth through Jehovah's mouth.'" Meeting the second test, he said to the tempter: "Again it is written, 'You must not put Jehovah your God to the test.'" Finally he thrust back the tempter with these words: "Go away, Satan! For it is written, 'It is Jehovah your God you must worship, and it is to him alone you must render sacred service.'"* In each test the Son of God quoted

---

*Quoting from Matthew 4:4, 7, 10, *New World Translation*. In these verses Jesus himself quotes from Deuteronomy 8:3; 6:16; 5:9; 6:13.

---

9. How well did he know God's name? What did his own name mean?

Moses' writings where God's name is used. The Son of God, in the very name given him on earth, bore his Father's name, for his Jewish followers knew that the name "Jesus" meant "Jehovah is salvation". This name indicates how necessary to our everlasting life it is to know Jesus as well as his Father. Jehovah sent his Son Jesus to be the Messiah, the promised Anointed King, and to that end the Father anointed his Son with holy spirit, immediately after his baptism in water. For that reason he is called Jesus Christ, because "Christ" means "Messiah" or "Anointed One" or "One consecrated by an anointing".

[10] The loving purpose of the Christ is to give everlasting life to all those whom his Father gives him by drawing them to Jesus through the power of knowledge. Knowing that the world would now heap tribulation upon them, Jesus prays for them, not for this world: "I make request concerning them; I make request, not concerning the world, but concerning those you have given me, because they are yours, and all my things are yours and yours are mine, and I have been glorified among them. Also I am no longer in the world, but they are in the world and I am coming to you. Holy Father, watch over them out of respect for your own name which you have given me, in order that they may be one just as we are. When I was with them I used to watch over them out of respect for your own name which you have given me, and I have kept them, and not one of them is destroyed

---

10. For whom did he then pray? What request did he make?

except the son of destruction, so that the scripture has been fulfilled."

[11] That "son of destruction" could have had life through Jesus if he had remained faithful. But though being so close to him as to take meals regularly with him like a dear friend, Judas Iscariot chose to lift up his heel against him. By this he doomed himself to destruction, cutting himself off from the Channel of life. Jesus felt no responsibility for the loss of this traitor. Psalm 41, verse 9, had foretold his treachery and, unforced, Judas had for selfish motives chosen to fulfill the prophecy. Yes, Jesus and his disciples had the Holy Scriptures back there in their day. Several centuries before Jesus' birth these sacred Hebrew writings had been completed, all together thirty-nine books, from the books of Moses to that of the prophet Malachi, and there were no apocryphal or deutero-canonical books included among them. These inspired Hebrew Scriptures were included under three heads, The Law, the Prophets, and the Psalms. Jesus here referred to the Psalms which headed the third section of the Scriptures. As a whole, those Hebrew Scriptures contained the divine name "Jehovah" 6,823 times. Out of respect for that holy name Jesus had watched over his disciples while with them. After Jesus' departure Jehovah God must watch over them for his own name's sake, because they were a people for his name.

---

11. What Scriptures did he have? Whose name did they set forth?

[12] "But," continues Jesus, "now I am coming to you, and I am speaking these things in the world in order that they may have my joy in themselves to the full. I have given your word to them, but the world has hated them, because they are no part of the world just as I am no part of the world." In addition to the Word of God already written in the Hebrew Scriptures, Jesus had brought his disciples a message or word from God, and this must in due time be added in writing to the Hebrew Scriptures. For accepting God's Word, including that brought by Jesus, the world hated his disciples, and the worst haters were the religious leaders. Jesus' disciples adhered to the Word of God rather than to this world. Hence they were no more part of this world than Jesus was. The world would like to get rid of them, but they had a work to do in the world. So Jesus did not want them removed.

[13] "I request you, not to take them out of the world, but to watch over them because of the wicked one. They are no part of the world just as I am no part of the world. Sanctify them by means of the truth; your word is truth. Just as you sent me forth into the world, I also sent them forth into the world. And I am sanctifying myself in their behalf, that they also may be sanctified by means of truth." The following morning Jesus was destined to tell the judge, the Roman gover-

---

12. What had Jesus given his disciples? Who hated them? Why?
13. What is it by which he prayed that they should be sanctified?

nor, Pontius Pilate: "For this purpose I have come into the world, that I should bear witness to the truth. Everyone that is on the side of the truth listens to my voice."* To Pilate's question, "What is truth?" the answer could have been made that it was the already written Hebrew Scriptures and the message from God which Jesus gave to his disciples. By the power of this truth God sanctifies those who accept and adhere to it. That is, he separates them from this unholy world and sets them apart to his sacred service. By adherence to divine truth Jesus sanctified himself. That was why he never became a part of this world. He was sending his disciples into the world on divine service, but they, too, would never become a part of it because their adherence to the truth would sanctify them and hold them away from it. In the world they must declare this sanctifying word of truth, that others might believe. Hence Jesus with loving foresight prays for such believers also:

[14] "I make request, not concerning these only, but also concerning those putting faith in me through their word, in order that they may all be one, just as you, Father, are in union with me and I am in union with you, that they also may be in union with us, in order that the world may believe that you sent me forth. Also I have given them the glory which you have given me, in order that they may be one just as we are one. I in union with them and you in union with me, in order that

---

* Quoted from John 18:37, *New World Translation*.

14. To what condition did he pray for them to come? In what sense?

they may be perfected into one, that the world may have the knowledge that you sent me forth and that you loved them just as you loved me." If Christ's believers were to adhere to this world, they would be divided among themselves by its religious sects, political parties, social distinctions and national pride and traditions, and racial prejudices. But by being sanctified away from worldliness by the power of God's truth they were to be welded into a perfect unity, regardless of race, color, language, or country of birth. They were to be at unity with one another, the same as Jehovah the Father and Jesus Christ the Son are at unity. No unexplainable, unscriptural "trinitarian" unity this, because all these believers in Christ were to be brought into perfect union with one another and also in union with God and Christ. Because of this unity of the believers in serving God and proclaiming his word, many in the world come to know that Jesus Christ is God's beloved Sent One.

[15] For the unification of his followers with him to be climaxed in heaven Jesus closes his prayer with these words: "Father, as to what you have given me, I wish that, where I am, they also may be with me, in order to behold my glory which you have given me, because you loved me before the world's foundation. Righteous Father, the world has, indeed, not come to know you, but I have come to know you, and these have come to know that you sent me forth. And I have made your name known to them and will make it known,

---

15. What knowledge did he come to bring them? With what end in view?

in order that the love with which you loved me may be in them and I in union with them." No, the world's hatred does not deny that God loves Jesus and his followers; it proves the contrary. Till Jesus' day there was world ignorance of the way to life. Jesus' own knowledge of the only true God meant everlasting life for him. His followers must now be given the vital knowledge of the heavenly Father and his Sent One. Jesus' mission to earth was one of bringing the knowledge necessary to the life of the people receiving and believing it. He knew God's name and disclosed it to his followers. He purposed to do so, not only down to his death, but also after his resurrection to heavenly life in glory. Those who come to know God's name and purpose and who become a people for his name have God's love rest on them and they are unified with Jesus for the sake of the divine name.

[16] The prayer of Jesus* points out the all-essentials for us to know. Nothing is sweeter and more precious than life with a knowledge of the great Life-giver and the beloved Son by whom He offers life to the dying. So in the following pages we continue on our absorbing quest for this knowledge. The world may focus its hate upon us for pursuing this course, but we know that this knowledge means something the world can never give, everlasting life.

---

* The prayer of Jesus in the foregoing paragraphs was quoted from John, chapter 17, *New World Translation*.

16. So what quest do we pursue, and why despite world hatred?

CHAPTER II

THE AUTHOR OF LIFE

LIFE has always existed in the universe. This is because God has always been. He has an eternal past, as he has also an eternal future, so that time measured by our clocks is as nothing to him. In inspired prayer the prophet Moses says: "LORD, thou hast been our dwelling place in all generations. Before the mountains were brought forth, or ever thou hadst formed the earth and the world, even from everlasting to everlasting, thou art God." (Psalm 90:1, 2) He had no beginning, and he will have no end. He challenges anyone to prove that there was any God before him. To those to whom he has revealed himself he says: "Ye are my witnesses, saith Jehovah, and my servant whom I have chosen; that ye may know and believe me, and understand that I am he: before me there was no God formed, neither shall there be after me. I, even I, am Jehovah; and besides me there is no saviour." (Isaiah 43:10, 11, *ASV*) It is idle to ask, Who made God? It is undignifying to his Godship. He is the one original Creator, and not a creature. His endless past agrees with his being the only true God. "But Jehovah is the true God; he is the living God, and an everlasting King." —Jeremiah 10:10, *ASV*.

---

1. Due to what fact has life always existed in the universe?

[2] To many minds it seems difficult to realize that Jehovah God is without a beginning, that he had an infinite existence before ever we came to life. But is that impossible? What about space and time? Where does space begin? When did time begin? The science of mathematics knows such a thing as infinity; and it should be no more difficult to accept that God always was than that time and space go on forever, into the past and into the future. It gives us some idea of God's eternal past to remember that in 1919, when the hundred-inch telescope on Mount Wilson, California, was the most powerful in the world, space was penetrated by human sight to a distance of five hundred million light years. That represents the distance light would travel in five hundred million of our solar years. Before all those five hundred million years Jehovah God was. But, measured by creation, that is not the limit of his past existence. Now with the 200-inch telescope atop Mount Palomar, California, the distance penetrated into space has been doubled, and the discernible universe has eight times the volume of the one disclosed by the Mount Wilson telescope. As the scientists who believe in relativity now tell us, the universe is expanding, even blowing up. According to the accepted theory the universe which we know began expanding 1,800 million years ago from the single, then created mass of densely packed matter. Even if we take that theory for what it is worth, then before all that time the ever-

2. What helps us to realize that God is without a beginning?

lasting true God was. Whither is this universe expanding, if it is expanding? Into further reaches of space. But into all that space the creative power of Jehovah God extends.

³ Lift up your eyes on high, the Creator invites, and consider all these heavenly works, with or without the aid of the telescope. All these are visible evidences that he is, even though unseen to us, and that from the eternal past he is God. These give mankind no excuse for doubting his existence and his Godship. "Because what may be known about God is manifest among them, for God made it manifest to them. For his invisible qualities are clearly seen from the world's creation onward, because they are understood by the things made, even his eternal power and Godship, so that they are inexcusable." (Romans 1:19, 20, *NW*) In the face of such overwhelming visible evidence it is only the self-conceited fool that says to himself: "There is no God." All these wonders tell of a Creator, and his name is Jehovah. The very name bespeaks his creatorship, for it means "He causes to be". Those who manufacture images of some created thing or imaginary thing and who kneel before them and worship them or worship what they are supposed to represent are called to their senses by these words of the true living God through his prophet:

⁴ "Can you not understand, cannot you see? Were you not told this from the first, have you

---

3. What visible evidences exist of a Creator and of his Godhood?
4. With what words does he call image-adorers to their senses?

not grasped this, since the world began?—that He sits over the round earth, so high that its inhabitants look like grasshoppers; he spreads the skies out like a curtain, and stretches them like a tent. 'To whom will you compare me, then, and equal me?' asks the Majestic One. Lift high your eyes, look up; who made these stars? he who marshals them in order, summoning each one by name. For fear of him, so mighty and so strong, not one fails to appear. Come now! Do you not understand, have you not heard, that the Eternal is an everlasting God, the maker of the world from end to end? He never faints, never is weary, his insight is unsearchable; into the weary he puts power, and adds new strength to the weak." —Isaiah 40:21, 22, 25, 26, 28, 29, *Moff.*

⁵ Since Jehovah God is the living Creator, from all past eternity, he is the one original source of life of all animate creatures. No life sprang spontaneously from dead matter. Death is not the source of life. "With thee is the fountain of life." (Psalm 36:9) Since God has an everlasting past and since numberless works which he has created throughout the vast depths of space have continued operating since the time of their creation, we can appreciate how the Creator could start human life on earth and could sustain it forever in perfection, constantly putting power into it and renewing its strength for all time to come.

⁶ The proper place for man to live is the earth,

---

5. What is the source of man's life? How long can it continue?
6. Where was mankind created to exist forever? Why there?

of which he is a part. "The first man is out of
the earth and made of dust." (1 Corinthians
15:47, *NW*) The earth from which the first man
was made was created to exist forever. Showing
the difference between the present human generations and the earth which moves around the sun,
the inspired Preacher says: "One generation pass-
eth away, and another generation cometh: but the
earth abideth for ever. The sun also ariseth, and
the sun goeth down, and hasteth to his place
where he arose." (Ecclesiastes 1:4, 5) According
to earth's eternal destiny Jehovah created it to be
inhabited by humankind forever. He says so. "I
have made the earth, and created man upon it:
I, even my hands, have stretched out the heavens;
and all their host have I commanded. For thus
saith Jehovah that created the heavens, the God
that formed the earth and made it, that established it and created it not a waste, that formed
it to be inhabited: I am Jehovah; and there is
none else." (Isaiah 45:12, 18, *ASV*) From the day
of the first man's creation to this day the earth
has never been without a human inhabitant, and
it never will be.

⁷ Mankind needs life, everlasting perfect human
life. For about six thousand years mankind has
been dying, and many generations of humans have
come and gone. When we remember the endless
happy existence that God promises for mankind,
it provokes a sympathetic smile to read the announcement from Washington, D.C., of the Na-

---

7. How do God's promises of life show up modern
science?

tional Office of Vital Statistics, that "the average life span in this country [U.S.A.] lengthened from 66.8 years in 1947 to 67.2 years in 1948. . . . The average length of life in 1900 was 49.2 years. Thus average life expectancy has lengthened eighteen years in approximately half a century. The decline in the death rate since 1940 has been greatest for children from 1 to 4 years of age." (New York *Times,* Feb. 16, 1950) That represents what modern medical and social science is supposed to have accomplished for the United States, one of the most progressive countries of the world. An increase of 18 years in the average age-length accomplished in fifty years! Unaided by modern science, the ark-builder Noah, who saw life on both sides of the global flood, lived to be 950 years old. Methuselah his grandfather died in the flood year at the age of 969 years.—Genesis 9:28; 5:27.

[8] Modern science cannot be depended upon to build man up to live forever. Look at the condition finally of any person whom it may have aided to live to a ripe old age beyond the general average! Modern science does not make for everlasting life. What with its development of bacteriological warfare and its invention of atomic bombs and the hydrogen or "hell" bomb and other weapons of mass destruction, modern science makes rather for death. It contradicts its own benevolent claims by prostituting itself to the aims of this world. Modern science is not the all-essential thing of which to gain knowledge in order to en-

---

8. Why is modern science not the essential thing to learn?

joy everlasting life. The warning to a faithful servant of God in the first century applies equally
to us today: "O Timothy, guard what is laid up
in trust with you, turning away from the empty
speeches that violate what is holy and from the
contradictions of the falsely called 'knowledge'.
For making a show of such knowledge some have
deviated from the faith."—1 Timothy 6:20, 21, NW.

⁹ All the investigations by modern science into
the heavens, the earth and the atom prove that
the entire universe was created by a great scientist of depthless wisdom. That great scientist of
the universe is Jehovah God the Creator. The
truth expressed by his wise Son Jesus Christ remains unchanged today: What means everlasting
life to us dying humans is our knowing first of all
the heavenly Father, "the only true God." As the
Father he is the Life-giver. This great Architect
of the universe is eternal in scientific knowledge.
He has the know-how and the power to create, yes,
re-create life by a resurrection and to protect and
renew and preserve it forever. His offer of everlasting life to mankind is the only one on which
to hope. That offer is through the one whom he
sent from heaven into this earth, Jesus Christ.
This one we must cultivate a knowledge of also.

¹⁰ You have the opportunity of life everlasting
in the righteous new world of happiness and peace.
But there is an enemy opposed to your getting it.
You must be warned of him.

---

9. So what truth concerning gaining knowledge remains
unchanged?
10. What opportunity do you have? Of whom must you
be warned?

CHAPTER III

THE ENEMY OF LIFE APPEARS

MAN was made to enjoy life on earth forever. In harmony with that Jehovah God made the original man perfect and placed him in a perfect garden spot on earth. It was a paradise located in Eden, and the name "Eden" indicates that it was a delightsome land. "And the Lord God formed man of the slime of the earth: and breathed into his face the breath of life, and man became a living soul. And the Lord God had planted a paradise of pleasure from the beginning: wherein he placed man whom he had formed. And the Lord God brought forth of the ground all manner of trees, fair to behold, and pleasant to eat of: the tree of life also in the midst of paradise: and the tree of knowledge of good and evil. And a river went out of the place of pleasure to water paradise, which from thence is divided into four heads."—Genesis 2:7-10, *Douay;* also the Latin *Vulgate* and Greek *Septuagint.*

[2] When God created this first man, from whom all of us have sprung, he made him perfect and not lacking any one of his proper human parts and qualities. To show how different from the perfect

---

1. How long was man made to enjoy life? What start was he given?
2. What disproves that life in material bodies is evil in itself?

Creator all mankind was more than twenty-five centuries after Adam's creation, the prophet Moses said under inspiration: "His work is perfect: for all his ways are judgment: a God of truth and without iniquity, just and right is he. They have corrupted themselves, their spot is not the spot of his children: they are a perverse and crooked generation." (Deuteronomy 32:4, 5) This fact makes it a religious lie to say that all visible, tangible matter is evil in itself and that all existence in material, human bodies is wretched and evil in itself. To say such a thing is to judge mankind's beginning merely by our present fallen condition. God did not give mankind such a start. After he finished preparing this earth for man's everlasting home and had put man in it he did not pronounce this material earth evil. To the contrary, Genesis 1:31 says: "God saw every thing that he had made, and, behold, it was very good." Only a perfect work would be a credit to a perfect, scientific God.

[3] The lower animals, fishes, birds and land animals, were created prior to man. Jehovah God made them animal souls. "And God said, Let the waters swarm with swarms of living souls, and let fowl fly above the earth in the expanse of the heavens. And God created the great sea monsters, and every living soul that moves with which the waters swarm, after their kind, and every winged fowl after its kind. And God saw that it was good. And God said, Let the earth bring forth living

---

3. What did God make the lower animals, created prior to man?

souls after their kind, cattle, and creeping thing, and beast of the earth, after their kind. And it was so. And God created Man in his image, in the image of God created he him; male and female created he them. And God said, Behold, I have

given you every herb producing seed that is on the whole earth, and every tree in which is the fruit of a tree producing seed: it shall be food for you; and to every animal of the earth, and to every fowl of the heavens, and to everything that creepeth on the earth, in which is a living soul, every green herb for food. And it was so."—Genesis 1:20, 21, 24, 27, 29, 30, *Dar.**

⁴ Jehovah God did not give the first man a soul that had transmigrated from some dead fish, bird or land animal. God's creating of every living thing "after its kind" is against any transmigration of souls. Souls do not mix, but stay to their kind. Man had dominion over lower animals, and so he would not descend to them nor they ascend up to him. Each kind is fixed by unchangeable divine law. God did not put in man an invisible soul that had till then been flitting around in heaven like a butterfly, the butterfly being to the pagan Greeks a symbol of their idea of a human soul. No; but the first man Adam was himself the soul. "And Jehovah God formed man of the dust of the ground, and breathed into his nostrils the breath of life; and man BECAME a living soul." (Genesis 2:7, *ASV*) Man's conscious existence as a living human creature is soul. He has no soul apart and distinct from his human body. Like the lower animal creatures, man alive is a living soul.

⁵ Instead of appointing man from the start to an existence of unavoidable wretchedness and misery

---

* See also the Septuagint translation, marginal readings, as published by S. Bagster and Sons Ltd., London, Eng. The text of *The Emphasised Bible* by J. B. Rotherham reads also like the above. See also the marginal readings of Genesis 1:20, 30 in the King James Version Bible for the application of the expression "living soul" to the lower animals, the way it is in the original Hebrew text.

---

4. Why does man not have any transmigrated soul?
5. What shows that man was not meant for a wretched existence?

such as mankind now experiences, God put Adam in the paradise of Eden. This name "Eden" literally means "pleasantness" or "delight". God afterward gave the man a wife, whom God made from a part of man's own body. She was a perfect human soul, the same as her husband Adam, privileged to share with him the delights and pleasantness of that garden of Eden. In this garden they could live forever in ideal happiness with all their sons and daughters, whom they could bring into this earth as perfect human souls. To that end God gave them his fatherly blessing, not his condemnation. "And God blessed them, and God said unto them, Be fruitful, and multiply, and replenish the earth, and subdue it: and have dominion over the fish of the sea, and over the fowl of the air, and over every living thing that moveth upon the earth."—Genesis 1:28.

[6] All this disproves the religious lie that God could not produce anything on earth but wretched, miserable, imperfect creatures, and that all this world of matter is simply an evil development and the best thing for us to do is to try to make our escape from it forever, and that to be restored to life on this earth in the new world would be a hard burden. God condemns the imperfect, wrong condition that has come to exist in the flesh. For this reason in the world to come he will people this earth with innocent, perfect men and women. He will not permit any other kind of

6. What religious lie does this disprove, and what conditions of life on earth will God produce in the new world?

population to inhabit this earth forever. He will accordingly remove all human wrong and imperfection. How so, we shall see.

[7] Man's everlasting life on earth is not based on his having an immortal soul inside him. It is dependent upon his perfect obedience to God, who can make full provision for sustaining man's life here forever. Man is a mortal soul, and to warn man of this the Creator said to Adam: "Of every tree of paradise thou shalt eat: but of the tree of knowledge of good and evil, thou shalt not eat. For in what day soever thou shalt eat of it, thou shalt die the death." (Genesis 2:16, 17, *Douay*) God did not appoint the perfect man to die, but God opened to him the opportunity of everlasting life in human perfection in the Edenic paradise. Only if the perfect man disobeyed would God sentence him to death, and he would cease to exist as a soul. This agrees with God's law stated over thirty-four centuries later: "The soul that sinneth, the same shall die." (Ezechiel 18:4, 20, *Douay*) God made no promise to take perfect man to heaven after he had proved his obedience. The scientific laws of God are against this: "The first man Adam was made into a living soul; . . . The first man was of the earth, earthly: . . . flesh and blood cannot possess the kingdom of God: neither shall corruption possess incorruption." (1 Corinthians 15:45, 47, 50, *Douay*) Man's death as a soul would not open up for him the door to heaven, turning the penalty of disobedience into a blessed oppor-

---

7. Why is man's eternal life not based on his having immortality?

tunity. Neither would the human soul survive a mere death of the body and be able to migrate to an invisible place of conscious torment. Death meant ceasing to exist as a soul, destruction. —Psalm 90:3.

[8] By making full provision for man's eternal life in the Edenic paradise and by warning him of the penalty for disobedience Jehovah God proved himself a friend of life to mankind. What, then, induced the perfect man and woman in Eden to rebel against their heavenly Life-giver and Friend and to provoke his sentence of death? An enemy of life turned up in Eden. This was not the serpent in Eden, the lowly creature that tempted Adam's wife Eve to eat the forbidden fruit of the tree of the knowledge of good and evil. It was the invisible spirit creature behind the serpent and that made the serpent speak enticingly. Presenting himself as an angel of light, he promised Adam and Eve wisdom and immortal life as gods, if they followed the course he suggested. Actually he worked for their death by leading them into being sentenced by God. "And the serpent said unto the woman, Ye shall not surely die: for God doth know that in the day ye eat thereof, then your eyes shall be opened, and ye shall be as gods, knowing good and evil." (Genesis 3:4, 5) So he denied that they were mortal souls and he held out to them divine life. By turning Eve and Adam into the course of rebellion against their God and Lawgiver, for which the penalty was death, he in

---

8. What induced man and woman in Eden to provoke the death sentence?

effect murdered them and their offspring. By contradicting God's stated law, he proved himself a liar.

⁹ The book of Genesis does not identify who this murderer was, but Jesus does so for us. Addressing his religious opposers who were inclined to kill him, Jesus said: "You are from your father the Devil and you wish to do the desires of your father. That one was a manslayer when he began, and he did not stand fast in the truth, because truth is not in him. When he speaks the lie, he speaks according to his own disposition, because he is a liar and the father of the lie." (John 8:44, NW) The name "Devil" means "slanderer, false accuser", and this agrees with Jesus' calling him a liar and the inventor of lies. The Devil lied against God to deceive the woman into disobeying God's true law. This was the same wicked one that tried to tempt Jesus in the wilderness. There Jesus called him "Satan", saying: "Go away, Satan! For it is written, 'It is Jehovah your God you must worship.'" (Matthew 4:10, NW) That name "Satan" means "opposer, adversary" and fits him because he was the first to oppose Jehovah God.

¹⁰ Who made Satan the Devil? Not Jehovah God, because He makes no creature in opposition to him and he makes no lie. A spirit son of God made himself Satan the Devil after God stationed him in Eden. When God fixed the foundation of our

9. Whom did Jesus identify that murderer of mankind to be?
10. Who made Satan the Devil? What prophecy shows this?

earth, there were spirit sons of God observing:
"When the morning stars sang together, and all
the sons of God shouted for joy." (Job 38:7) One
of these sons of God he assigned to the garden of
Eden, to do a protective or covering work over
God's interests with respect to mankind. Long
after this cherub son of God had become Satan,
the king of Tyre became a servant and representative of him. Speaking to Satan the Devil through
the king of Tyre, God shows how his cherub son
went wrong: "Thus saith the Lord Jehovah: Thou
sealest up the sum, full of wisdom, and perfect in
beauty. Thou wast in Eden, the garden of God;
. . . Thou wast the anointed cherub that covereth: and I set thee, so that thou wast upon the
holy mountain of God; thou hast walked up and
down in the midst of the stones of fire. Thou wast
perfect in thy ways from the day that thou wast
created, till unrighteousness was found in thee.
Thy heart was lifted up because of thy beauty;
thou hast corrupted thy wisdom by reason of thy
brightness."—Ezekiel 28:12-15, 17, *ASV*.

[11] This explains how sin or unrighteousness
started in the universe, although the cherub son
of God was perfect from the day he was created
and there was then no evil or temptation to evil-
doing in the universe. How, then, could evil suggest itself to a perfect creature in a sinless universe? The temptation to become Satan the Devil
came, not from outside, but from inside. The Bible
writer James describes it: "When under trial, let

---

11. How could evil suggest itself to a perfect creature
in a sinless universe?

no one say: 'I am being tried by God.' No; for
with evil things God cannot be tried nor does he
himself try anyone. But each one is tried by being
drawn out and enticed by his own desire. Then
the desire, when it has become fertile, gives birth
to sin; in turn, sin, when it has been accomplished,
brings forth death."—James 1:13-15, *NW*.

¹² In Eden, the anointed cherub that covers had
a pure and clean assignment, to serve God's sovereignty over the earth in connection with man. This
was no temptation to wrong-doing, but an opportunity for showing love to God and man and for
vindicating Jehovah God's righteous sovereignty
over earth and mankind. But the chance for one
to pervert the divine favor and his position of
power and influence was also there as an opposite
of the course of obedience. The anointed covering
cherub saw this chance; by it he could exalt himself over all the race of mankind with which Jehovah commanded Adam and Eve to fill the earth.
Yes, he could replace Jehovah as ruler and god
over mankind. Desire for this formed in the covering cherub's heart. He became tempted when he
was drawn out and enticed by his own selfish desire. The desire, being cultivated and yielded to,
became fertile. It produced or gave birth to sin,
the sin of rebelling against Jehovah's Godship and
universal sovereignty. The sin turned him into
Satan. How he fell through pride the apostle Paul
suggests, when he warns against elevating novices
in the congregation, saying: "Not a newly con-

12. How did this prove true of the anointed cherub that
covers?

verted man, for fear that he might get puffed up with pride and fall into the judgment passed upon the Devil."—1 Timothy 3:6, *NW*.

[13] Adam and Eve, being perfect, could have resisted the temptation Satan the Devil put in their way. The perfect man Jesus showed such was possible. It meant subjecting themselves in faith to Jehovah's universal sovereignty and opposing the one that suggested rebellion. "Subject yourselves, therefore, to God; but oppose the Devil, and he will flee from you." (James 4:7, *NW*) In willfully giving way to the temptation by Satan the Devil, they went over on his side. They stood with him in rebellion against God's universal sovereignty and so became his subjects. "He who practices sin originates with the Devil, because the Devil has been sinning from when he began. For this purpose the Son of God was made manifest, namely, to break up the works of the Devil." (1 John 3:8, *NW*) Satan the Devil being first to sin, every one making a practice of sin after him, copies him, as a child does his father. God is not the producer of sinners. The Devil is.

[14] "Sin, when it has been accomplished, brings forth death." By leading off in sin and inducing other perfect creatures of God to sin, Satan the Devil caused death to invade the universe. The enemy of life had now appeared. His first victims were mankind.

13, 14. (a) How could Adam and Eve have resisted temptation? (b) What did Satan produce? What did he cause to invade the universe?

CHAPTER IV

DIVINE PROMISES
OF BLESSING

SATAN'S rebellion against the universal sovereignty of Jehovah God brought cursings upon himself and mankind. Almighty God did not then cast Satan out of heaven, forever thereafter closing the holy realms above to him. Neither did God then create a subterranean place called "hell" for the torture of souls in fire and brimstone after death and put Satan the Devil in charge of it. This accounts for it that Satan was able to corrupt many angels of heaven and transform them into demons and make himself their ruler.—Matthew 12:24, NW.

[2] God's written Word discloses that about twenty-four centuries after the rebellion in Eden Satan the Devil was still above the earth and still had free entry into the courts of heaven. This was in the days of Job. "And that man was perfect and upright, and one that feared God, and turned away from evil." Plainly stating that God's great adversary had access to the heavenly courts in contact with the holy angels, the account of Job, evidently written by the contemporary Moses, says: "Now it came to pass on the day when the sons of God came to present themselves before

---

1, 2. (a) Did God at once cast Satan out of heaven for his rebellion? (b) What proof of this do we have in Job's days?

38

Jehovah, that Satan also came among them."
Next showing that Satan was not confined to an
underground hell of torment, the inspired record
says: "And Jehovah said unto Satan, Whence
comest thou? Then Satan answered Jehovah, and
said, From going to and fro in the earth, and from
walking up and down in it. And Jehovah said
unto Satan, Hast thou considered my servant
Job? for there is none like him in the earth, a
perfect and upright man, one that feareth God,
and turneth away from evil." Then Satan, mindful of his success in Eden, challenged God to let
him tempt Job to rebel against God and thus show
that this man had been serving God only for selfish motives.

[3] Although Satan reduced Job to a childless,
poverty-stricken state, he failed to make Job rebel
against God's universal sovereignty and curse
Him in renunciation. Still Satan was not cast out
of heaven; he made another appearance before
God for larger powers respecting Job. Unwilling
to admit defeat, "Satan answered Jehovah, and
said, Skin for skin, yea, all that a man hath will
he give for his life. But put forth thy hand now,
and touch his bone and his flesh, and he will renounce thee to thy face. And Jehovah said unto
Satan, Behold, he is in thy hand; only spare his
life." (Job 1:1 to 2:6, *ASV*) This restriction on
Satan proves he had the power of death toward
mankind. He had just caused the death of Job's
ten children. He had long before induced Adam's
son Cain to put his younger brother Abel to death.

---

3. What proves Satan then had the power of death?

"Cain, who originated with the wicked one and slaughtered his brother. And for the sake of what did he slaughter him? Because his own works were wicked, but those of his brother were righteous." (1 John 3:12, *NW*) The issue on which Job was being proved was Jehovah's universal sovereignty. Satan failed to shake Job's loyalty.

⁴ The last book of the Bible, the Revelation or Apocalypse, was written about sixty-two years after Jesus' death, resurrection and ascension to heaven. It shows Satan the Devil would not be cast out of heaven and confined to the earth until God's kingdom was set up over earth, with His Son on the throne. Describing the birth of the Kingdom, the Revelation tells what was then due to happen in the invisible realms: "And there was war in heaven: Michael and his angels fought against the dragon; and the dragon fought and his angels, and prevailed not; neither was their place found any more in heaven. And the great dragon was cast out, that old serpent, called the Devil, and Satan, which deceiveth the whole world: he was cast out into the earth, and his angels were cast out with him. And I heard a loud voice saying in heaven, Now is come salvation, and strength, and the kingdom of our God, and the power of his Christ: for the accuser of our brethren is cast down, which accused them before our God day and night. . . . Therefore rejoice, ye heavens, and ye that dwell in them. Woe to the inhabiters of the earth and of the sea! for

_____
4. When does the Revelation show he was due to be cast out?

the devil is come down unto you, having great wrath, because he knoweth that he hath but a short time. And . . . the dragon saw that he was cast unto the earth."—Revelation 12:7-13.

⁵ This account and that of Job show who is behind all the sorrows and afflictions upon mankind for the past six thousand years, and especially since A.D. 1914, the year World War I began. Why God has permitted wickedness to rage over earth since the rebellion of Satan also becomes clear. The malicious purpose of Satan in bringing all the calamitous woes upon humankind has been the same as in the case of Job, to turn all men, even the righteously disposed, God-fearing ones, to bitterness and revolt against the Creator and rightful Sovereign, Jehovah God. The issue during all these millenniums of the prevalence of wickedness has been the universal sovereignty of the Most High God. Therefore he has let the wicked one have ample opportunity in the earth and even access to the holy courts of heaven to back up his claimed ability to turn all living creation against the universal Sovereign. Only by letting Satan have all this time and such a wide range of action could the supreme issue be settled for all eternity.

⁶ This has been hard upon mankind. But the hardness of the experience is due to Satan. For God's part, it has been very merciful to mankind, for while sinners have been let live on earth God

5. Why has God permitted wickedness to rage since Satan rebelled?
6. Why has this been very merciful for mankind on God's part?

has used the time to work out his great purpose of saving those who will win everlasting life in the righteous new world. God could justly have destroyed Adam and Eve at once for their sin, without letting them bring children into the earth. Then none of us would have been born and had the opportunity to learn of the only true God and Jesus Christ, to know both of whom means everlasting life. But Satan had raised an issue that touched God and affected all the universe. To destroy Satan at once would not have settled it to the satisfaction of all living creation. That he would settle it in his fixed time he gave his unconditional promise in the hearing of Satan and Adam and Eve.

⁷ The great Judge turned to Satan who had used the serpent to deceive Eve into death-dealing sin. "And Jehovah God said unto the serpent, Because thou hast done this, cursed art thou above all cattle, and above every beast of the field; upon thy belly shalt thou go, and dust shalt thou eat all the days of thy life: and I will put enmity between thee and the woman, and between thy seed and her seed: he shall bruise thy head, and thou shalt bruise his heel." (Genesis 3:14, 15, *ASV*) This language is unmistakably symbolic and seals up a mystery. After more than four thousand years God unlocked the mystery. The woman meant is not Eve or any of her daughters, but is God's holy universal organization which he has used as a mother to provide or bring forth the

---

7. How did God promise in Eden to settle the supreme issue?

promised Seed. (Galatians 4:26-31) The Seed is primarily the Son whom God sent forth from his heavenly organization to become a man on earth and to be subject to the great test of loyalty to Jehovah's universal sovereignty amid Satan's world. Under test by everything that Satan had to bring to bear against him, the Seed would vindicate Jehovah's sovereignty by proving true to the death, the bruising of his heel. In fulfillment of the divine curse upon him Satan the Devil, that "old Serpent", would be destroyed with all his wicked seed in heaven and in earth. The Seed of God's "woman" would crush the wicked one's head like that of a snake under his heel.

[8] Till then wickedness must be let continue. Persons who looked ahead during 4,000 years to the Seed and persons who became his followers must all be tested by it for some personal share in vindicating Jehovah's sovereignty over all creation, including our earth. But the clearing out of wickedness from the universe is certain. The death and resurrection of the Seed, Jesus Christ, guarantee it will be accomplished, and that shortly now. This means also the deliverance of all those who become the children of God and brothers of Christ. "Therefore, since the 'young children' are sharers of blood and flesh, he also similarly partook of the same things, that through his death he might destroy the one having the means to cause death, that is, the Devil, and might emancipate all those who for fear of death were subject

---

8. So what do Christ's death and resurrection now guarantee?

to slavery all through their lives." (Hebrews 2:14, 15, *NW*) "For this purpose the Son of God was made manifest, namely, to break up the works of the Devil." (1 John 3:8, *NW*) God has had to endure much by permitting wickedness for settling the supreme issue, and we can count his patience as adding up to our everlasting salvation.

⁹ Pronouncing sentence upon Adam and Eve, God assured Eve that she would not immediately be put to death but would give birth to many children, subject to her husband's rule. For Adam's guilt God pronounced a curse on the ground outside of Eden and added: "In the sweat of thy face shalt thou eat bread, till thou return unto the ground; for out of it wast thou taken: for dust thou art, and unto dust shalt thou return." (Genesis 3:16-19) He pronounced no condemnation to eternal torment in a hell of fire and brimstone after Adam and Eve's death. That would have required eternal life for them. God's unchangeable law must stand and be enforced: "In the day that thou eatest thereof thou shalt surely die." (Genesis 2:17) For the very purpose that the sinner rebels might not live forever God drove them out of the paradise of pleasure into the cursed earth. "And he said: Behold Adam is become as one of us, knowing good and evil: now, therefore, lest perhaps he put forth his hand, and take also of the tree of life, and eat, and live for ever. And the Lord God sent him out of the paradise of pleasure, to till the earth from which he was taken. And

---

9. How did God judge Adam and Eve and then execute judgment?

he cast out Adam; and placed before the paradise of pleasure Cherubims, and a flaming sword, turning every way, to keep the way of the tree of life." —Genesis 3:22-24, *Douay.*

[10] For his treachery that made him Satan the Devil the "anointed cherub that covereth" lost his position in Eden as guardian of God's interests in the earth. He would have led man, if allowed to remain in the paradise of pleasure, to that "tree of life" for him to eat and live on in spite of God's sentence. But now other cherubs were stationed at the entrance to that pleasant garden to prevent the rebellious anointed cherub from leading man back to eat of the tree of life. Terrible destruction awaits the traitor under the heel of the Seed of God's "woman". Speaking prophetically as though it was already accomplished, God says to him: "By the abundance of thy traffic they filled the

10. What did the anointed covering cherub lose? What awaits him?

midst of thee with violence, and thou hast sinned: therefore have I cast thee as profane out of the mountain of God; and I have destroyed thee, O covering cherub, from the midst of the stones of fire. All they that know thee among the peoples shall be astonished at thee: thou art become a terror, and thou shalt nevermore have any being." —Ezekiel 28:16, 19, *ASV*.

[11] Everlasting life in a fiery, sulphurous hell of torment did not now enter into the world for sinful mankind, but death did. "Through one man sin entered into the world and death through sin, and thus death spread to all men because they had all sinned." (Romans 5:12, *NW*) This is why sin is common to all mankind. Satan the enemy of life was responsible in the first degree for this. Sin is not merely a harming of oneself or of some other person. It is a violation of the law of the great Creator and Lawgiver. Sin is a missing or failure to live up to the mark of perfection which He sets for his creatures. The wages that sin pays is death to the sinner. Satan the Devil, who has the power of death, has induced some religionists to think that death is a blessing. In fact, he has induced some to believe that total extinction is the very climax of a creature's experience, the ideal state of happiness, because it relieves one of the worries, burdens and pains of living under imperfect conditions. The soul's being blended into a universal state of unconsciousness these religionists call "nirvana". But destruction or annihila-

---

11. Why is sin common to all men? What is it? What does it pay?

tion out of all existence is a curse, not a blessing. Jehovah is not an unconscious quiescent God. He is "the living God", and the gift which he gives to human creatures who want to escape from the undersirable conditions of existence in this present evil world is perfect life everlasting in a righteous new world.

¹² The crushing of the Serpent's head by the Seed of God's "woman" means the deliverance of mankind from the domination of the great enemy of life. It means for them an opportunity for everlasting life in a new world. It means a lasting blessing from God through his promised Seed. His Edenic promise of the Seed links up with his promise made over two thousand years later to an earthly friend, Abraham the Hebrew. Showing that the Seed for bringing blessing to men was to come through this man of faith, Jehovah said: "I will make of thee a great nation, and I will bless thee, and make thy name great; and thou shalt be a blessing: and I will bless them that bless thee, and curse him that curseth thee: and in thee shall all families of the earth be blessed." (Genesis 12:2, 3) Both of these promises were Jehovah's irretractable declarations of his purpose to destroy all wickedness and its evil results and to bless all families of the earth.

---

12. With what later promise does God's Edenic promise link up?

CHAPTER V

NO SELF-SALVATION
BY THE LAW OF MOSES

"SALVATION belongeth unto Jehovah: thy blessing be upon thy people." (Psalm 3:8, *ASV*) With these words the royal psalmist of ancient Israel teaches us that man's eternal salvation can never come from man himself. This lesson had to be taught even to those whom God chose as his people for Abraham's sake. Abraham was a man of unshakable faith in Jehovah. He proved this by his works of obedience toward God. One night after God had led Abraham into the promised land of Palestine he said to him: "Look now toward heaven, and number the stars, if thou be able to number them: and he said unto him, So shall thy seed be." Did the aged childless Abraham believe that divine promise? God's own inspired Record answers Yes. "And he believed in Jehovah; and he reckoned it to him for righteousness."—Genesis 15:5, 6, *ASV*.

[2] Not for human perfection and sinlessness, but for his obedient faith toward God Abraham had righteousness counted to him. About fifteen years after this, when Almighty God announced the

---

1. From whom alone can man's salvation come? Who were taught this?
2. (a) What connection had circumcision with Abraham's righteousness? (b) Through whom was his seed to be reckoned?

coming birth of Abraham's son Isaac, God laid upon Abraham and his descendants the obligation to be circumcised. But Abraham had had righteousness reckoned to him long before circumcision. The circumcision was given him merely as a sign of the righteousness which he already had through faith and obedience. Abraham had now a son named Ishmael by Hagar the slavegirl of his wife. Yet Abraham's seed was not to be reckoned through Ishmael, but to be reckoned through the coming son, Isaac. When God told Abraham that Ishmael was rejected as the channel of Abraham's promised seed, God said: "In Isaac shall thy seed be called."—Genesis 17:9-27; 21:12; Romans 9:7.

[3] Righteousness is now counted to imperfect humans through faith in Jehovah God. In proof the apostle writes: "Since we say, 'His faith was counted to Abraham as righteousness.' Under what circumstances, then, was it counted? When he was in circumcision or in uncircumcision? Not in circumcision, but in uncircumcision. And he received a sign, namely, circumcision, as a seal [confirmation] of the righteousness by the faith he had while in his uncircumcised state, that he might be the father of all those having faith while in uncircumcision, in order for righteousness to be counted to them." (Romans 4:9-11, *NW*) Further showing that a righteous standing with the God of perfection is possible now only through faith in him coupled with works to correspond, the in-

---

3. How is righteousness now counted to men? What illustrates it?

spired James writes: "Was not Abraham our father declared righteous by works after he had offered up Isaac his son upon the altar? You behold that his faith worked along with his works and by his works his faith was perfected, and the scripture was fulfilled which says: 'Abraham exercised faith in Jehovah, and it was counted to him as righteousness,' and he came to be called 'Jehovah's friend'."—James 2:21-23, NW.

⁴ The privilege of being a benefactor of all mankind God gives to his friends and lovers, and not to his enemies. This was why the divine promises were made to faithful Abraham and his seed or offspring. To make his promise of blessing through Abraham and his seed even stronger for those who hope in the promise, the Most High God backed it up with an oath. He swore by himself, the Supreme Sovereign of the universe. How and when did this come about? To test Abraham's faith still further God commanded him to sacrifice his miraculously born son Isaac. With faith that God Almighty was able to raise Isaac from the dead, if necessary, and still carry out blessings to all mankind through him, Abraham proceeded to sacrifice the young man on Mount Moriah. When Abraham had Isaac bound on the altar and was about to kill him with the knife, Jehovah's angel stopped him and said: "By myself have I sworn, saith Jehovah, because thou hast done this thing, and hast not withheld thy son, thine only son, that in blessing I will bless thee, and in multiply-

---

4. How did God make his promise of blessing stronger for the heirs?

ing I will multiply thy seed as the stars of the heavens, and as the sand which is upon the seashore; and thy seed shall possess the gate of his enemies; and in thy seed shall all the nations of the earth be blessed; because thou hast obeyed my voice."—Genesis 22:15-18, *ASV*.

[5] This promise harmonizes with Abraham's name, which means "father of a multitude". Abraham was here a type or prophetic picture of the great Life-giver himself, Jehovah. His only son by his beloved wife Sarah was a typical picture of God's only-begotten Son Jesus Christ. Abraham's wife was a picture of God's symbolic woman, his holy organization of heavenly creatures from whom the heavenly Father brings forth that beloved Seed for blessing all the nations of the earth. But that blessing does not come without the sacrifice of God's only-begotten Son as a perfect man. That fact was what God here foreshadowed by the living drama which he called upon faithful Abraham to enact with his son Isaac. Abraham practically received Isaac back from the sacrificial death, to continue Abraham's line of descendants. Likewise, God centuries later raised his faithful Son from the dead to carry out the promised blessings and to make it possible for others to be adopted as sons of God and become part of the symbolic seed of Abraham. This privilege has come to people of all nations only through their faith. Such faith has resulted in their being declared righteous like Abraham. Certainly persons

---

5. Who is Abraham's Seed? How do persons become part of the Seed?

not justified by faith like Abraham could never be rightly called part of Abraham's seed. This is necessary, too, for them to gain everlasting life, for God will never give the gift of eternal life to anyone except to a person justified or declared righteous by faith in God and through Christ.

[6] That is not our interpretation of this vital arrangement, but God's. Through his inspired apostle Jehovah showed that this was the way the blessings of the Abrahamic promise would begin and that Abraham's Seed of blessing was primarily Jesus Christ. God had all this interpretation put in sacred Scripture for our education. "Surely you know that those who adhere to faith are the ones who are sons of Abraham. Now the Scripture, seeing in advance that God would declare people of the nations righteous due to faith, declared the good news beforehand to Abraham, namely: 'By means of you all the nations will be blessed.' Consequently, those who adhere to faith are being blessed together with faithful Abraham. Now the promises were spoken to Abraham and to his seed. It says, not, 'And to seeds,' as in the case of many such, but as in the case of one, 'And to your seed,' who is Christ. Moreover, if you belong to Christ, you are really Abraham's seed, heirs with reference to a promise." (Galatians 3:7-9, 16, 29, *NW*) It is an unspeakable blessing to become a part of the seed of Abraham with Christ Jesus. All the seed of Abraham must first be produced before the blessings promised can go to mankind in general.

------

6. To whom does the blessing of the promise go first? Why so?

⁷ For over fifteen centuries of time God taught the natural descendants of Abraham that they could gain a righteous standing with God only in the way that their forefather did, by faith. Men cannot have righteousness legislated into them by some imperfect human political government, and neither can they justify themselves or prove themselves righteous by their own works of self-righteousness. To teach this, Jehovah God established a covenant with the Israelites four hundred and thirty years after he first made his promise to Abraham concerning the blessing of all families of the earth by means of him. This was in the third month after the Israelites had celebrated the first passover in Egypt and Jehovah had rescued them from that land. These Israelites were Abraham's natural descendants through his son Isaac and his grandson Jacob, whose name God changed to Israel. The twelve tribes of Israel were now at the base of the Mount of God, Mount Sinai in Arabia, and the prophet Moses was acting as their mediator between God and man. Through Moses Jehovah God said to them: "Ye have seen what I did unto the Egyptians, and how I bare you on eagles' wings, and brought you unto myself. Now therefore, if ye will obey my voice indeed, and keep my covenant, then ye shall be mine own possession from among all peoples: for all the earth is mine: and ye shall be unto me a kingdom of priests, and a holy nation." The Israelites agreed to enter this covenant

---

7. What covenant did God establish to show righteousness is not by self-works? With whom and when?

with God to be his holy nation. The third day
after that he gave them the Ten Commandments,
the fundamental law of his covenant or compact
with them.—Exodus 19:1 to 20:18, *ASV*.

⁸ Jehovah God continually laid stress on the
need of a great sacrifice acceptable to him. He
showed that when he commanded Abraham to
offer his son for sacrifice. The passover was made
a feature of the Law covenant with the Israelites, and so that covenant with them was really
made down in Egypt when they sacrificed the
passover lamb and sprinkled its blood on their
doorposts and lintels. When this Law covenant
was inaugurated at Mount Sinai, Moses had more
sacrifices offered and he sprinkled their blood.
The inspired apostle makes the following comment
on this:

⁹ "Consequently neither was the former covenant inaugurated without blood. For when every
commandment according to the Law had been
spoken by Moses to all the people, he took the
blood of the young bulls and of the goats with
water and scarlet wool and hyssop and sprinkled
the book itself and all the people, saying: 'This
is the blood of the covenant which God has laid
as a charge upon you.' And he sprinkled the tent
and all the vessels of the public service likewise
with the blood. Yes, nearly all things are cleansed
with blood according to the Law, and unless blood
is poured out no forgiveness takes place."—Hebrews 9:18-22, *NW*.

8, 9. How did God continually lay stress on the need of
a sacrifice?

[10] To carry out their part of the covenant and be Jehovah's holy nation the Israelites were commanded to keep clean from this world and its pollutions. This was required for attaining to life in God's way: "And ye shall observe my statutes and my judgments, by which the man that doeth them shall live: I am Jehovah." (Leviticus 18:5, *Dar.*) The Israelites disobeyed and failed to keep separate from this world; they adopted the ways of this world and became stained with its sins and practices in violation of the Ten Commandments. The honest-hearted among the Israelites found that God's law was good but that they could not keep it perfectly. Instead of proving to be a means of gaining life for them by deeds of self-righteousness, the Law condemned them as sinners. It gave to them the knowledge of what sin was by naming and describing it, and it therefore more forcefully proved to them that they were just as much sinners as people who were not natural descendants of Abraham. Jews today cannot deny the charge.

[11] "For above we have made the charge that Jews as well as Greeks are all under sin; just as it is written: 'There is not a righteous man, not even one; there is not a one that understands, there is not a one that seeks for God. All men have deflected, all of them together have become worthless; there is not a one that does good, there is not so much as one.' Now we know that all the things

---

10, 11. (a) Did the Law prove to be a means for Jews to gain life? (b) By the Law what came to them? How so?

the Law says it addresses to those under the Law, so that every mouth may be stopped and all the world may become liable to God for punishment. Therefore by works of law no flesh will be declared righteous before him, for by law is the accurate knowledge of sin. For all have sinned and fall short of the glory of God."—Romans 3:9-12, 19, 20, 23, *NW*.

¹² Since the Law covenant was given to Abraham's natural descendants, did it set aside the Abrahamic covenant given four hundred and thirty years earlier? Thank God, no! And neither did it set aside or nullify the unconditional promise God gave still earlier in Eden concerning the woman's Seed who would bruise the Serpent's head. From the giving of the Law of Moses to the coming of that Seed the time was more than fifteen centuries. For what purpose, then, was the Law added to God's covenant with Abraham concerning the Seed of blessing? Hear the inspired interpretation:

¹³ "As to the covenant previously validated by God, the Law that has come into being four hundred and thirty years later does not invalidate it, so as to abolish the promise. For if the inheritance is due to law, it is no longer due to promise; whereas God has kindly given it to Abraham through a promise. Why, then, the Law? It was added to make transgressions manifest, until the seed should arrive to whom the promise had been

12. Did the Law do away with the covenant with Abraham?
13. Why, then, was the Law added to the Abrahamic covenant?

made, and it was transmitted through angels by the hand of a mediator [Moses]. Consequently, the Law has become our tutor leading to Christ, that we might be declared righteous due to faith. But now that this faith has arrived, we are no longer under a tutor. You are all, in fact, sons of God through your faith in Christ Jesus."—Galatians 3:17-19, 24-26, *NW*.

¹⁴ So every person that claims he is trying to keep the Ten Commandments and that he is therefore all right and does not have to worry is deceiving himself. He can no more gain self-righteousness by this attempt and justify himself than the Israelites could during their fifteen cen-

14. How, then, must righteousness come to the Jews, and to others?

turies under the Law. The Jews today who profess to keep the Mosaic Law and who refuse to exercise faith in Christ Jesus as the promised Seed are keeping themselves under the curse of the Law: "For all those who depend upon works of law are under a curse, for it is written: 'Accursed is every one that does not continue in all the things written in the scroll of the Law in order to do them.' Moreover, that by law no one is declared righteous with God is evident, because 'the righteous one will live by reason of faith'. Now the Law does not adhere to faith, but 'he that does them shall live by them'. Christ by purchase released us from the curse of the Law by becoming a curse instead of us, because it is written: 'Accursed is every man hanged upon a stake.' The purpose was that the blessing of Abraham might come to be by means of Jesus Christ for the nations, that we might receive the promised spirit through our faith."–Galatians 3:10-14, *NW*.

[15] All hope of proving worthy of the right to everlasting life by keeping the Law covenant has vanished for the natural Israelites as well as for all proselytes to the Mosaic Law covenant. "For there is not a just man upon earth, that doeth good, and sinneth not." (Ecclesiastes 7:20) God foresaw this, and so he promised to provide the perfect Seed of deliverance. The hope of all mankind, Jew and Gentile alike, rests in the Seed of God's woman and in God's kingdom by him.

---

15. So where does mankind's hope for everlasting life rest?

CHAPTER VI

"THE APPOINTED TIMES
OF THE NATIONS"

AFTER the global flood of Noah's day the nations of the earth were formed from the descendants of his three sons, Shem, Ham and Japheth. "These are the families of the sons of Noah, after their generations, in their nations: and by these were the nations divided in the earth after the flood." (Genesis 10:32) The first human king reported on earth was Nimrod, son of Cush, son of Ham, son of Noah. The city with which Nimrod began in the plains of Shinar was the first center of defiance to Jehovah's rule of the earth. It was a city destined to become a Biblical symbol of the very organization of the Devil itself, Babylon! "He was a mighty hunter before Jehovah: wherefore it is said, Like Nimrod a mighty hunter before Jehovah. And the beginning of his kingdom was Babel, and Erech, and Accad, and Calneh, in the land of Shinar." (Genesis 10:8-10, *ASV*) All the kingdoms of this world have since then drawn their inspiration from Babylon and its invisible ruling power, "the god of this world," the foe of Jehovah.

² Suddenly in the Bible record of kingdoms ap-

1. From whom were the nations formed? Who was their first king?
2. Who was Melchizedek? What relations had he with Abraham?

pears a king in the land of Canaan, the land promised to Abraham and his descendants. It is the king of Salem, the city which later becomes Jerusalem, the capital of the ancient kingdom of Israel. Without offering us any information about his ancestry or his posterity, the Bible announces his name as Melchizedek. His name means "king of righteousness", and the name of his city means "peace". In bright contrast with Nimrod king of Babylon, Melchizedek is a worshiper of Jehovah. In fact, he is his earthly great priest as well as a king on a throne. He met Abraham, who was returning from the victory over the aggressive alliance of four invader kings, including Amraphel king of Shinar and Tidal king of nations. The brief Bible record of this royal priest of Jehovah says: "And Melchizedek king of Salem brought forth bread and wine: and he was priest of God Most High. And he blessed him, and said, Blessed be Abram of God Most High, possessor of heaven and earth: and blessed be God Most High, who hath delivered thine enemies into thy hand." Recognizing Melchizedek as Jehovah's priest of those days, Abraham gave him tithes of the spoils of victory, as Jehovah's dues. "And he gave him a tenth of all."—Genesis 14:18-20, *ASV*.

[3] Melchizedek was the first king on earth who met God's approval. Because he also combined in himself the office of priest, he was used to picture prophetically the promised Seed of God's "woman" as High Priest and King. The divine Interpre-

---

3. Of whom was Melchizedek a prophetic picture? How so?

ter of this Bible record says: "For this Melchizedek, king of Salem, priest of the Most High God,
who met Abraham returning from the slaughter
of the kings and blessed him and to whom Abraham apportioned a tenth from all things, is first of
all, by translation, 'King of righteousness,' and is
then also king of Salem, that is, 'King of peace.'
In being fatherless, motherless, without geneal-
ogy, having neither a beginning of days nor an
end of life, but having been made like the Son of
God, he remains a priest perpetually. Behold,
then, how great this man was to whom Abraham,
the family head, gave a tenth out of the chief
spoils."—Hebrews 7:1-4, *NW*.

⁴ The Israelite descendants of Abraham, under
Moses' successor Joshua, crossed the Jordan river
by Jehovah's miracle and entered the Promised
Land of "milk and honey". There they destroyed
thirty-one of the local kings, after which the
land was distributed by lot to the twelve tribes
of Israel. The tribe of Levi, as a sort of thir-
teenth tribe, was dedicated to Jehovah's service at his tabernacle or temple. Jehovah set up
over them a Theocratic government. That is to
say, God was their invisible Ruler or King. But
the Israelites neglected to clear out all the heathen kings from the Promised Land and frequently
they fell away from the worship of the only true
God to worshiping the idol and demon gods of
their tolerated heathen neighbors. Resisting no
longer the desire to copy their untheocratic neigh-

---

4. What kind of government did Israel get? What did
they request?

bors, the Israelites came to the prophet Samuel
and asked him to appoint a visible earthly king
over them. Jehovah God commanded Samuel to
carry out their wishes, saying: "They have not
rejected thee, but they have rejected me, that I
should not be king over them." So under Jehovah's guidance Samuel anointed Saul of the tribe
of Benjamin as Israel's first human king.—1 Samuel 8:7; 10:1; 11:14, 15, *ASV*.

⁵ Because of King Saul's disobedient failures
Jehovah God removed him from the throne and
had the shepherd of Bethlehem, David, a man
agreeable to His heart, anointed and installed
as king of the Theocratic kingdom. David completed the conquest of the city of Jerusalem
and made it the capital city of Israel. He established his throne at its citadel called Zion, and
there also he brought the most sacred article of
Jehovah's worship, the ark of the covenant. To
the prophet Nathan he bared his heart's desire
to build a magnificent temple to house the precious ark of the covenant. Jehovah overruled this
desire because David had been a man of war and
blood in Theocratic warfare against Jehovah's
foes; but David's peaceful son was to have the
privilege of carrying out David's wish to build
the temple.

⁶ Jehovah God now unfolded wider his purpose
to have an everlasting kingdom by the Seed of
His "woman". He had raised up for a prophetic

5. Who next became king? What did he desire to build?
6. What did God establish with David? What did this
disclose?

shadow the king-priest Melchizedek. Also to Abraham he had said: "I will make nations of thee, and kings shall come out of thee." And when he overthrew the mightily armed Egyptian pursuers in the Red sea and delivered his chosen people Israel, he inspired Moses to sing: "Jehovah shall reign for ever and ever." (Genesis 17:6; Exodus 15:18, *ASV*) Now he disclosed that the Seed of his "woman" would have royal lineage and be king forever. To that end he established a covenant for the Kingdom with King David, that the royal privilege to sit upon the throne of Jehovah as his representative king would never pass from the line of David. Jehovah made this covenant promise to David: "I will set up thy seed after thee, that shall proceed out of thy bowels, and I will establish his kingdom. He shall build a house for my name, and I will establish the throne of his kingdom for ever. I will be his father, and he shall be my son: . . . And thy house and thy kingdom shall be made sure for ever before thee: thy throne shall be established for ever." (2 Samuel 7:12-16, *ASV*) This covenant for the everlasting kingdom could be fulfilled only by having the Seed of God's "woman" become permanent heir of the covenant.

⁷ So the Kingdom Seed must be David's descendant, a son of David. Jesus was just that. Since he as Heir of the covenant died childless, he could leave no human heir or successor. But since God gave him immortality at his resurrection

---

7. How is Jesus the Permanent Heir and the "root of David"?

from the dead, he lives forever and needs no successor, but remains Permanent Heir. He calls himself "the root of David". This expression, when taken to mean "the lineage of David", means that because of Jesus the royal lineage of David can never end. Or, taken to mean the life-giving root of David, the expression means that Jesus as Priest-King gives everlasting life to David by means of his ransom sacrifice and the resurrection of the dead.—Revelation 22:16; 5:5.

[8] David was of the tribe of Judah, and the making of the Kingdom covenant with him harmonized with the blessing pronounced by the dying Jacob upon his son Judah: "The sceptre shall not depart from Judah, nor the ruler's staff from between his feet, until Shiloh come; and unto him shall the obedience of the peoples be." (Genesis 49:10, ASV) The permanent heir of the Kingdom covenant would be a "son" of David, yet he was to be higher than his forefather David. He was to be a heavenly king, sitting at God's own right hand. David had been only a king on the earthly Mount Zion and after a reign of forty years he had died like all descendants of the sinner Adam. But the Permanent Heir of the Kingdom covenant was to combine in himself the office of both king and priest, as Melchizedek had done. He was to be a king and priest for all time. For this reason David was inspired to prophesy of this coming Son as his Lord and Superior and to foretell Jehovah's oath by which he was to be made priest

---

8. What kind of king was he to be? How did David prophesy this?

and king forever. Sang David: "Jehovah saith unto my Lord, Sit thou at my right hand, until I make thine enemies thy footstool. Jehovah will send forth the rod of thy strength out of Zion: Rule thou in the midst of thine enemies. Jehovah hath sworn, and will not repent: Thou art a priest for ever after the manner of Melchizedek." (Psalm 110:1, 2, 4, *ASV*, margin) The role predicted for this heavenly heir of the Kingdom covenant showed he was to be the one to crush the head of the enemy Serpent and destroy all his wicked seed.

⁹ Accordingly, after David's death, the line of David went on ruling at Jerusalem. "Then Solomon sat on the throne of Jehovah as king instead of David his father, and prospered; and all Israel obeyed him." Because the Judean king was merely a representative of the real invisible Ruler Jehovah God, it was a Theocratic kingdom. Solomon was the wisest of the human kings of Israel and he built the glorious temple at Jerusalem. During his years of faithful reigning he brought great peace and prosperity to the nation. Like under the coming kingdom of God, the Israelites were as the sand of the seashore for number and ate and drank to their heart's content and enjoyed themselves, every man sitting safely under his own vine and fig tree. Hence Solomon, the direct natural son of David, was used to prefigure the Greater than Solomon, the royal Seed of God's "woman", the permanent Kingdom Heir. —1 Chronicles 29:23; 1 Kings 4:20-25; 6:1-14, *ASV*.

---

9. Whom did King Solomon prefigure? Why?

¹⁰ But long before, in the Mosaic Law covenant, Jehovah had warned the Israelites: "And if notwithstanding this ye will not hearken unto me, but walk contrary unto me: then will I also walk contrary unto you in fury; and I, even I, will chastise you, sevenfold for your sins. And I will surely make desolate the land: and your enemies who dwell therein shall be astonished at it. And you will I scatter among the nations, and I will draw out after you the sword; and your land shall be a desolate wild, and your cities shall be a waste. Then shall the land satisfy its sabbaths, all the days of its desolation, when ye are in the land of your enemies: then shall the land rest, and satisfy its sabbaths." (Leviticus 26:27, 28, 32-34, Lees.; Dar.) "Jehovah will bring thee, and thy king whom thou shalt set over thee, unto a nation that neither thou nor thy fathers have known, and there shalt thou serve other gods, wood and stone." (Deuteronomy 28:36, Dar.) Such a national disaster occurred after the kingdom of the line of David, with capital at Jerusalem, had stood for about five hundred years. The last and twenty-first king from David to sit on the Theocratic throne at Jerusalem was King Zedekiah.

¹¹ Shortly before Zedekiah was dethroned and carried captive to Babylon he was given this message: "And thou, O deadly wounded wicked one, the prince of Israel, whose day is come, in the

10. How had God warned he would punish the kingdom for repeated disobedience? When did this national disaster occur?
11. What showed God did not then renounce his Davidic covenant?

time of the iniquity of the end, thus saith the Lord Jehovah: Remove the mitre, and take off the crown; this shall be no more the same; exalt that which is low, and abase that which is high. I will overturn, overturn, overturn it: this also shall be no more, until he come whose right it is; and I will give it him." (Ezekiel 21:25-27, *ASV*) This meant to say that, although Jehovah then caused the active rule of Jerusalem's kings to be overturned, yet he did not renounce his everlasting covenant with David for the Kingdom. In due time the permanent heir of that Kingdom covenant would come. Then Jehovah would anoint this Son of David as the rightful Heir and would give The Theocratic Government to him.

[12] Jehovah God used Nebuchadnezzar king of Babylon to overturn the Jewish kingdom. This took place in 607 B.C. That year, on the 9th day of the 4th Jewish month (or Tammuz 9), the Babylonian besiegers breached Jerusalem's walls, following which King Zedekiah and his army fled the city, but only to be captured. Next month, on Ab 10, corresponding to August 3 to 4 (Gregorian calendar), sundown to sundown, the Babylonians came and began burning down the temple, the king's palace and other houses of Jerusalem, broke down its walls, and took the surviving Jews captive to carry most of them to Babylon hundreds of miles away. Later the poor Jews that were left in the territory became frightened and some time in the latter half of the seventh Jewish

---

12. How and when did Jerusalem and Judah become desolate?

month of 607 B.C. they fled down to Egypt. So the land of Judah and Jerusalem was not left desolate without human inhabitant to enjoy seventy sabbath years until along in October, 607 B.C.

¹³ There a period of time began during which there was to be no Theocratic kingdom on the earth and no ruler of David's line would sit upon the "throne of Jehovah" to represent Jehovah's sovereignty over any part of the earth. There in the fullest sense Satan the Devil became, what 2 Corinthians 4:4 calls him, "the god of this system of things." (NW) Since Jehovah had used Nebuchadnezzar to destroy Jerusalem, he indicated to him how long that period of total domination of the earth without divine interference would be. Through an inspired dream to Nebuchadnezzar which the prophet Daniel interpreted Jehovah showed that the period was to be "seven times". (Daniel 4:16, 23, 25, 32) Each of these "times" corresponds to a year, and hence some transla-

13, 14. (a) What period of domination there began? (b) How long did Jehovah show that period would be?

tions render the expression "seven years". (*Moff.*; *AAT*) Seven literal years of loss of reason did pass over King Nebuchadnezzar in miniature fulfillment of the prophetic dream; but the full-scale fulfillment of the uninterrupted mad Gentile domination of the earth proved to be a much longer period.

[14] The "seven times" that Nebuchadnezzar spent were seven years of twelve lunar months, or of 360 days to a year. That would multiply up to 2,520 days (7×360 days) for the seven literal times. Such 2,520 days of his "seven times" of beastlike madness were symbolic of the period of Gentile world-domination during which Jerusalem or what it represented was trodden underfoot by the non-Jewish nations. Jehovah himself gives us the rule for interpreting the symbolism by saying regarding punishment upon Israel: "Each day for a year." (Numbers 14:34) "I have appointed thee each day for a year." (Ezekiel 4:6) So calculated, the 2,520 days of Jerusalem's destroyer in beastlike madness symbolized 2,520 years counting from 607 B.C.—Compare Revelation 12:6 and 14.

[15] So the "seven times" did not end in 537 B.C. when the land of Judah and Jerusalem had finished its seventy sabbath years of lying desolate without man or domesticated beast and when the Israelite captives returned from Babylon and rebuilt Jerusalem and Jehovah's temple there. Centuries later when Jesus Christ was predicting the

15. How did Jesus show those times had not ended in 537 B.C.?

second destruction of Jerusalem, this time by the pagan Roman imperial armies A.D. 70, he referred to those seven times of world domination by Gentile nations as having to continue much longer. He called that period of seven times the "appointed times of the nations", saying: "There will be great necessity upon the land and wrath on this people, and they will fall by the edge of the sword and be led captive into all the nations, and Jerusalem will be trampled on by the nations, until the appointed times of the nations are fulfilled."—Luke 21:23, 24, *NW*.

[16] Since those "appointed times of the nations" began with the desolating of Judah and Jerusalem by the Gentiles in October of 607 B.C., the end of their 2,520 years' duration would fall in October, A.D. 1914. What was destined to happen that year according to the divine purpose, not only with respect to our earth but also with respect to all the universe of Jehovah's sovereignty, we must leave to a later chapter to tell.

16. How do we figure when those times ended?

CHAPTER VII

THE BOOK
OF LIFE-GIVING KNOWLEDGE

THE destruction of Jerusalem and of so many of its inhabitants in the year 607 B.C. was largely due to the king's failure to read and heed the words of the book of life-giving knowledge, the Bible. Centuries before the setting of a human king over his chosen people Jehovah in his foresight moved the prophet Moses to write these words for the king's guidance:

[2] "When you reach the land that the LORD your God is giving you, and occupy it, and settle down in it, and then declare, 'I must place a king over me like all the nations surrounding me,' you must be sure to make him king over you whom the LORD your God chooses. You must make one of your own countrymen king over you; you may not put a foreigner over you, who is not a countryman of yours. . . . As soon as he has taken his seat on his royal throne, he must write for himself in a book a copy of this code as approved by the Levitical priests; he must keep it with him, and peruse it all the days of his life, that he may learn to stand in awe of the LORD his God, by being careful to observe all the provisions of this code and these statutes, that he may not consider himself more exempt than his fellow-countrymen, and that he may not swerve from

1, 2. Through neglect of what provision was the kingdom overturned?

71

the charge to the right or to the left, in order
that he with his descendants may continue long
on the throne in Israel."—Deut. 17:14-20, *AAT*.

[3] That instruction was given especially for the
benefit of the permanent heir of God's Kingdom covenant, Jesus Christ. He, above all, must
be a student of God's written Word, the Bible.
Did he have the books of the Bible in his day?
Yes, the majority of them, thirty-nine of the
present-day sixty-six inspired books. The Bible
he had was entirely a Jewish or Hebrew book,
written in Hebrew and the related language of
Aramaic, and it had been collected by devoted
Hebrews. The writing of the book of Moses in its
five sections now known as Genesis, Exodus,
Leviticus, Numbers and Deuteronomy, began at
God's command in the year he delivered the Hebrews from Egypt. That was in 1513 B.C., or at
least 760 years before the traditional date
(753 B.C.) of the founding of the city of Rome.
(Exodus 17:14) Before ever Rome began expanding its power in the third century B.C. to
become something of a pagan universal empire,
all the books of the inspired Hebrew Scriptures
had been written, completing their canon. Also
the translation of these Hebrew Scriptures in
Greek to form the Greek Septuagint Version was
begun (280 B.C.). The last books of the Hebrew
Scriptures, namely, Chronicles and the prophecy
of Malachi, were written about the fifth century
B.C. The canon of the entire Bible was completed

---

3. Why must Jesus study the Bible? Did he have it in
his day?

by the writing of the Christian Greek Scriptures before the end of the first century after Christ, and those who wrote these were, even including Luke, Hebrews who had changed their faith from Judaism to Christianity. (Romans 3:1, 2; Galatians 1:13-17) So the city of Rome had no hand in the producing of the Bible, and the Book cannot be called "Roman" in any sense.

⁴ The prophet Moses compiled his writings in the book of Genesis from earlier written records. In Genesis he indicates he consulted and incorporated part of eleven historical documents.* After giving us the general account of the seven creative days Moses indicates he drew on old written records by saying: "These are the histories of the heavens and the earth, when they were created, in the day that Jehovah Elohim made earth and heavens." Then, marking the second written record from which he drew information, Moses writes: "This is the book of Adam's history." (Genesis 2:4 and 5:1, *Dar.*, margin) In this way Moses did not depend upon verbal tradition. Being Jehovah's prophet, he was guided and inspired by God's spirit in compiling the record of events before his time and also in writing the account of his own times. He embodied into his writings a copy of that which had been written by the "finger of God" on stone, the Ten Commandments. Besides this, the writing of the book

---

* Genesis 2:4; 5:1; 6:9; 10:1; 11:10; 11:27; 25:12, 19; 36:1, 9; and 37:2.

---

4. On what did Moses depend for writing his record? What shows it?

of Job and of Psalms 90 and 91 is attributed to him. Malachi, the last book of the Hebrew canon, refers us back to the first part of the Bible as authentic and inspired, saying: "Remember ye the law of Moses my servant, which I commanded unto him in Horeb for all Israel, even statutes and ordinances."—Malachi 4:4, *ASV*.

[5] Did Jesus read the Bible? The word "Bible" is drawn from the Greek word *bi·bli'a,* which means "little books". Jesus had all thirty-nine inspired books of the Hebrew Scriptures available in either the original tongue or the Greek Septuagint translation. Being the Son of David and Heir of the Kingdom covenant to whom God's instructions for anointed kings at Deuteronomy 17:14-20 applied, he read those Scriptures privately and publicly. "He came to Nazareth, where he had been reared, and according to his custom on the sabbath day he entered into the synagogue, and he stood up to read aloud. So the scroll of the prophet Isaiah was handed him, and he opened the scroll and found the place where it was written, 'Jehovah's spirit is upon me, because he anointed me to declare good news to the poor, . . . to preach Jehovah's acceptable year.' With that he rolled up the scroll, handed it back to the attendant and sat down." Then he said: "Today this scripture that you just heard is fulfilled." (Luke 4:16-21, *NW*) He not only read the Scriptures, but knew them by heart and quoted them. In his temptation by the Devil in the wilderness

---

5, 6. Did Jesus study the Law, Prophets and Psalms? What is the proof?

he three times repelled the enemy by quoting from memory three texts from the Mosaic book of Deuteronomy, each time saying: "It is written."—Matthew 4:4, 7, 10.

⁶ Proving the resurrection of the dead, he said to the Sadducees: "Did you not read in the book of Moses, in the account about the thorn-bush, how God said to him: 'I am the God of Abraham and God of Isaac and God of Jacob'?" (Mark 12:26, *NW;* Exodus 3:6) In a controversy with the scribes he said: "How is it they say that the Christ is David's son? For David himself says in the book of Psalms, 'Jehovah said to my Lord, Sit at my right hand until I make your enemies a stool for your feet.' David, therefore, calls him 'Lord'; so how is he his son?"—Luke 20:41-44, *NW;* Psalm 110:1.

⁷ Jesus is thus proved to have read and familiarized himself with the book of Moses, the Prophets, and the Psalms. As the record shows, not only did he copiously quote the Scriptures in support of the truth and in proof of his identity, down to the hour of his death, but after his resurrection he continued to direct his disciples to the Scriptures: "And commencing at Moses and all the Prophets he interpreted to them things pertaining to himself in all the Scriptures." "He now said to them: 'These are my words which I spoke to you while I was yet with you, that all the things written in the law of Moses and in the Prophets and Psalms about me must be fulfilled.'

7. Did he refer to them only till his death? What is the proof?

Then he opened up their minds fully to grasp the meaning of the Scriptures, and he said to them: 'In this way it is written that the Christ would suffer and rise from among the dead on the third day." (Luke 24:27, 44-46, *NW*) All the inspired Hebrew Scriptures were included under the three heads, the Law, the Prophets, and the Psalms. Jesus thus referred to the entire Hebrew Bible.

⁸ From all this we note the remarkable fact that the Bible preceded the founding of Christianity and the establishing of the Christian congregation. The preaching by Jesus and his apostles and disciples did not do away with the written Bible. The life and work of Jesus Christ and the founding of the Christian congregation upon him was the fulfillment of the Bible prophecies. Yes, Christ and his disciples of the first century as well as those of this twentieth century prove the basis for their Christian faith to be laid in the inspired Hebrew Scriptures. Hence all through the writings of Jesus' inspired disciples they quote from the old Hebrew Bible. In his first letter Peter makes 34 quotations, from 10 books of the Law, the Prophets and the Psalms. In his second letter he quotes 6 times from three different books. The apostle Matthew, in his gospel account, makes 122 quotations from Genesis to Malachi. Out of those 39 books he quotes 20 and altogether ignores the Apocryphal books, Macchabees, Wisdom, etc.

⁹ As for the Christian Greek Scriptures in their entirety, from Matthew to Revelation, in those 27

8, 9. Did the Bible precede Christianity? What do inspired Christian writers show?

books we find 365 direct quotations from Genesis to Malachi, and about 375 more references to those Hebrew Scriptures; or a total of about 740. The quotations are from 35 different books, or from all except Ruth, Ezra, Ecclesiastes, and Song of Solomon. How could this be if those early Christians did not have the Bible? They both had it and refused to belittle its importance.

[10] When Paul went out on missionary work he generally found the Hebrew Bible ahead of him in the Jewish community. At Antioch in Pisidia Paul and Barnabas took a seat in the Jewish synagogue. What happened? "After the public reading of the Law and of the Prophets the presiding officers of the synagogue sent out to them," inviting them to speak. (Acts 13:15-27, NW) In Paul's speech in which he quoted from the Psalms and Prophets, he spoke, too, of the "Prophets which are read aloud every Sabbath". At the conference of apostles and older brothers in Jerusalem, the disciple James quoted the Prophets and said: "From ancient times Moses has had in city after city those who preach him, because he is read aloud in the synagogues on every sabbath." (Acts 15:15, 21, NW) In the synagogue at Thessalonica, Macedonia, the apostle Paul reasoned for three sabbaths from the Hebrew Scriptures, and when he went from there to Beroea, he found the Scriptures ahead of his preaching of Christianity. Though he was an apostle, he submitted to, yes, he encouraged, having his preaching

_____

10. How did Paul and James verify that the Bible preceded Christianity?

examined in the light of the pre-Christian Bible. His traveling companion, Luke, says of the Beroean Bible students: "Now the latter were more noble-minded than those in Thessalonica, for they received the word with the greatest readiness of mind, carefully examining the Scriptures daily as to whether these things were so." (Acts 17:11, NW) It is gross error for any religious cult to claim that the Christian church preceded the Bible, scheming by this false argument to undermine the influence of God's written Word and to turn people from it to religious traditions.

[11] Acknowledging the precedence of the Hebrew Bible, the apostle Peter speaks of the effect of Christ's transfiguration before him and others on the mountaintop, saying: "Consequently, we have the prophetic word made more firm, and you are doing well in paying attention to it as to a lamp shining in a dark place, until day dawns and a daystar rises, in your hearts. For you know this first, that no prophecy of Scripture springs from any private release. For prophecy was at no time brought by man's will, but men spoke from God as they were borne along by holy spirit." Finally Peter shows that the writings of Paul and the other inspired disciples were added to the Hebrew canon to complete the body of authentic Scripture, the complete Bible. "Our beloved brother Paul according to the wisdom given him also wrote you, speaking about these things as he does also in all his other letters. In them, however, are

---

11. How did Peter verify this? Did he condemn Bible study?

some things hard to understand, the meaning of which the untaught and unsteady are twisting, as they do also the rest of the Scriptures, to their own destruction." Hence Peter's admonition to his readers to pay close attention to the prophetic writings of pre-Christian centuries. (2 Peter 1:19-21 and 3:15, 16, *NW*) Just because some were twisting the Scriptures, Peter did not ban or condemn reading of the Bible.

[12] The apostle Paul, too, writes of the precedence of the Bible over Christianity and of the benefits that Christians receive from studying it rather than religious traditions of false shepherds. He quotes the pre-Christian Psalms when he writes: "Just as it is written: 'The reproaches of those who were reproaching you have fallen upon me.' For all the things that were written aforetime were written for our instruction, that through our endurance and through the comfort from the Scriptures we might have hope." (Romans 15:3, 4, *NW*) Do you want light, comfort and hope? Then read those inspired ancient writings. Do you want to be wise for gaining salvation? Then read and heed those Scriptures. Paul's words to the young man Timothy are for your information and assurance: "From infancy you have known the holy writings which are able to make you wise for salvation through the faith in connection with Christ Jesus. All Scripture is inspired of God and beneficial for teaching, for reproving, for setting things straight, for disciplining in righteousness, that the man of God

12. How did Paul write showing the Bible's precedence?

may be fully competent, completely equipped for every good work."—2 Timothy 3:15-17, *NW*.

¹³ When you read the Bible, prove the pre-Christian Hebrew writings by the fulfilled facts and inspired interpretations in the Christian Greek Scriptures. In turn, find your support for these latter inspired Scriptures by searching the former, and prove the harmony of the entire Bible as the One Book of the One infallible Author, Jehovah God. As you read and search the Scriptures, be honest and open to conviction by them. Do not be like the Jews who had the Hebrew Bible and to whom Jesus said: "You are searching the Scriptures, because you think that by means of them you will have everlasting life; and these are the very ones that bear witness about me. And yet you do not want to come to me that you may have life. In fact, if you believed Moses you would believe me, for that one wrote about me. But if you do not believe the writings of that one, how will you believe my sayings?" He added: "The sayings that I have spoken to you are spirit and are life."—John 5:39, 40, 46, 47 and 6:63, *NW*.

¹⁴ The Bible is the book of life-giving knowledge. By it we gain knowledge of the true God and of Jesus Christ whom he sent, and our knowing them is required for everlasting life. The Bible is the Word of truth that proceeds out of God's mouth. Feed upon it with heart and mind, and grasp the life that really is life.

---

13. How should we handle the Bible, unlike those men Jesus exposed?
14. What essential for life should we gain from the Bible? How?

CHAPTER VIII

COUNTING THE WEEKS TILL THE CHIEF AGENT OF LIFE

THE perfect mathematics of the divine Constructor of the universe is displayed not only in his inanimate creation but also in his timing of the various features of his purpose. By the sun, moon and stars he provides the means for his creatures on earth to measure time, seasons, days, and years. (Genesis 1:14-18) Jehovah, who has purposed the vindication of his own universal sovereignty and the salvation of mankind, "is doing these things which he has known from of old." Not alone does he foreknow those things themselves but he knows exactly the time they are scheduled to occur. He has placed the times and seasons in his own jurisdiction for the outworking of his wonderful purpose, and we may know and learn of his times and seasons only as he unveils them to us in his Word by his spirit. (Acts 15:17, 18 and 1:7, *NW*) His timing of events has been particularly in connection with his beloved Son, the Seed of Jehovah's "woman". This Jesus appeared exactly at God's fixed time, and we can Scripturally prove it. We are spurred to the proof by the words: "But when the full limit of the time arrived, God sent forth his Son, who was produced out of a woman and who came to

---

1. Besides foretelling the events, what also has God done?

81

be under law, that he might release by purchase those under law, that we in turn might receive the adoption as sons."—Galatians 4:4, 5, *NW*.

² By the time prophecy which he gave, Jehovah's people could count the weeks to the appearance of his Chief Agent for giving life and a perfect government to mankind. Babylon under Nebuchadnezzar's grandson Belshazzar had just fallen, on October 7, 539 B.C.,* to the Medes and Persians led by Darius and Cyrus. About two years more and the seventy years of desolation of Judah and Jerusalem ordained by Jehovah would be due to terminate. The prophet Daniel was keenly interested and wrote of himself: "In the first year of Darius the son of Ahasuerus, of the seed of the Medes, who was made king over the realm of the Chaldeans, in the first year of his reign, I Daniel understood by the books that the number of the years, whereof the word of Jehovah came to Jeremiah the prophet, for the accomplishment of the desolations of Jerusalem, was seventy years. And I set my face unto the Lord God." (Daniel 9:1-3, *Dar.*) While Daniel penitently continued to pray and fast, Jehovah sent his angel Gabriel with a message which looked far beyond the rebuilding of desolated Jerusalem.

³ Gabriel said to Daniel: "Mark then the word, and have understanding in the revelation: Seven-

---

* October 13, 539 B.C., Julian Calendar.

2. Was Daniel interested in time features? What is the proof?
3. What time prophecy did Gabriel give Daniel? Covering what time?

ty weeks have been divided concerning thy people and concerning thy holy city—to put an end to the transgression, and fill up the measure of sin, and put a propitiatory-covering over iniquity, and bring in the righteousness of ages, and affix a seal to vision and prophecy, and anoint the holy of holies." (Daniel 9:23, 24, *Roth.*) Gabriel not mentioning days, the weeks are not to be viewed as weeks of days, totaling 490 days. The weeks are made up of seven years each,* and so very modern translators render it: "Seventy weeks of years are destined for your people," etc. (*AAT*) "Seventy weeks of years are fixed for your people and for your sacred city," etc. (*Moff.*) Hence the seventy weeks multiply up to 490 years. They were divided up into three periods, (1) seven weeks, (2) sixty-two weeks, and (3) one week; that is to say, (a) 49 years, (b) 434 years, and (c) 7 years; totaling 490 years. When do they begin to count?

⁴ Gabriel continued: "Thou must know then and understand: From the going forth of the word to restore and to build Jerusalem—unto the Anointed One the Prince shall be seven weeks, and sixty-two weeks,—the broadway and the wall shall again be built, even in the end of the times." (Daniel 9:25, *Roth.*) The starting point of the seventy weeks is the going forth of the word or command "to restore and to build Jerusalem".

*Compare Genesis 29:27.

4, 5. (a) Why did not that time period begin counting in 537 B.C.? (b) Why not in the 7th year of Artaxerxes?

When did such a word go out? Not two years
after Gabriel's message; that is to say, not in
537 B.C., for the decree of Cyrus which went forth
that year was specifically for rebuilding Jehovah's temple on its old site. Cambyses, next the
usurper Smerdis, and then Darius II followed on
the throne, and during Darius' reign the temple
was finished. (Ezra 6:15) His son Xerxes I succeeded him and reigned, not 21 years, but 12
years, and was succeeded by Artaxerxes III.
(Esther 3:7) The historian Thucydides lived during his reign, and, taken in conjunction with a
later table of chronology by Diodorus, who lived
in the first century B.C., Thucydides' writings fix
the disputed end of Xerxes' rule and beginning of
Artaxerxes' rule at 474 B.C.

[5] In the 7th year of Artaxerxes the Jewish
scribe Ezra went up to Jerusalem with a special
letter of commission from the Persian king, but
this did not authorize him to rebuild Jerusalem.
It had as its purpose, "to beautify the house of
Jehovah which is in Jerusalem." (Ezra 7:27,
ASV) In the thirteen years following Ezra's visit
Jerusalem, somewhat rebuilt, came into the condition that some refugees described to Nehemiah,
the royal butler, in the 20th year of Artaxerxes'
reign. (Nehemiah 1:1-3) This 20th year counted
really from October 5, 456, and continued through
twelve lunar months to sundown of September 23,
455 B.C. (Gregorian Calendar) In the spring of
455 B.C., in the Jewish month Nisan, Nehemiah
received from Artaxerxes the command to restore
and rebuild Jerusalem.

[6] Nehemiah 2:1 reads: "And it came to pass in the month Nisan, in the twentieth year of Artaxerxes the king, that wine was before him: and I took up the wine, and gave it unto the king." Asked the reason for his sadness, Nehemiah said to the king: "If it please the king, and if thy servant have found favour in thy sight, that thou wouldest send me unto Judah, unto the city of my fathers' sepulchres, THAT I MAY BUILD IT." Then he asked for timber "for the gates of the palace which appertained to the house, and for the WALL of the city, and for the house that I shall enter into." He tells us: "And the king granted me, according to the good hand of my God upon me." —Nehemiah 2:1-8.

[7] The king's decree really went into effect when Nehemiah rebuilt Jerusalem's wall. After some months of travel he arrived at Jerusalem toward the beginning of the 5th Jewish month (Ab). Work began on the 3d day of that month, July 29, Gregorian Calendar,* and was finished the following month (Elul) in 52 days. "So the wall was finished in the twenty and fifth day of the month Elul, in fifty and two days." (Nehemiah 2:11, 18; 6:15) That was September 18, 455 B.C.,† if that year was a normal lunar year with no intercalary lunar month inserted near spring's beginning.‡

---

* August 3, Julian Calendar.
† September 23, 455 B.C., Julian Calendar.
‡ See *Babylonian Chronology 626 B.C.—A.D. 45*, by Richard A. Parker and Waldo H. Dubberstein, 2d edition of June, 1946, page 30, under Artaxerxes.

---

6. When and how did Nehemiah receive his commission?
7. When did the king's decree really go into effect?

⁸ Counting from 455 B.C. forward for sixty-nine weeks (or 483 years), we come to A.D. 29. What must happen that year? Daniel 9:25 answers: "From the going forth of the word to restore and to build Jerusalem till Messiah the Leader is seven weeks, and sixty and two weeks." (*Yg.*) The appearance of the long-promised Messiah or Anointed One must occur that year. History shows that the 15th year of Roman Emperor Tiberius Caesar overlapped on A.D. 29. He began reigning in Rome at Augustus' death on August 19, A.D. 14. Hence the 15th year of Tiberius' reign extended from August 19, A.D. 28, to August 18, A.D. 29. Luke 3:1-6 tells us that in Tiberius' 15th year John the baptizer appeared and began baptizing and announcing God's kingdom. John was about six months older than his cousin according to the flesh, Jesus. John the son of a temple priest rightly began his public ministry at thirty years of age. (Numbers 4:1-47) On this basis Jesus came to John to be baptized about six months later, for Jesus was thirty years old when baptized. Jesus must become Messiah or Anointed One that year, A.D. 29, according to Daniel's prophecy. He did become such then by being anointed with the spirit of God: "Now when all the people were baptized, Jesus also was baptized and, as he was praying, the heaven was opened up and the holy spirit in bodily shape like a dove came down upon him, and a voice came out of heaven: 'You are my Son, the beloved; I have approved you.' Furthermore, Jesus himself, when he commenced

8. What must and did occur at the end of the 69 weeks?

his work, was about thirty years old." (Luke 3:21-23, *NW*) Messiah had appeared exactly on time.

⁹ Daniel's prophecy also tells us the length of Jesus' public ministry on earth and hence the time of his death "to put an end to the transgression, and fill up the measure of sin, and put a propitiatory-covering over iniquity, and bring in the righteousness of ages, and affix a seal to vision and prophecy, and anoint the holy of holies". The weeks of years had been divided up into 7 and 62 and 1, or 70 in all. Now telling what was to happen after 69 weeks (7 plus 62) were up, Daniel 9:26 says: "And after the sixty-two weeks shall Messiah be cut off, and shall have nothing; and the people of the prince that shall come shall destroy the city and the sanctuary; and the end thereof shall be with an overflow, and unto the end, war,—the desolations determined."—*Dar.*

¹⁰ By saying that after the sixty-two weeks Messiah would be cut off, the prophecy means that at some time after the close of that second division of weeks, or some time after A.D. 29, the Messiah's death could be expected. The final verse of the prophecy indicates when. His being cut off was not to be for any sin of his own or because he had any part in this world. He said his kingdom was not of this world and that the Devil, the ruler of this world, had nothing in common with him and had no hold upon him. The people,

---

9. What was prophesied to occur after the 69 weeks?
10. How was Messiah to be "cut off" and to "have nothing"?

except a small believing Jewish remnant, would have none of him. He was cut off, as "the Lamb of God that takes away the sin of the world". —John 1:29, *NW*.

[11] Because Messiah was thus innocently "cut off", being rejected by the Jewish religious leaders and turned over to Gentile hands to be executed, the things described in the rest of Daniel 9:26 came as a judgment from God upon Jerusalem and the unbelieving Jews. Not, of course, in the final week of the seventy weeks of years. After Messiah was cut off, the difficulties of the Jews with themselves and with the Roman government continued and increased. History shows that, thirty-seven years after Messiah the Prince was cut off as a martyr, the Roman prince and general Titus, son of Emperor Vespasian, came with a host of warrior people against rebellious Jerusalem and destroyed both it and its profaned temple. This took place August 31, A.D. 70 (Gregorian Calendar), about forty-one years after Messiah was anointed. Truly war to the end and the "desolations determined" by the Supreme Judge came upon them.

[12] The final week, or seventieth week, of the foretold period was unquestionably meant when the angel Gabriel said, in the last verse of the prophecy: "And he shall make a firm covenant with many for one week: and in the midst of the

---

11. When did the other things of Daniel 9:26 occur, and how?
12. When, to whom, and for how long was the covenant made firm?

week he shall cause the sacrifice and the oblation to cease; and upon the wing of abominations shall come one that maketh desolate; and even unto the full end, and that determined, shall wrath be poured out upon the desolate." (Daniel 9:27, *ASV*) The covenant that is made firm is the Abrahamic covenant concerning the Seed in whom all families of the earth are to be blessed. The Jews, Abraham's natural seed, were the first ones to whom the benefits and opportunities of that covenant were to go and did go. (Acts 3:25, 26) Confirming that covenant or making its application strong to "many" of the natural Jews means, therefore, restricting first its benefits to the Jews exclusively during this final "one week", from A.D. 29 to 36. The "midst" of that week is a critical time.

[13] When the prophecy says, "In the midst of the week he shall cause the sacrifice and the oblation to cease," it means Messiah the Prince will do so. How? "Cause to cease" means literally "cause to sabbath, to rest, to desist from working". The "sacrifice and the oblation" which he causes to cease are not Jesus' ransom sacrifice offered at Calvary, but are the sacrifices and oblations offered by the Jews at the temple in Jerusalem according to Moses' law. Jesus' death on the torture stake at Calvary took place on the afternoon of Passover day, Nisan 14, of A.D. 33, and this proved to be the very midst of the seventieth week of years. That time is generally fixed as

---

13, 14. What was made to cease in the midst of the week? How?

Friday afternoon, April 1, A.D. 33.* Jesus and his apostles celebrated the passover the preceding night, March 31. Since Jesus was thirty years old when he was anointed at the close of the sixty-ninth week, he added three and a half years to his earthly life by the middle of the seventieth. So, since he was thirty-three and a half years old when he died, he must have been born the night of about October 1, B.C. 2.

[14] By Jesus' own sacrifice he fulfilled the type of the Jewish sacrifices. Fifty-one days later, at Pentecost of A.D. 33, he offered up the antitypical oblation or offering to God by anointing his faithful disciples on earth with the holy spirit. Though Jewish priests kept offering sacrifices and oblations at Herod's temple in Jerusalem till A.D. 70 saw it destroyed, Jesus caused such sacrifice and oblation to cease or desist from having typical value or any divine recognition. God now accepted only the realities of true value.

[15] The middle or midst of the seventieth week was marked by cutting off Messiah in sacrificial martyrdom. The end of that week in the fall of A.D. 36 must likewise be marked. All through that week the Abrahamic covenant of blessing continued confirmed to the "many" of the Jewish remnant who accepted Jesus as "Messiah the Prince". The anointing of the holy of holies, God's sanctuary class, continued during that final week

---

* April 3, A.D. 33, Julian Calendar.

---

15. How was the end of that week marked? And to confirm what?

to its end exclusively upon consecrated Jewish or circumcised flesh. At the end of that week the anointing would be free to go to the uncircumcised believing non-Jews or Gentiles. So at the exact time marked by the great Timekeeper, the conversion of Gentile Cornelius and his household, followed at once by their being anointed with holy spirit, must have taken place at the final end of the seventieth week in the fall of A.D. 36. The accomplishment of all things foretold in the exact time-order served to affix a seal of confirmation to this vision and prophecy given to Daniel and it vindicated Jehovah God as a Prophet and Timekeeper.

[16] We may be sure that also at God's decreed time the desolation by the Roman legions and the end of the Jewish nation in Palestine came upon the unbelieving Israelites after the end of the seventy weeks. Jerusalem with her temple was wiped out A.D. 70, and the last Jewish stronghold, at Masada, on the west shore of the Dead sea, fell to the Romans at Passover time, A.D. 73. Thus God's appointed doom fell upon the abomination as represented by the erstwhile Jewish alliance with Rome against Messiah the Prince. God's wrath was poured out upon that desolate nation. He baptized them with a baptism of fire of destruction. (Matthew 3:10-12) But the life-giving blessings that were secured by the coming and sacrifice of Messiah the Prince continue till this day for all believing and obedient people.

---

16. After that upon whom was God's wrath poured out? How? When?

CHAPTER IX

WHEN LIFE
AND INCORRUPTION
WERE BROUGHT TO LIGHT

MEN who accept the religious traditions of this world rest their hope of eternal life and incorruption upon the teaching that immortality dwells in the human soul. Whether they realize it or not, they follow the lie told in the paradise of Eden by the inventor of lies, Satan the Devil. When that old Serpent said to Adam's wife Eve, "Ye shall not surely die," and induced her to break God's command not to eat of the forbidden fruit, he did not lead her into the path of life and incorruption. He steered her into God's sentence to destruction.

[2] Death was no thing unavoidable for the original parents of the human family and hence unavoidable for all of us their offspring. Religious teachers who claim so quote Hebrews 9:27, 28: "And as it is reserved for men to die once for all time, but after this a judgment, so also the Christ was offered once for all time to bear the sins of many, and the second time that he appears it will be apart from sin and to those earnestly looking for him for their salvation." (*NW*) It is unscriptural for anyone to think from this state-

---

1. What lie did Satan invent? By it where did he steer Eve?
2. Was death unavoidable for Adam? For what was he on trial?

ment that the perfect Adam and Eve in Eden were appointed to death before they sinned and that their living on earth was meant to be for a time and, after they proved faithful in Eden during a trial period, they would die and be judged worthy of resurrection and go to heaven and be like the angels. In Eden the first man and woman were on trial, neither for heaven nor for a fiery place of torment, but for eternal life on earth or for eternal death in earth's dust from which they were taken. They were never destined for heaven, if faithful. Till Jesus' day, four thousand years later, no man had gone to heaven, for the Son of God from heaven said: "No man has ascended into heaven but he that descended from heaven, the Son of man."—John 3:13, *NW*.

[3] It is impossible for man of flesh and blood to go to heaven. The Creator, who made creatures after their kind and for their place, made mankind to be forever on earth. "As the one made of dust is, so those made of dust are also; . . . flesh and blood cannot inherit God's kingdom, neither does corruption inherit incorruption." (1 Corinthians 15:48, 50, *NW*) Jesus went to heaven only after he sacrificed his human life forever and then was resurrected to spirit life, "he being put to death in the flesh, but being made alive in the spirit." (1 Peter 3:18, *NW*) As *he* was changed, so the apostle Paul says to Jesus' faithful followers, "we shall be changed." Before ever these can inherit the heavenly kingdom of God, there must

---

3. Only by what change can Christians go to heaven? Why?

be a change in the nature of his followers, resulting in their changing to spirit creatures in the resurrection.—1 Corinthians 15:51-54, *NW*.

⁴ Before our first parents there was set the opportunity for everlasting life on earth, with never a promise of being taken body and soul to heaven. If they never ate of the forbidden fruit they were merely promised a continuance of life as human souls, in earthly perfection and under the rulership of the universal Sovereign, Jehovah God. But in unmistakable language God said: "Of the tree of the knowledge of good and evil, thou shalt not eat of it: for in the day that thou eatest thereof thou shalt surely die." (Genesis 2:16, 17) It follows that if Adam never ate of it as long as God's prohibition rested on it, he would never die off the earth of which he was a living part. For him the test must result in either life or death, existence or non-existence.

⁵ Adam and Eve's children were born outside the paradise of Eden. They never had a chance to eat of the forbidden fruit, and so they were not directly on trial in Eden. Adam and Eve's judgment was over with in Eden before their being driven out, but not so with their unborn offspring. Hence inescapably these were born dying, or with death reserved for them. But God's own Word shows when and why they were appointed to die and after this to have a judgment. This appoint-

---

4. What was the opportunity set before Adam for faithfulness?
5. How was it reserved for men once to die, followed by judgment?

ment was made only after Adam and Eve had sinned. Because their children born outside Eden could only come forth sinners, they were appointed to death. "The wages sin pays is death." (Romans 6:23, *NW*) Not having been directly on trial and responsible before God in Eden, a future judgment would be possible for them by God's merciful arrangement. When God announced to the Devil in Eden that the Seed of God's "woman" would bruise the Serpent's head, this proved God has purposed the arrangement. The bruising of that wicked one's head would open up the way for Adam's offspring to be resurrected out of the graves of death and be given the opportunities and benefits of a judgment day on their very own responsibility.—Ezekiel 18:20-23.

⁶ It is only "once for all time" that Adam's descendants can die because of what he disobediently did in Eden before their birth. When born as his offspring it unavoidably awaited them to die or merely exist under the inherited condemnation of death. Honest-hearted David expressed their condition when he said: "Behold, I was shapen in iniquity; and in sin did my mother conceive me." (Psalm 51:5) When put personally on judgment before God, then they cannot hold Adam responsible for whether they gain eternal life then or suffer everlasting destruction, "the second death." (Revelation 2:11; 20:6) It does not unavoidably await men nor is it appointed to them to die AFTER they enter the period of judgment. Everlasting salvation is possible for them, and

6. Need they die after entering upon judgment? Why?

many will gain this gift, because life and incorruption have been brought to light by God's provision.

⁷ Adam's descendants did not have the same standing as transgressors before God that Adam had, because they had not been individually on trial in Eden. Just the same, they were sinners, even if they did not have the Law of Moses to point out what sin was, so that they could be charged with sin for violating that Law. But being sinners from birth, they were all under a reign of death. "That is why, just as through one man sin entered into the world and death through sin, and thus death spread to all men because they had all sinned—. For until the Law sin was in the world, but sin is not charged against anyone when there is no law. Nevertheless, death ruled as king from Adam down to Moses, even over those who had not sinned after the likeness of the transgression by Adam, who bears a resemblance to him that was to come." (Romans 5:12-14, NW) That is why, too, a future judgment with life possibilities for them was within the range of God's loving-kindness.

⁸ Let no person think he can earn the right to endless life in sublime happiness by keeping the Ten Commandments, the fundamental law of Jehovah's covenant with Israel through the mediator Moses. Why, many Israelites also thought that by this Law compact they could develop self-

---

7. Why did death reign from Adam to Moses, without the Mosaic Law?
8. How was the Law found to be to death, and sin made more sinful?

righteousness that would win divine approval and God's judgment to eternal life. They thought they could meet the requirement: "Ye shall therefore keep my statutes, and mine ordinances; which if a man do, he shall live in them: I am Jehovah." (Leviticus 18:5, ASV) The honest-hearted finally had to admit that the Law only condemned them, exposing them as imperfect sinners, and they came under its curse: "Really I would not have come to know sin if it had not been for the Law, and, for example, I would not have known covetousness if the Law had not said, 'You must not covet.' But sin, receiving an inducement through the commandment, worked out in me covetousness of every kind, for apart from law sin was dead. In fact, I was once alive apart from law; but when the commandment arrived, sin came to life again, but I died. And the commandment which was to life, this I found to be to death. For sin, receiving an inducement through the commandment, seduced me and killed me through it." God's holy Law was in itself not death to them. The sin in them, which that Law condemned, earned death for them. So sin worked their death, "that sin might become far more sinful through the commandment."—Romans 7:7-13, NW.

⁹ Neither can money or wealth buy eternal life or heaven for any person. Jesus, who did not indulge in material riches, said: "It will be a difficult thing for a rich man to get into the kingdom of the heavens. Again I say to you, It is easier for a camel to get through a needle's eye than for

9. As to gaining life, why have the rich no advantage?

a rich man to get into the kingdom of God." (Matthew 19:23, 24, NW) The rich have no advantage over the poor materially in gaining life: "Those who trust in their wealth, . . . boast of the abundance of their riches. But no man can at all ransom himself, or give a price for himself to God; since the ransom of his person forever and ever is too costly, that he should continue to live forever, without seeing the Pit. But see if he shall! Even wise men die; the fool and the brutish alike perish, and leave their wealth to others." (Psalm 49:6-10, AAT) The poor have no reason to envy the rich at all.

[10] A sacrifice for the complete removal of death-dealing sin was needed. But the animal sacrifices which the Israelites offered continually throughout the fifteen centuries of their holy tabernacle or temple could not remove human sin or ransom a single man. Why, the value of any or of all those animals together was less than the value of the perfect human life that Adam had lost for himself and his descendants by his sin in Eden. Those sacrifices offered under the Mosaic Law merely foreshadowed the good and perfect sacrifice to come. They regularly reminded the Israelites of their need of that human sacrifice by the Seed of Abraham.

[11] "For since the Law has a shadow of the good things to come, but not the very substance of the things, men can never with the same sacrifices

---

10, 11. (a) Of what value were the sacrifices offered under the Mosaic Law? (b) Why could none from Abel to John offer the ransom?

from year to year which they offer continually make those who approach perfect. Otherwise, would the sacrifices not have stopped being offered, because those rendering sacred service who had been cleansed once for all time would have no consciousness of sins any more? To the contrary, by these sacrifices there is a reminding of sins from year to year, for it is not possible for the blood of bulls and of goats to take sins away." (Hebrews 10:1-4, *NW*) No man, from Abel to John the Baptist, could offer the needed human sacrifice, because they all drew their existence from sinner Adam and were condemned for inborn sin. So they had no right to perfect human life which they could sacrifice for others. Moreover, no man could ascend to heaven to pay the needed human ransom to God. No man of flesh and blood can approach glorious Jehovah God and yet live. —Exodus 33:20.

[12] Were it not for the promises of Jehovah God from Eden forward, the prospect of life and incorruption for human creatures would have been absolutely dark. What, then, brought the opportunity for life and incorruption to the light of reality? The sending of God's Son from heaven four thousand years after Eden did so. Then he was manifested to be the Seed of God's "woman", the Seed who suffers the heel-wound from the Serpent but who is to crush the Serpent's head and bless all families of the earth. So with the apostle Paul all his fellow Christians can say: God

---

12. How was light shed upon life and incorruption for us?

"saved us and called us with a holy calling, not by reason of our works, but by reason of his own purpose and undeserved kindness. This was given us in connection with Christ Jesus before times long lasting, but now it has been made clearly evident through the manifestation of our Savior, Christ Jesus, who has abolished death but has shed light upon life and incorruption through the good news".—2 Timothy 1:9, 10, *NW*.

[13] What the dying human race needs is primarily life on earth, not life in heaven, where they do not belong. But incorruption, which corresponds with immortality, is something more than human life and is to be enjoyed only by those at-

---

13. With what is incorruption linked? What opened the way to it?

taining the heavenly kingdom of God. That is why the apostle links incorruption with the Kingdom, saying: "Flesh and blood cannot inherit God's kingdom, neither does corruption inherit incorruption." And concerning Jesus' resurrection to heavenly life he says: "And that fact that he resurrected him from the dead destined no more to return to corruption, he has stated in this way: 'I will give you people the loving-kindnesses of David which are dependable.' Hence he also says in another psalm, 'You will not grant your man of loving-kindness to see corruption.'" (1 Corinthians 15:50 and Acts 13:34, 35, *NW*) The fact that Jesus was resurrected from the dead proved that he had laid down the perfect sacrifice to ransom mankind and afford them everlasting life on earth. By being raised from death he was recovered from the wound with which the Serpent bruised him. Because he was raised from the dead, not flesh and blood, but a spirit clothed with immortality, he could not return to corruption, but he could ascend to God's heavenly presence and there present the value of his ransom sacrifice. By his own resurrection change and entry into heaven, he shed light upon incorruption for his faithful followers and opened the way to immortal life in heaven for them. What good news this provided!

CHAPTER X

A NEW COVENANT FOR GOD'S PEOPLE

FORTY years before the first destruction of Jerusalem in 607 B.C., God raised up his prophet Jeremiah. He inspired him to say to the natural Jews under the old Mosaic covenant: "Behold, the days come, saith Jehovah, that I will make a new covenant with the house of Israel, and with the house of Judah: not according to the covenant that I made with their fathers in the day that I took them by the hand to bring them out of the land of Egypt; which my covenant they brake, although I was a husband unto them, saith Jehovah. But this is the covenant that I will make with the house of Israel after those days, saith Jehovah: I will put my law in their inward parts, and in their heart will I write it; and I will be their God, and they shall be my people. And they shall teach no more every man his neighbor, and every man his brother, saying, Know Jehovah; for they shall all know me, from the least of them unto the greatest of them, saith Jehovah: for I will forgive their iniquity, and their sin will I remember no more." —Jeremiah 31:31-34, *ASV*.

---

1. By whom and in what terms did God foretell the new covenant?

[2] On the passover night thirty-seven years before the second destruction of Jerusalem A.D. 70, Jesus Christ started the Memorial evening meal with his eleven faithful apostles and, as he handed them the cup of wine, he said: "Drink out of it, all of you; for this means my 'blood of the covenant' which is to be poured out in behalf of many for forgiveness of sins." Luke's account of it says: "Also the cup in the same way after they had the evening meal, he saying: 'This cup means the new covenant by virtue of my blood, which is to be poured out in your behalf.'" (Matthew 26:27, 28 and Luke 22:20, *NW*) By these words Jesus indicated that the making of a new covenant was at hand and that he was the sacrifice required for it.

[3] The old Law covenant had been made with the blood of the passover lamb in Egypt. About fifty days later it had been ratified or inaugurated with the blood of young bulls and of goats at Mount Sinai in Arabia. Moses had acted by divine appointment as mediator between Jehovah God and natural Israel. But the blood of all those animal sacrifices had not been able to wash away human sins and give the Israelites a conscience free from sin. And so animal sacrifices were offered continually year after year upon a literal altar. God remembered their sins, and for that reason found it necessary to make a new and better covenant. Jesus did not offer the sacrifice of

---

2. At the Memorial what did Jesus indicate about the new covenant?

3, 4. (a) Why did God remember sins under the old Law covenant? (b) What sacrifice did Jesus offer? With what effect on that covenant?

lower animals, but offered himself, because he was a perfect human, with right to everlasting life as a man. By his baptism in water at John's hands Jesus symbolized his dedication to do God's will in behalf of a new covenant and the rest of God's purpose. At that time of coming to baptism he fulfilled prophecy as follows:

⁴ "Hence when he comes into the world he says: ' "You did not desire sacrifice and offering, but you prepared a body for me. You did not approve of whole burnt-offerings and sin offering." Then I said, "Look! I am come (in the roll of the book it is written about me) to do your will, O God." ' After first saying, 'You did not desire nor did you approve of sacrifices and offerings and whole burnt-offerings and sin offering'—sacrifices which are offered according to the Law—then he actually says, 'Look! I am come to do your will.' He does away with what is first that he may establish what is second. By the said 'will' we have been sanctified through the offering of the body of Jesus Christ once for all time."—Hebrews 10:5-10, NW.

⁵ Moses and the other Israelites down in Egypt offered a literal passover lamb without power to remove human sins. But Jesus, in offering himself, died as "the Lamb of God that takes away the sin of the world". (John 1:29, NW) The new covenant rested thus upon a better sacrifice. Because it was written about him in the "roll of the book", the pre-Christian Hebrew Scriptures, Je-

5. By his sacrifice what did Jesus become, like Moses?

sus became the mediator of the promised new covenant by virtue of the perfect sacrifice of himself. Moses had been the mediator of the Law covenant with Israel, and because he was an imperfect descendant from Adam he could not offer the better sacrifice for a covenant that actually could take human sins away. Moses prophesied that Jehovah God would raise up from the Israelites a prophet like Moses but far greater than Moses. (Deuteronomy 18:15-18) Jesus became

that prophet greater than Moses. Like Moses he became the mediator of a covenant, but a perfect mediator of a better covenant. "But now Jesus has obtained a more excellent public service, so that he is also the mediator of a correspondingly better covenant, which has been legally established upon better promises." (Hebrews 8:6, *NW*) "For there is one God, and one mediator between God and men, a man Christ Jesus, who gave himself a corresponding ransom for all—this is what is to be witnessed to at its own particular times." —1 Timothy 2:5, 6, *NW*.

⁶ Under the old Law covenant there was a priesthood in the Levite family of Aaron, with Aaron as high priest, and all the rest of the tribe of Levi were made temple servants of this Aaronic priesthood. These priests of the tribe of Levi were all sinful descendants of Adam and under the condemnation of death. Moreover, because they were under the Mosaic law and were condemned as violators of it, they were under the curse of the Law. The animals they sacrificed on the altar could not take away sins. So those priests could not individually continue in office forever, but died off and had to be replaced by new priests. Certainly, then, the old Law covenant could not make anything perfect, because of the weakness, imperfection and sinfulness of the human flesh contaminated by Adam's sin. So Jesus was made Jehovah's High Priest for a better ministry, not by being descended from the tribe of Levi and family of Aaron, but by Jehovah's oath at Psalm 110:4 concerning the priesthood like Melchizedek's. By his perfect sacrifice of himself he proved

---

6. How did Jesus become a better priest than Levite priests?

himself the satisfactory High Priest. The new
covenant needed just such a High Priest; he is
exactly suitable for persons brought into the new
covenant:

7 "(For there are indeed men that have become
priests without a sworn oath, but there is one
with an oath sworn by the one that said respecting him, 'Jehovah has sworn, and he will not feel
regret: "You are a priest forever," ') to that extent also Jesus has become the one given in pledge
of a better covenant. Furthermore, many had to
become priests in succession because of being pre-
vented by death from continuing as such, but he
because of continuing alive forever has his priesthood without any successors. Consequently he is
able also to save completely those who are approaching God through him, because he is always
alive to plead for them. For such a high priest
as this was suitable for us, one of loving-kindness,
guileless, undefiled, separated from the sinners,
and become higher than the heavens. He does not
need daily, as those high priests do, to offer up
sacrifices, first for his own sins and then for those
of the people: (for this he did once for all time
when he offered himself up;) for the Law appoints men high priests having weakness, but the
word of the sworn oath that came after the Law
appoints a Son, who is perfected forever."—Hebrews 7:21-28, *NW*.

8 By foretelling a new covenant with his chosen

---

7. How can Jesus be a priest forever? With what benefit to us?
8. How was the old covenant canceled? With what was
it replaced?

people Jehovah made the covenant of Moses' law old and he indicated that it was to pass away with the coming of the Mediator greater than Moses, and a High Priest greater than Aaron. The old Law covenant, however, foreshadowed the new. The natural Israelites had no reason to resent the taking away of the old Mosaic Law covenant. Why not? Because it is replaced by the new covenant with better promises based on a better mediatorial sacrifice, and it does lead to perfection. When the mediatorial sacrifice of Jesus was laid down by his death on the stake at Calvary, Jehovah God canceled the Law covenant and took it away and established the better new covenant. Jesus gave his flesh for the life of mankind: "By means of his flesh he abolished the hatred, the Law of commandments consisting in decrees, that he might create the two peoples [Jew and Gentile] in union with himself into one new man and make peace, and that he might fully reconcile both peoples in one body to God through the torture stake, because he had killed off the hatred by means of himself."—Ephesians 2:15, 16, NW.

⁹ Explaining further how God could forgive sins and remember them no more under the new covenant, the apostle writes of the abolishing of the Law covenant: "Furthermore, though you were dead in your trespasses and in the uncircumcised state of your flesh, God made you alive together with him. He kindly forgave us all our trespasses and blotted out the handwritten document against

9. To what did God nail the old covenant? With what effect?

us which consisted of decrees and which was in opposition to us [by condemning us as sinners and by dividing off Israelite from Gentile], and He has taken it out of the way by nailing it to the torture stake. . . . Therefore let no man judge you in eating and drinking or in respect of a feast day or of an observance of the new moon or of a sabbath, for those things are a shadow of the things to come, but the reality belongs to the Christ." (Colossians 2:13-17, *NW*) God canceled the old covenant of the Law as if by nailing it to Jesus' torture stake at Calvary.

[10] For the benefit specifically of the natural Israelites under the old covenant it was necessary for Jesus to die as a man accursed on the torture stake. By agreeing to the terms of the Law covenant and then failing to live up to its requirements, the natural Israelites came under the curse of the Law, something which never applied to the Gentiles not bound by that Law. Worse still, that Law was meant to be a tutor to lead them to Christ, Jehovah's anointed King, and yet they refused the leadings of the Law and rejected the permanent Heir of Jehovah's Kingdom covenant. So the curse descended upon them: "Cursed be he that confirmeth not all the words of this law to do them." (Deuteronomy 27:26) To remove this special curse from the Israelites, the Law-keeping innocent Jesus must not only die, but die on the stake like an accursed lawbreaker. "For all those who depend upon works of law are

---

10. Why was it necessary that Jesus' death be on a stake?

under a curse, for it is written: 'Accursed is every one that does not continue in all the things written in the scroll of the Law in order to do them.' Christ by purchase released us from the curse of the Law by becoming a curse instead of us, because it is written: 'Accursed is every man hanged upon a stake.' " (Galatians 3:10, 13, *NW*) Every natural Israelite believing on the impaled Jesus gets out from under that curse.

[11] Jehovah God announced that he would make the new covenant with a people, a Theocratic organization. The new covenant is not a personal covenant that some believing individual makes with God. No; but it is an organizational covenant. It is made through an individual, Christ Jesus the Mediator, but with an organization of people delivered by the Most High God. Jesus' sacrifice is the only sacrifice that puts the new covenant into force, and thus it is God's covenant made with them over Christ's sacrifice. Jehovah says to those in the covenant: "Gather yourselves unto me—ye my men of lovingkindness, who have solemnised my covenant over sacrifice." (Psalm 50:5, *Roth.*) The old covenant was made with the rescued nation of Israel, and through Moses its mediator God said to them: "Now then, if you will but heed my injunctions, and keep my covenant, you shall be my very own out of all the peoples (for all the earth is mine), and you shall be a kingdom of priests to me, and a holy nation." So the purpose of that Law covenant was to take out

---

11. With whom is the new covenant made? Through whom? Over what?

from among the worldly nations a people for God's name.—Exodus 19:5, 6, *AAT*.

[12] The purpose of the new covenant is to take out of the nations a people for Jehovah's name, a people on whom his name is called. The natural Israelites were given the first opportunity to enter into the new covenant, escaping from the curse of the old covenant through faith in the impaled Jesus Christ, the Mediator of the new covenant. Only a remnant of some thousands of natural Israelites did so, but not enough of them to make up the full number of people for Jehovah's name. For a week of years following Christ's appearing Jehovah extended the natural Jews the exclusive privilege, and then God sent Symeon Peter to convert the first Gentile to Christianity. "Symeon has related thoroughly how God for the first time turned his attention to the nations to take out of them a people for his name." (Acts 15:14, *NW*) All those taken into the new covenant, natural Jew and natural Gentile, were anointed with God's spirit and made spiritual Israelites. The natural Jews that did not believe proved they were not real Israelites: "for he is not a Jew that is one on the outside, nor is circumcision that which is on the outside upon the flesh. But he is a Jew that is one on the inside, and his circumcision is that of the heart by spirit, and not by a written code." (Romans 2:28, 29, *NW*) These spiritual Israelites constitute Jehovah's "very own out of all the peoples" and become a "kingdom of

12. What is its purpose? Who have been brought into it?

priests" and a "holy nation" to him. At the annual Memorial celebration of our Lord's evening meal, these rightly eat the bread and drink of the cup which Jesus said "means the new covenant by virtue of my blood".—1 Corinthians 11:25, NW.

[13] Moses ratified or inaugurated the old Law covenant at Mount Sinai, the mountain of God, when he sprinkled both the book of the Law and the people with the blood of the sacrificial animals. In behalf of the new covenant the Mediator Jesus ascended to heaven forty days after his resurrection from death and presented to God the value or merit of his earthly human sacrifice. Ten days after ascending, Jesus applied to his devoted followers on earth the benefit of the blood of his human sacrifice, manifesting this by pouring out upon them the holy spirit which he had received from God who accepted his sacrifice. Thus Christ Jesus on the heavenly mountain of God inaugurated the new covenant toward his faithful disciples on that day of Pentecost. (Exodus 24:1-8; Hebrews 9:15-20; Acts 2:1-18) Today, after nineteen centuries of operation, the new covenant is nearing its end in full success, taking out the full number of people for Jehovah's name from among all the nations. From the least of these to the greatest of these, they "know Jehovah", whom to know means everlasting life through Jesus Christ, the Mediator whom he sent forth.—Jeremiah 31:34, ASV.

---

13. When and how was the new covenant inaugurated? Toward whom?

CHAPTER XI

THE WAY TO HEAVENLY LIFE

THE way to life in heaven God opened up by Jesus Christ. That was why Jesus could say to the inquiring Jewish ruler Nicodemus: "No man has ascended into heaven but he that descended from heaven, the Son of man." At the moment that Jesus died a miracle occurred; the curtain separating the first compartment or "holy" of the temple from the second compartment, the "most holy", was torn from top to bottom. The most holy represented heaven itself, and this rending of the curtain was a symbol that till Jesus' death the way from earth to heaven had not been opened: "Thus the holy spirit makes it plain that the way into the holy place had not yet been made manifest while the first tent was standing." "For Christ entered, not into a holy place made with hands which is a copy of the reality, but into heaven itself, now to appear before the person of God for us." (Hebrews 9:8, 24, NW) Building up confidence on this fulfilled prerequisite, the apostle says: "Therefore, brothers, since we have boldness for the way of entry into the holy place by the blood of Jesus, which he inaugurated for us as a new and living way through the curtain, that is, his flesh, and since

1. By whom and when was the way from earth into heaven opened?

113

we have a great priest over the house of God, let us approach with sincere hearts in the full assurance of faith." (Hebrews 10:19-22, *NW*) With such confidence we can take up this study of the ones who go to heaven.

[2] Before Jesus Christ began preaching, "The kingdom of heaven is at hand," no creature on earth had basis for hoping to go to heaven and live there as a spirit person. No creature from earth could precede Jesus Christ into heaven. As God's High Priest, he must be the first to enter, the forerunner. Then only could his followers have hope of following him there. "This hope we have as an anchor for the soul, both sure and firm, and it enters in within the curtain, where a forerunner has entered in our behalf, Jesus, who has become a high priest after the likeness of Melchizedek forever."—Hebrews 6:19, 20, *NW*.

[3] What requirements must we meet to walk in the way that leads to heavenly life? Speaking to Nicodemus one night, Jesus set out the general requirements: "Unless anyone is born again, he cannot see the kingdom of God." Man has already been born human, fleshly, earthly, bearing the image of Adam. What kind of birth must this second birth be to put him into God's heavenly kingdom? Not another human birth, Jesus explained to Nicodemus: "Unless anyone is born from water and spirit, he cannot enter into the kingdom of God. What has been born from the flesh is flesh, and what has been born from the spirit

2. Why could none precede Christ Jesus into heaven?
3. What kind of birth is needed to enter heaven?

is spirit." (John 3:3, 5, 6, *NW*) It must be a spiritual birth, a birth by God's spirit to become his spiritual sons. Parents of flesh and blood have nothing to do with these sons of God, for they are "born not from blood or from a fleshly will or from man's will, but from God".—John 1:13, *NW*.

⁴ Not only God's spirit or invisible active force performs a part in this birth to heavenly life, but also what Jesus called "water" plays its part first. Not the water of baptism, although heirs of heaven must copy their Forerunner and be immersed in water; but the water of the truth. Water has cleansing, purifying power, and so does the word of truth: "You have purified your souls by your obedience to the truth." "The Christ also loved the congregation and delivered up himself for it, that he might sanctify it, cleansing it with the bath of water by means of the word." "Sanctify them by means of the truth; your word is truth." —1 Peter 1:22 and Ephesians 5:25, 26 and John 17:17, *NW*.

⁵ The person favored with the heavenly opportunity must first hear the truth concerning the only true God and Jesus Christ whom he sent forth. True knowledge is the foundation for the real faith that leads to right works. God's Word strictly tells us that "without faith it is impossible to win his good pleasure, for he that approaches God must believe that he is and that he becomes the rewarder of those earnestly seeking

---

4. Besides spirit, by means of what else must one be born?
5. How is birth by such water accomplished?

him". (Hebrews 11:6, *NW*) A person's faith is tested by the truth as to whether he will believe, accept and apply it. The experience of the natural Jews with the Law of Moses for fifteen centuries illustrates that by our own works of self-righteousness we cannot be justified with God. We can be declared righteous by God only by our faith in him together with his Son Jesus Christ, the sin-removing Lamb of God. So the faith-inspiring truth plays an initial part in a person's being born for entry into God's kingdom. In harmony with that, those who are born again are told: "Because he willed it, he brought us forth by the word of truth, for us to be a certain firstfruits of his creatures." (James 1:18, *NW*) "For you have been given a new birth, not by corruptible, but by incorruptible reproductive seed, through the word of the living and enduring God. ' . . . the word spoken by Jehovah endures forever'. Well, this is the 'word spoken', this which has been declared to you as good news."—1 Peter 1:23-25, *NW*.

⁶ Having now heard the truth, how does a person prove by his deeds that he accepts it and has faith in God and his Christ? When Jesus had preached the truth to those who were to become his disciples, how did he prove their faith? By saying to them: "Be my follower." Those men were already members of the Jewish nation, a people already dedicated to Jehovah God under the terms of the Law covenant by Moses. But now that was

---

6. How did Jesus show what dedication one must make and symbolize?

not enough. They must dedicate or devote themselves to following Jesus the rest of their days.
That meant copying him as their Leader. He, too,
was born under the Law and was a member of the
dedicated nation. Yet at thirty years of age he
personally dedicated himself to God to carry out
the realities which the Law covenant foreshadowed. So he presented himself to obey God's will
now due to be revealed; and he fulfilled the prophecy: "Then I said, 'Look! I am come (in the roll
of the book it is written about me) to do your will,
O God.'" (Hebrews 10:7, *NW;* Psalm 40:7, 8) It
was like a burial of himself into God's will. To
symbolize his becoming dead to his own will,
Jesus insisted upon being submerged under the
waters of the Jordan river by God's prophet, John
the Baptist. As he was thus immersed, he was
praying, not confessing any sins, for he had none.
His baptism was not for the forgiveness of sins,
but was for symbolizing his dedication of himself
to do God's will. To the end of his earthly days his
prayer was: "Not as I will, but as you will."
—Matthew 26:39, *NW.*

⁷ To prove faith in the word of truth, the hearer
must now become Christ's follower, copying him
by making an unconditional, irrevocable presen-
tation of himself to God to do the divine will. He
does this with full faith in God's Son as his ransom and as his sole means of gaining righteousness from God. Does he then get baptized in water to symbolize this dedication of himself to

7. So, to prove faith in the word of truth, what does
one do?

God's sacred service? Yes, in imitation of Jesus and in obedience to his command, he gets bap-

tized at the earliest opportunity, as believers on the day of Pentecost did and as Saul of Tarsus and Cornelius did.—Acts 2:41; 9:18; 10:46-48.

⁸ Where, now, does being born from spirit come in? Just as the water from which a believer is born is not a person, neither is the spirit. But the believer is born from God and by means of his spirit or life-giving active force. When the perfect man Jesus was baptized in water, God brought him forth or begot him as his spiritual son and acknowledged him with words which Jesus as well as John the Baptist heard: "You are my Son, the beloved; I have approved you." (Luke 3:21, 22, *NW*) He was now begotten from God by means of His spirit, and there was a manifestation of that spiritual force in the form of a dove. He was now a spiritual son of God and was now definitely on his way back to heaven where he had been God's only-begotten spirit Son. It was as a newly

8. How is a believer born from spirit, as illustrated by Jesus?

begotten spiritual Son that he was also anointed with God's spirit and so became the Messiah or Anointed One. At Nazareth he declared this fact, saying: "Jehovah's spirit is upon me, because he anointed me."—Luke 4:16-18, *NW*.

⁹ That water baptism of Jesus was only a symbol. It was not the main baptism for him. He must undergo a baptism into death, by which he proved his complete integrity, obedience and faithfulness to God to the limit and by which also he laid down his human life as a ransom sacrifice for condemned mankind. Three years after his water baptism he said: "I have a baptism with which to be baptized, and how I am being distressed until it is finished!" (Luke 12:50, *NW*) A half year later it was finished in his death at Calvary. But a person baptized is raised up to a future course of life, and likewise Jesus was raised up to life, but not to human life again. He had forever sacrificed that in behalf of mankind. If he had taken it back on the third day after dying, he would have sacrificed it for only three days, and mankind would not be entitled to enjoy perfect human life forever. But at Jordan river he had been begotten of God to be a spiritual Son and had heavenly promises set before him. So when he was raised from death he was resurrected an immortal spirit Son of God. That is directly stated: "Christ died once for all time concerning sins, a righteous person for unrighteous ones, that he might lead you to God, he being put to death

9. What main baptism did Jesus undergo? How was he raised from it?

in the flesh, but being made alive in the spirit."
(1 Peter 3:18, *NW*) Because his disciples could
not see spiritual creatures, the resurrected Jesus
manifested himself to them in flesh, materializing
a human body for each occasion, just as the spirit
angels did on his resurrection day and his day
of ascension to heaven.

[10] Can believers be baptized into Christ's death
and be resurrected like him to heavenly life? Yes.
Jesus told his disciples they could, saying: "The
cup I am drinking you will drink, and with the
baptism with which I am being baptized you will
be baptized." (Mark 10:38, 39, *NW*) This means
they must sacrifice their human lives in God's
service, forever giving up the prospect of living
as human creatures perfected in the righteous
new world. That they may be counted as laying
down such perfect human life privileges, the right
to perfect human life which Jesus by his sacrifice
bought for them is counted to them because of
their faith in him as Ransomer. God's reckoning
of human perfection to them, his imputing of
righteousness in the flesh to them, is their justification in his sight. It is their being declared
righteous by him through his Son, who lived a
perfectly righteous human life. Persons thus justified or declared righteous in order to be sacrificed
with Christ have hope of heavenly glory: "Therefore, now that we have been declared righteous
as a result of faith, let us enjoy peace with God
through our Lord Jesus Christ, through whom
also we have gained our approach by faith into

---

10. Can believers be thus baptized and raised? How?

this undeserved kindness in which we now stand, and let us exult, based on hope of the glory of God. Much more, therefore, since we have been declared righteous now by his blood, shall we be saved through him from wrath."—Romans 5:1, 2, 9, *NW*.

[11] When Jesus was accepted for sacrifice at his baptism in water he was begotten to heavenly life by God's spirit and was from then on counted as his spiritual Son. At his resurrection from death he was perfected as a spirit creature and was clothed upon with deathlessness, immortality. When God justifies or declares any believers in Jesus Christ righteous he counts such justified believers acceptable for the sacrifice of all things human and earthly. Then it is that God begets them by his spirit, adopting them as his spiritual sons. They are now in the way to heavenly life and are a new creation: "Consequently, if anyone is in union with Christ, he is a new creation; the old things passed away, look! new things have come into existence." (2 Corinthians 5:17, *NW*) They do not yet have immortality, but have a hope of it set before them and so seek it as a prize: "everlasting life to those who are seeking glory and honor and incorruptibleness by endurance in work that is good." (Romans 2:7, *NW*) To gain that incorruptible prize they must be loyal to God even at the cost of their human lives. The deathless resurrected Jesus encourages them to complete integrity: "Prove yourselves faithful even with the danger of death, and I will give you

11. By God's begettal what are they now? What hope have they?

the crown of life." (Revelation 2:10, *NW*) They do not know what it is to be a spirit or what they will be like in the resurrection, but they do know they are now God's adopted sons, "born from water and spirit." With confidence they say: "Now we are children of God, but as yet it has not been made manifest what we shall be. We do know that whenever he is made manifest we shall be like him, because we shall see him just as he is." —1 John 3:2, *NW*.

¹² When believers are justified or declared righteous for their faith and by means of Jesus' blood, they are then devoted to sacrifice and their baptism into his death begins. To such ones the apostle writes: "Do you not know that all of us who were baptized into Christ Jesus were baptized into his death? Therefore we were buried with him through our baptism into his death, in order that, just as Christ was raised up from the dead through the glory of the Father, we also should likewise walk in a newness of life. For if we have become united with him in the likeness of his death, we shall certainly also be united with him in the likeness of his resurrection; . . . if we have died with Christ, we believe that we shall also live with him. For we know that Christ, now that he has been raised up from the dead, dies no more; death is master over him no more." (Romans 6:3-9, *NW*) So since Jesus' resurrection as a glorious spirit to heavenly life he is immortal, incorruptible. By being raised from death in the

---

12. When does baptism into death begin? To what are they raised?

likeness of his resurrection, his faithful followers gain immortality. Jesus slept in death in the tomb for three days. When the baptism of his followers into his death is fully carried out, they too sleep in death and must await his return in glory, his coming in his kingdom. Then he raises them, but not to the human life which they sacrificed. No; they are changed to spirit, and they enter into heavenly life with him. Explaining why they must be changed and to what, the apostle writes:

[13] "Flesh and blood cannot inherit God's kingdom, neither does corruption inherit incorruption. Look! I tell you a sacred secret: We shall not all fall asleep in death, but we shall all be changed, in a moment, in the twinkling of an eye, during the last trumpet. For the trumpet will sound, and the dead will be raised up incorruptible, and we shall be changed. For this which is corruptible must put on incorruption, and this which is mortal must put on immortality. But when this which is corruptible puts on incorruption and this which is mortal puts on immortality, then the saying will take place that is written: 'Death is swallowed up forever.' "—1 Corinthians 15:50-54, NW.

[14] The Christian remnant who die faithful after his return or during his second presence do not need to sleep on in death waiting for his second coming. With him invisibly present, they are changed instantly after dying as humans to immortal life above.

---

13. How does the apostle explain it at 1 Corinthians 15:50-54?
14. Who do not fall asleep at death? Why?

CHAPTER XII

THEOCRATIC ORGANIZATION

A SCANNING of the starry heavens by night should convince an intelligent person that the apostle's statement to the Christian congregation is true: "God is a God, not of disorder, but of peace." He should appreciate the practical application which the apostle makes of that principle to the congregation, saying: "Let all things take place decently and by arrangement." That requires organization according to the God of peace, Theocratic organization, for "theocratic" means "ruled by God".—1 Corinthians 14:33, 40, NW.

[2] The congregation of Christ's justified followers who are in the way to heavenly life is a Theocratic organization. The word "organization" comes from the Greek word used at James 1:4 (NW): "Let endurance have its work complete," namely, the word "ergon", which means "work" or "deed". The electrical term erg is taken from that word and means a unit of work or energy. Just as an organ is an instrument with which to accomplish a particular work or do a thing, whether it be an organ in our human body or be a musical instrument which an organist plays to produce har-

---

1. Why does the congregation require organization? What kind?
2. From what is the word *organization* drawn? What is God's organization?

monious, melodious sounds, just so an organization is an arrangement with which to work or do a deed. God's organization is an orderly, well-connected arrangement of his devoted, obedient creatures in order for them to work together toward a common end and in harmony with his purpose, doing so in peace and oneness, without clash or conflict, with efficiency and a comfortable state of heart and mind. God's organization is at one with itself. All its members are at one with its great Organizer, Jehovah God, and at one with their obedient fellow members. God's perfect wisdom made his holy universal organization that way.

[3] The organization of the Christian congregation is Theocratic, because God is its organizer and is its top director at all times. It operates Theocratically, because it functions by taking orders from God down through his Son Jesus Christ, and not up from the organization members below. Nineteen centuries ago God by his Son Jesus Christ set up this Theocratic organization among men. Being on earth, it is an organization visible to men. But as it is composed of those begotten by God to heavenly life it is a part of Jehovah's great universal organization which he governs. Being Theocratic, it is not nationalistic nor infected with any kind of national politics, whether democratic, communistic, Nazi, fascistic, imperialistic, or otherwise. Though drawn from all nations, its members obey the divine command to

---

3. How is the congregation Theocratic as to organization?

keep on seeking first God's kingdom and his righteousness.—Matthew 6:33.

[4] Jehovah the great Theocrat made his obedient Son Jesus Christ the Head member of the new Theocratic organization. "He also subjected all things under his feet, and made him head over all things to the congregation, which is his body." (Ephesians 1:22, 23, NW) When he likens those of the congregation under Jesus the Head to a human body, it shows that the true congregation must be organized Theocratically, for God's creation of the perfect human body is a marvelous organization, with many parts, all performing their special functions and yet all knit together in one harmonious whole. When a justified believer is baptized into the "body of Christ" and so becomes a member of the Theocratic organization, he comes under Christ Jesus the Head and so comes under certain responsibilities and cannot act independently of the one whom God has made Head of the organization to direct it. He must submit himself to organization instructions, "holding fast to the head, to the one from whom all the body, being supplied and harmoniously joined together by means of its joints and ligaments, goes on growing with the growth which God gives."—Colossians 2:19, NW.

[5] Now as the perfect human body of Jesus had just so many members to make it complete, no more, no less, so the complete "body of Christ",

---

4. Who was made its Head? How does a member act Theocratically?
5. How was the number of its members foretold and disclosed?

which is the congregation, has a perfect number of members, foreordained by the Theocratic Creator, Jehovah God. Before Christ's time he left their number unrevealed and hence likened the members to the stars of heaven and the sands of the seashore which no man can number. But through Christ Jesus he at last revealed their number to be 144,000, and likened them to the twelve tribes of ancient Israel, allowing 12,000 to each tribe of spiritual Israel. (Genesis 22:16-18; Revelation 7:1-8) Their being pictured as divided into twelve tribes, with no partiality to any tribe as to numbers, symbolizes that the Theocratic congregation is completely organized in a well-balanced way. "And I saw," says the apostle John, "and look! the Lamb standing upon the mount Zion, and with him a hundred and forty-four thousand having his name and the name of his Father written on their foreheads. . . . And they are singing as if a new song . . . and no one was able to master that song but the hundred and forty-four thousand, who have been purchased from the earth." With the Lamb Jesus Christ they total one and a hundred forty-four thousand, and they are all the creatures that are finally taken from earth to heaven. "These are the ones that keep following the Lamb no matter where he goes. These were purchased from among mankind as a firstfruits to God and to the Lamb." —Revelation 14:1-4, *NW*.

⁶ Their being symbolized as of twelve tribes

---

6. How do the numbers of their tribes and foundations agree?

agrees with their resting upon the twelve prophet-ic apostles of the Lamb as foundation stones. "You . . . are members of the household of God, and you have been built up upon the foundation of the apostles and prophets, while Christ Jesus himself is the foundation cornerstone. In union with him the whole building, being harmoniously joined to-gether, is growing into a holy temple for Jehovah. In union with him you, too, are being built up together into a place for God to inhabit by spirit." (Ephesians 2:19-22, *NW*) "And he showed me the holy city Jerusalem coming down out of heav-en from God . . . The wall of the city also had twelve foundation stones, and on them the twelve names of the twelve apostles of the Lamb."—Rev-elation 21:10-14, *NW*.

⁷ Jesus Christ the Head chose his twelve apos-tles, appointed them to positions and delegated to them special powers in the organization. They, to-gether with the older brothers in the congrega-tion at Jerusalem, formed a visible presiding or governing body for the entire congregation throughout the earth during the first century of its existence. (Acts 15:6-23) Jesus Christ only is the congregation's Head under God and he left no apostle or any other man on earth as his vice-gerent or vicar to act as a totalitarian ruler to the congregation.

⁸ While Jesus the only Head is invisible, he is not powerless or inoperative toward his congrega-

---

7. Who were the governing body in the first century?
8. Who is liaison officer? What are the basic organiza-tion instructions of the congregation world-wide?

tion on earth. He is the Theocratic liaison officer between all members and all local groups of the congregation all over the earth. We still have with us apostles and older brothers of the congregation of the first century in their inspired writings of the Christian Greek Scriptures. But the inspired Scriptures of God's *complete* Bible form the basic Theocratic organization instructions for the congregation at all times until its glorification in heaven.

⁹ Appointments of official servants in the congregation are from the Theocratic Creator and through Christ Jesus. Servants must be put in position under the guiding influence of God's spirit of holiness and must have the qualifications laid down in God's Word. So the appointments are not by a democratic or popular election, as when the people of Rome used to vote to elect a pope, nor by a political government of this world. But appointments are through the Theocratic organization from the Top down.—1 Corinthians 12:18, 28.

¹⁰ Those appointed to positions are older brothers, older, not in physical age, but in Christian spiritual growth. The apostle Peter said: "I, too, am an older man like them." (1 Peter 5:1, *NW*) The apostle Paul and the Levite Barnabas were appointed under the power of the holy spirit to go out on missionary work, establishing congregations of believers in new territories. In such new congregations they appointed older men to the

9. How are appointments of official servants made?
10. Who are appointed to office? Is there an ordination service?

various congregational offices that needed to be filled: "They appointed older men to office for them in the congregation and, offering prayer with fastings, they committed them to Jehovah in whom they had become believers." (Acts 13:2-4 and 14:23, *NW*) The inspired Scriptures give no description or instructions concerning any ordination. So all the lengthy, pompous, formalistic, ritualistic ceremonies of ordination in Christendom's religious systems are mere inventions of men, human traditions, and unscriptural. They are not Theocratic and so are not recognized by God.

[11] The Scriptures give instructions for the appointment of overseers and ministerial servants to assist them. Timothy, a young man physically but a mature person spiritually, was made an overseer by the laying on of the hands of Paul and possibly the body of older men with him. (Acts 16:1-3; 1 Timothy 4:14; 2 Timothy 1:6) The apostle Paul, a member of the governing body of that century, told his assistant Timothy what requirements the ones he appointed to service in the congregation must meet in order to have apostolic or Theocratic approval. "The overseer [*e·pis'ko·pos,* Greek] should therefore be irreprehensible, . . . not a newly converted man, for fear that he might get puffed up with pride and fall into the judgment passed upon the Devil. . . . Ministerial servants [*di·a'ko·noi,* Greek] should likewise be serious, . . . let these be tested as to fitness first, then let them serve as ministers [*di·a·ko·nein',*

---

11. What requirements must overseers and ministerial servants meet?

Greek verb], as they are free from accusation. Let ministerial servants be husbands of one wife, presiding in a right manner over children and their own households. For the men who minister in a right manner are acquiring for themselves a right standing and great freeness of speech in the faith in connection with Christ Jesus."—1 Timothy 3:1-10, 12, 13, NW.

¹² Titus, a Gentile believer evidently much younger than Paul, was made an overseer and was instructed by the apostle: "For this reason I left you in Crete, that you might correct the things that were defective and might make appointments of older men in city after city, as I gave you orders, if there is any man free from accusation, a husband of one wife, having believing children that were not under a charge of debauchery nor unruly. For an overseer [e·pis'-ko·pos] must be free from accusation as God's steward, . . . able both to exhort by the teaching that is healthful and to reprove those who contradict." (Titus 1:5-9, NW) No instructions as to any ordination ceremony are given.

¹³ En route to Jerusalem Paul, when near Ephesus, "called for the older men of the congregation" and exhorted them: "Pay attention to yourselves and to all the flock, among which the holy spirit has appointed you overseers [e·pis·ko'pous], to

12. Did instructions include an ordination ceremony for an overseer?
13. How many overseers were appointed to a congregation? How many ministerial assistants? How was the appointing done?

shepherd the congregation of God, which he purchased with the blood of his own [Son]." This record, at Acts 20:17-28 (*NW*), shows that there were a number of overseers in the congregation of Ephesus, and not just one so-called "bishop" superintending a so-called "episcopal diocese" with a lot of lesser clergymen. Besides having a number of overseers, a local congregation could have a number of ministerial servants, or assistants. In assigning seven men to look after certain material needs of the local flock, the congregation at Jerusalem indicated their choice of seven, but the apostles did the final appointing of the recommended men to service: "They placed them before the apostles, and after having prayed these laid their hands upon them."—Acts 6:2-6, *NW*.

[14] Scripturally examined, the Christian congregation was set up as a Theocratic organization and it is regulated and operated Theocratically from the great Universal Sovereign Jehovah God and through the congregational Head Jesus Christ down. Those believers today who discern the true Christian congregation and who have the Scriptural evidences that they are members of it strive more and more to have the congregation conducted Theocratically in all the earth. God's guiding spirit helps them to that end.

---

14. How do we seek to have the congregation conducted now? Why?

CHAPTER XIII

HOW TO BECOME
A PREACHER OF GOOD NEWS

BEING a real preacher of good news is the work of greatest importance and good on earth today. The bogus man-made preachers of religious sects have misrepresented the ministry of preaching and have brought scorn, ridicule and reproach upon it. The true preachers of good news are made and sent forth by Jehovah God, the Giver of every good gift and every perfect present.

[2] The apostle Paul was ridiculed and thought foolish and weak for being a preacher of the good news about Jesus Christ who had died on a torture stake. But the superiority of preaching over everything else on earth as to vital importance can be judged by this statement: "The speech about the torture stake is foolishness to those who are perishing, but to us who are being saved it is God's power. . . . Did not God make the wisdom of the world foolish? For since, in the wisdom of God, the world through its wisdom did not get to know God, God saw good through the foolishness of what is preached to save those believing. For both the Jews ask for signs and the

---

1, 2. (a) What work on earth is of greatest importance and good? (b) Who makes and sends such ones as do this work?

Greeks look for wisdom; but we preach Christ impaled, to the Jews a cause for falling but to the nations foolishness; however, to those who are the called, both Jews and Greeks, Christ the power of God and the wisdom of God. Because a foolish thing of God is wiser than men, and a weak thing of God is stronger than men."—1 Corinthians 1:18-25, *NW*.

³ Now, more so than at any other time since Pentecost A.D. 33, is the day in which to come to know Jehovah God and to call upon his name for rescue from impending doom. It is now most urgent for people to hear the good news about Jehovah's purpose through Jesus Christ. But if they are to hear this life-giving good news it is necessary for Jehovah to raise up his preachers and send them out into the field of activity. "For 'everyone that calls upon the name of Jehovah will be saved'. However, how will they call upon him in whom they have not put faith? How, in turn, will they put faith in him of whom they have not heard? How, in turn, will they hear without someone to preach? How, in turn, will they preach unless they have been sent forth? Just as it is written: 'How beautiful are the feet of those who declare good news of good things!'" (Romans 10:13-15, *NW*) Realizing the criticalness of the time and the need of the people who long for righteousness and deliverance, Jehovah God in his mercy has raised up his preachers and

---

3. (a) In this critical time on whose name must people call? (b) What progressive steps must be taken to help them do so?

moved their feet to go to all the nations and declare the good news for all people to hear. To the ones who hear and believe it, their coming is beautiful, oh, "how beautiful!"

[4] To be a preacher of good news is to follow and copy Messiah the Prince. Jesus Christ is the model for all of God's true preachers since. He was not a man-made preacher, attending a theological seminary to learn religious traditions and receiving an ordination from sectarian religious leaders. Up till thirty years of age he was not attending a theological seminary or rabbinical school but was a carpenter. At God's appointed time for Messiah the Prince to appear he left carpentry forever and came to John the Baptist to begin doing God's will then due to be carried out. He was baptized beneath Jordan's waters to symbolize his devoting of himself to do that divine will. God's will was for Jesus to be a preacher the rest of his days on earth. So then and there God appointed and consecrated Jesus to be a preacher. How? When Jesus came up out of the baptismal waters, God poured out his holy spirit upon him and thus anointed him with it. The manifestation of the spirit under the visible form of a dove was the initial evidence of it. When Jesus returned to Nazareth where he was brought up, it was not as a carpenter, but as a preacher made by the Most High God. He had already begun performing miracles and preaching, "The kingdom of the heavens has drawn near." Now

4. Who is the model for all preachers? How was he made such?

he would preach to his own townspeople and show them his commission from God to do so.

⁵ "On the sabbath day he entered into the synagogue, and he stood up to read aloud. So the scroll of the prophet Isaiah was handed him, and he opened the scroll and found the place where it was written, 'Jehovah's spirit is upon me, because he anointed me to declare good news to the poor, he sent me forth to preach a release to the captives and a recovery of sight to the blind, to send the crushed ones away with a release, to preach Jehovah's acceptable year.' With that he rolled up the scroll, handed it back to the attendant and sat down; and the eyes of all in the synagogue were intently fixed upon him. Then he started to say to them: 'Today this scripture that you just heard is fulfilled.' "—Luke 4:16-21, *NW*.

⁶ The commission and ordination of Jesus, the Leader of all Christian preachers, was from Jehovah God. There was no religious ceremony connected with it. Jesus dedicated himself to do God's will and was immersed in water to symbolize this, and God accepted his self-dedication and anointed him with the holy spirit. God anointed him, not only to be Messiah the Prince, the Permanent Heir of the Kingdom covenant, but also to be a preacher, declaring the good news of God's kingdom. Jesus found his divine commission recorded in the Holy Scriptures, which he quoted (Isaiah

5. How did he show the people of Nazareth his commission?
6. How did God ordain him? Where did He state his commission?

61:1, 2), and he also had the evidence that Jehovah's spirit was upon him and was operating through him in his ministry as a preacher.

[7] What is true of the Leader and Exemplar is true also of his disciples or followers. True Christian preachers who follow and imitate their Master Jesus need no university, college or seminary schooling, nor is any degree, title, diploma or ceremonious ordination by clergy operators of a theological seminary required by them. Religious clergymen have all such impressive things, but not one has fulfilled God's requirements for becoming one of His ordained, anointed preachers. Compared with the religious clergy of his day, Jesus was what they call a "lay preacher". But he was really God's ordained preacher, and they were not.

[8] According to Jesus' example, then, what is required is for the believer to dedicate himself unconditionally to God to do the divine will. The believer must do this with full faith in Jesus Christ as the ransom sacrifice by which his sins against God can be canceled and forgiven. This dedication of himself he properly symbolizes by being immersed in water. Once made, that dedication holds and is beyond recall; it binds the believer forever to do God's will. God's will is that, to make good his salvation to everlasting life, the believer must be a preacher in this world. "For if you publicly

---

7. What worldly requirements do real preachers not need? Why?
8. What must a believer do first to become a preacher?

declare that 'word in your mouth', that Jesus is Lord, and exercise faith in your heart that God raised him up from the dead, you will be saved. For with the heart one exercises faith for righteousness, but with the mouth one makes public declaration for salvation."—Romans 10:9, 10, *NW*.

⁹ The believers whom Jehovah God accepts for sacrifice, for baptism into Christ's death, he declares to be righteous for having faith in Jesus' blood. The faithful apostles and other disciples of Jesus became justified in that way. (Romans 5:1, 9; 3:24-30) When Jesus started the annual Memorial supper with his faithful apostles, he said to them: "You are the ones that have stuck with me in my trials; and I make a covenant with you, just as my Father has made a covenant with me, for a kingdom, that you may eat and drink at my table in my kingdom, and sit on thrones to judge the twelve tribes of Israel." (Luke 22:28-30, *NW*) On the day of Pentecost, ten days after Jesus' ascension to heaven, the holy spirit which Jesus received from Jehovah God he poured out upon his true followers on earth. They were thus anointed with this spirit, not only to be heirs with Jesus of the Kingdom covenant, but also to be preachers of the good news on earth. They did preach at once, from a private home, and about three thousand people believed the message, dedicating themselves to God through Christ. These were baptized, received the anointing of the holy spirit and took up preaching.—Acts 2:1-47.

---

9. How were those Jews accepted for sacrifice made preachers?

[10] Three and a half years later the apostle Peter preached at a private home to those who were the first uncircumcised Gentiles to believe the message and find acceptance with Jehovah God. While Peter was preaching to those Gentiles at the home of Cornelius, God through the glorified Jesus poured out the holy spirit upon those Gentile believers. At once they began preaching, in miraculously bestowed foreign tongues. In the case of these first Gentile believers their baptism in water followed their being anointed with the spirit and ordained to preach. Just the same, their water baptism followed the thing which it symbolized, namely, their believing the message and dedicating themselves to God through the righteousness of Jesus Christ.—Acts 10:1-48.

[11] Proving that it is God through Jesus that ordains and anoints his consecrated preachers, 2 Corinthians 1:21, 22 (NW) says: "But he who guarantees that you and we belong to Christ and he who has anointed us is God. He has also put his seal upon us and has given us the token of what is to come, that is, the spirit, in our hearts." That spirit or active force of God is an instructive, enlightening force that opens up the Scriptures to the preachers and also guides and strengthens them to proclaim the truth. The apostle John makes that point: "And you have an anointing from the holy one; all of you have knowledge. I write you, not because you do not know the truth,

_____

10. How were the first Gentile believers made preachers?
11. Who anoints preachers? What does his spirit do for them?

but because you know it, and because no lie originates with the truth. These things I write you about those who are trying to mislead you. And as for you, the anointing that you received from him remains in you, and you do not need anyone to be teaching you; but, as the anointing from him is teaching you about all things, and is true and is no lie, and just as it has taught you, remain in union with him." (1 John 2:20, 21, 26, 27, NW) They must be faithful, fearless preachers of the truth before they can gain the covenanted Kingdom.

[12] Before they were given the divine appointment to announce his message they had to come to a knowledge of the truth, to know what to announce. Now that they have been ordained by God, they must more diligently than ever study God's Word under the guidance of his spirit of truth in order to learn and preach the full counsel of God, advancing the education of their listeners with the advancement of the truth. Since the ones anointed with the spirit are heirs of the heavenly kingdom jointly with Christ Jesus, they, like him, must fulfill the divine requirement of kings of Israel. They must study God's Word and abide by it, adding no contradictory doctrines to it nor taking away any of its truths. (Deuteronomy 17:18-20) This is very necessary to the saving of the preachers themselves as well as the saving of those hearing them. "Continue applying yourself to public reading, to exhortation, to teach-

---

12. What are anointed preachers required to study? Why so?

ing. Pay constant attention to yourself and to your teaching. Stay by these things, for by doing this you will save both yourself and those who listen to you."—1 Timothy 4:13, 16, *NW*.

 ¹³ But where are the congregation and place of preaching of these Scripturally ordained minis-

ters? The correct answer can be gained by answering the question, Where were Jesus' congregation and his place of preaching? Not at some fixed building with steeple and bells and pulpit and the same old paying audience, who had to come there if they wanted to hear preaching. Jesus' congregation was the "lost sheep of the house of Israel" to whom God sent him forth. Before leaving his disciples for heaven he made the world's population their congregation, saying: "Go therefore and make disciples of people of all the nations,

---

13. Where were Jesus' congregation and place of preaching?

baptizing them in the name of the Father and of
the Son and of the holy spirit, teaching them to
observe all the things I have commanded you."
(Matthew 15:24 and 28:19, 20, *NW*) Jesus went
out to the people with God's message. He went
not only to the synagogues and temple, where he
accepted invitations to preach to the crowds, but
for a large part to the homes of the people. All
comers to him he considered his congregation,
also all people with whom he came in touch,
whether singly or in groups. Anywhere and
everywhere he preached, by wellside, seaside,
mountainside, in the lonely wilderness, in popu-
lous city streets, in public temple and synagogue
and in private home. And he never embarrassed
his audience with holding out a money-itching
palm or passing the collection plate under their
noses.

[14] Jesus' example shows where God's organized
preachers of good news are to find their congregation today. They must bring increase of fruitage
to God and must expand their congregation. This
they do largely or for most of the time by going
daily to the private homes of all people, regardless of religion, race, color, occupation or station
in life, political persuasion, or language. Paul, who
copied Jesus, did so: "I did not hold back from
telling you any of the things that were profitable
nor from teaching you publicly and from house
to house. But I thoroughly bore witness both to

14. How must preachers expand their congregation, as
Paul showed?

Jews and to Greeks about repentance toward God and faith in our Lord Jesus."—Acts 20:20, 21, *NW*.

[15] There is world-wide need for such true preachers of good news today. Delivering his prophecy on the sign of the end of this wicked system of things, Jesus said: "Nation will rise against nation and kingdom against kingdom, . . . And this good news of the kingdom will be preached in all the inhabited earth for the purpose of a witness to all the nations, and then the accomplished end will come." (Matthew 24:7, 14, *NW*) Many persons of good-will who hear and believe are devoting themselves to do God's will. Whereas God may not *anoint* these with his spirit because he does not call them to be joint heirs with Jesus of the heavenly kingdom, yet they must be God's preachers of good news. They vowed to do his will, and his will for this most critical time is that the Kingdom good news be preached. His command to all those dedicating themselves to do His will constitutes the ordination of such persons of good-will. He backs them up with his spirit or active force, just as he put his spirit upon his prophets and witnesses before the anointing of Jesus, our model Preacher.

---

15. (a) Why is there world-wide need for preachers now? (b) How are believing persons of good-will now ordained to preach?

CHAPTER XIV

MARRIAGE
AMONG THE HEIRS OF LIFE

MARRIAGE was the means by which Jehovah God the Creator purposed that our earth should be peopled. He himself performed the first marriage by creating the first woman and bringing her to the man Adam with whose rib as a base God had made her. He put them together, and, says Jesus, "what God has yoked together let no man put apart." (Matthew 19:6, NW) Approving the marriage and stating its purpose, "God created Man in his image, in the image of God created he him; male and female created he them. And God blessed them; and God said to them, Be fruitful and multiply, and fill the earth, and subdue it." When the earth's population was reduced to only four men and four women by the global flood, and these came out of the ark of their salvation, "God blessed Noah and his sons, and said to them, Be fruitful and multiply, and fill the earth." (Genesis 1:27, 28 and 9:1, Dar.) Thus 1,656 years after Adam's creation, God showed that his purpose concerning marriage had not changed, namely, the producing of children to spread humankind over all the globe that it might be comfortably inhabited.

1. By what method did God purpose the peopling of the earth?

² God gave Adam only one woman to be his wife, his helpmate or helper to suit him. This was the original and perfect standard for a married man. It was recognized and adhered to by the Christian congregation established by Jesus Christ. Hence the following requirement of the older brothers who were appointed to official service in the congregation and who should be examples of the believers: "The overseer [e·pis'ko·pos] should therefore be irreprehensible, a husband of one wife, . . . a man presiding over his own household in a right manner, having children in subjection with all seriousness; . . . Let ministerial servants [di·a'ko·noi] be husbands of one wife, presiding in a right manner over children and their own households."—1 Timothy 3:2-4, 12, NW.

³ No taking of a vow of celibacy and to lead a single life was required of those appointed to the services of overseer and ministerial servant. The only requirement was that, if married, they should have but one wife. Although married and with his mother-in-law still living, Peter (Cephas) was chosen to be one of the twelve apostles of the Lamb Jesus Christ. Also Paul claimed the right to lead about a wife in the course of his service as apostle, saying: "We have authority to lead about a sister as a wife, even as the rest of the apostles and the Lord's brothers and Cephas, do we not?" (1 Corinthians 9:5, NW; AAT; Moff.;

2, 3. (a) What original standard for a married man did the Christian congregation hold? (b) Were its servants forbidden to marry?

Roth.) One of the signs of a falling away by some from true faith in later times was foretold to be their "forbidding to marry". (1 Timothy 4:3) The married Christians were not required to oppose the purpose of marriage, childbearing. But to qualify for appointed service in the congregation it was required of overseers and ministerial assistants to preside over their children in a right way, controlling them in such a way as to let no reproach be brought upon the congregation and its representatives.—Titus 1:5, 6.

4 In this way, although polygamy, a man's having two or more living wives, with even concubines besides, was allowed among Jehovah's ancient people, and the Mosaic Law covenant sanctioned it for natural Hebrews, it was disposed of for the Christian congregation. Jesus ruled that a man would have two living wives if he divorced a wife on improper grounds and then married another. The Jewish Pharisees asked him: "Is it lawful for a man to divorce his wife on every kind of grounds?" Jesus replied that in Eden God provided for no divorce of the perfect man from his wife. "They said to him: 'Why, then, did Moses prescribe giving a certificate of dismissal and divorcing her?' He said to them: 'Moses, out of regard for your hardheartedness, made the concession to you of divorcing your wives, but such has not been the case from the beginning. I say to you that whoever divorces his wife except on the grounds of fornication and marries another

---

4. What did Jesus rule concerning polygamy and adultery?

commits adultery.' " In his sermon on the mountain he had commented similarly on the subject: "I say to you that everyone divorcing his wife except on account of fornication makes her a subject for adultery, seeing that whoever marries a divorced woman commits adultery."—Matthew 19:3-9 and 5:31, 32, NW.

⁵ This is a serious matter for Christians, for the apostle Paul plainly says that fornication, moral uncleanness, and loose conduct are works of sinful flesh and that "neither fornicators, nor idolaters, nor adulterers, nor men kept for unnatural purposes, nor men who lie with men, . . . will inherit God's kingdom". So if they are called to that kingdom and fail to inherit it for immoral reasons, it means their destruction.—Galatians 5:19-21 and 1 Corinthians 6:9, 10, NW; Romans 1:24-32.

⁶ Death dissolves the marriage union: "a married woman is bound by law to her husband while he is alive; but if her husband dies, she is discharged from the law of her husband. . . . she is free from his law, so that she is not an adulteress if she becomes another man's." (Romans 7:2, 3, NW) The person that marries takes on a responsibility, therefore, that fences in his personal freedom and he takes on the most intimate care of a lifelong mate. Because a Christian marriage cannot be dissolved by divorce except if one

5. Why are the consequences of his ruling serious for Christians?
6. (a) What definitely dissolves the marriage union? (b) Hence why may marriage be inadvisable? When may it be advisable?

of the mates proves unfaithful, it is a matter for sober thought whether a single Christian who wants to be a preacher of good news as freely and as fully as possible should marry or remarry. If, through weakness in an immoral worldly society, a single or widowed person is subject to attacks of passion, such one might consider marriage as a safeguard. Says Paul: "It is well for them that they remain even as I am. But if they do not have self-control, let them marry, for it is better to marry than to be inflamed with passion." (1 Corinthians 7:8, 9, NW) But by prayerfully applying himself to the things that keep his mind off marriage and sexual relations a Christian can cultivate the gift of singleness and make himself a eunuch for the interests of the New World. As to the inadvisability of marrying in this world Jesus said: "Not all men make room for the saying, but only those who have the gift. For . . . there are eunuchs that have made themselves eunuchs because of the kingdom of the heavens. Let him that can make room for it make room for it." —Matthew 19:10-12, NW.

⁷ In encouraging singleness and showing why it allows greater freedom of mind and body for directly serving the interests of God's kingdom, the apostle says: "Further, the single woman, and the virgin, is anxious for the things of the Lord, that she may be holy both in her body and in her spirit. However, the married woman is anxious for the things of the world, how she may gain

---

7. How does the apostle contrast the married state and virginity?

the approval of her husband. But this I am saying for your personal advantage, not that I may cast a noose upon you, but to move you to that which is becoming and that which means constant attendance upon the Lord without distraction. But if anyone thinks he is behaving improperly toward his virginity, if that is past the bloom of youth, and this is the way it should take place, let him do what he wants; he does not sin. Let them marry. But if anyone stands settled in his heart, having no necessity, but has authority over his own will and has made this decision in his own heart, to keep his own virginity, he will do well. Consequently, he also that gives his virginity in marriage does well, but he that does not give it in marriage will do better. A wife is bound during all the time her husband is alive. But if her husband should fall asleep in death, she is free to be married to whom she wants, only in the Lord. But she is happier if she remains as she is, according to my opinion. I certainly think I also have God's spirit."—1 Corinthians 7:34-40, *NW; Roth.; Dar.*

⁸ If a person does not follow the apostle's counsel for a believer to marry "only in the Lord", such person must suffer the consequences of thus mismating himself spiritually with an unbeliever or one not devoted to God. Finding oneself poorly mated or unequally yoked with an unbelieving person is not Scriptural grounds for divorce. If

---

8. (a) Why should a believer marry "only in the Lord"? (b) Why is separation of married mates allowed and yet not encouraged?

they agree to a separation, legal or not, this does not dissolve the marriage in God's sight. And so the separated ones must remain single, having no sex relations with another, or else get reconciled and come together again in a better understanding and with the needed concessions made to each other. If an unbelieving person is agreeable to living on with the marriage mate, then the believing mate should not leave home for a life of separation. But if the unbelieving mate wants to separate, let him do so in the interests of Christian peace. "For [by not separating], wife, how do you know but that you will save your husband? Or, husband, how do you know but that you will save your wife?"—1 Corinthians 7:10-16, *NW*.

⁹ Continuing to live with an unbelieving mate may subject the believing one to trialsome disagreeableness at home or to some form of domestic persecution. But, rather than separate, the believer can accept this as suffering for Christ's sake and can strive to show the unbelieving mate what good Christian fortitude and endurance are. "If, when you are doing good and you suffer, you endure it, this is a thing agreeable with God. In fact, to this course you were called, because even Christ suffered for you, leaving you a model for you to follow his steps closely. In like manner, you wives, be in subjection to your own husbands, in order that, if any are not obedient to the word, they may be won without a word through the conduct of their wives, because of having been eye-

9. How is hardship for refusing to separate to be viewed and met?

witnesses of your chaste conduct together with deep respect." (1 Peter 2:20, 21; 3:1, 2, *NW*) The winning of a mate to a Christian life would be a victory for one's faithful integrity and would improve home conditions to the desirable state. It also provides another preacher of the good news.

[10] Whether subjection to a husband wins him from unbelief or not, the subjection of the believing wife proves her faithfulness to God's law, "The head of a woman is the man." (1 Corinthians 11:3, *NW*) Her suffering under such circumstances is for righteousness' sake and has God's approval and reward. Subjection to a believing husband should be observed by a believing wife not only because it is easier to do but because it is the divine arrangement: "Let wives be in subjection to their husbands as to the Lord, because a husband is head of his wife as the Christ also is head of the congregation, he being a savior of this body. In fact, as the congregation is in subjection to the Christ, so let wives also be to their husbands in everything." The headship of a husband, especially of a believing husband, should by no means take on oppression and an abuse of marriage dues and privileges to the point of harming the body, mind and spiritual condition of the wife. The headship should express itself in love, like that of Christ for his congregation, his spiritual body. "In this way husbands ought to be loving their wives as their own bodies. He who loves

---

10. (a) Why should a wife be subject to her husband whether a believer or not? (b) How should a husband exercise headship Christlike?

his wife loves himself, . . . let each one of you individually so love his wife as he does himself; on the other hand, the wife should have deep respect for her husband." (Ephesians 5:22-33, *NW*) So Christian husbands should deal considerately with their Christian wives, having in mind their highest interests, "since you are also heirs with them of the undeserved favor of life." The wife is just as much an heir of life as the husband. In closest neighbor-love each mate should help the other to win it.—1 Peter 3:7, *NW*.

[11] If a believer contemplates marriage, then wisdom and faithfulness to God dictate that it should be marriage only to another person in devoted relationship with the Lord. Not only does the apostle warn against a Christian's yoking himself up unequally with an unbeliever, but also Jehovah's Law covenant with the Israelites foreshadowed a warning against this in forbidding his chosen people to marry with heathen neighbors. It endangers faithfulness.—Exodus 34:14-16; Deuteronomy 7:3, 4; Numbers 25:1-8.

[12] In all Biblical accounts of marriages, there is no record of a religious priest or clergyman's being needed or having any part in completing the marriage. This does not mean a person should not be married by an officer of the law of the land and have the marriage legally acknowledged, confirmed and recorded and published beyond all denial. The Bible record argues for this, because

---

11. Why do wisdom and faithfulness dictate marrying in the Lord?
12. Should marriage be legalized? Why Scripturally so?

back there the marriage was arranged between the parents of the bridegroom and bride by means of a go-between friend. Through him the marriage was agreed to by the parents or caretakers on both sides and the betrothal of male and female was formally made with the customary considerations passing from one side to the other. Then on the day the marriage was consummated, the bridegroom amid great publicity and happy arrangements took his bride to her new home. (Genesis 24:1-67; Matthew 25:1-10; 22:1-14; John 3:29) Hence anyone who dedicates himself to God and who has been living in common law marriage

till then should get the marriage legalized or legally performed. This works for the protection of each one before the law of the land. By it also each party to the marriage acknowledges his responsibility to the other. It shows consideration also for the children born to such a union. God blesses this action. He removes reproach from those involved and opens up larger privileges to them in his blessed service.

CHAPTER XV

WOMAN'S PRIVILEGES IN THE CONGREGATION

T HERE are no sexes in heaven. But there are now women in the congregation, which is the "body of Christ", and these rightfully have hope of heaven. In creating woman on earth to be man's suitable helper God did not copy any sex distinctions among the heavenly angels, for Jesus said in discussing the raising of the dead: "In the resurrection neither do they marry nor are they given in marriage, but are as angels in heaven." (Matthew 22:30, *NW*) All the angels whom the Bible reports appearing to mankind materialized as men, not women. When Paul tells his anointed fellow Christians, "But the Jerusalem above is free, and she is our mother. Wherefore, brothers, we are children, not of a servant girl, but of the free woman," he is not referring to a literal woman up in heaven. Neither is John doing so, when he says, "And a great sign was seen in heaven, a woman arrayed with the sun." (Galatians 4:26, 31 and Revelation 12:1, *NW*) Paul and John were referring to God's holy universal organization and were symbolizing it as a woman who becomes a mother.

[2] However, all this is not saying that persons

---

1. What proves there are no sexes in heaven?
2. May women become heirs of God's kingdom? How will they enter it?

who are now women cannot become heirs of the heavenly kingdom. The Christian Greek Scriptures report many women who became joint heirs with Christ. But it is not as creatures of flesh and blood of the female sex that they will finally enter God's kingdom. They have now been born from water and spirit and are a "new creation" in union with Christ. When they die a sacrificial death with Christ, they cease forever from the flesh, and in the resurrection to heavenly life, the apostle Paul says, they as well as their faithful brothers will be "changed" to spirit creatures, females no longer. All will form Christ's bride.

[3] In proof that all those now in spiritual union with Christ are a "new creation" Galatians 3:26-29 reminds them: "You are all, in fact, sons of God through your faith in Christ Jesus. For all of you who were baptized into Christ have put on Christ. There is neither Jew nor Greek, there is neither slave nor freeman, there is neither male nor female; for you are all one in union with Christ Jesus. Moreover, if you belong to Christ, you are really Abraham's seed, heirs with reference to a promise." (*NW*) There is no distinction as to male and female, in that all were privileged to accept the true faith, devote themselves to God, be declared righteous and be baptized into union with Christ Jesus. Equally with the males, the female Christians hold hopes of living and ruling as kings with Christ for a thousand years and being priests of God and of Christ. All are "living

---

3. In what respects is there neither male nor female in Christ?

stones" now being built up into a spiritual house in which God dwells by his spirit, that they may offer up spiritual sacrifices, acceptable to God by Christ. All alike are anointed with the spirit and may serve God now, imitating Jesus, suffering reproach with him, and praising God daily as his ministers. All anointed believers, male and female, have God's adoption as his sons.

[4] Nevertheless, these believers united with Christ are still in the flesh, and the great Theocratic Ruler of the Christian congregation takes recognition of that fact and lays down rules accordingly. Because he recognizes the sex distinctions in their flesh the great Theocrat grants them the privilege of becoming husband and wife and of raising children. At the same time he warns members of the congregation against committing any sexual abuses. Likewise God takes sex into account in ordering certain arrangements within the congregation. By so doing he does not make any unrighteous, unwarranted discrimination. He does no one any injury but makes provision for the good and happiness of all. The Theocratic Creator has the right to do with his own creatures and organization what his perfect will dictates, and no creature has the right to complain and say: "Why did you make me this way and put me here or there?" It is a great privilege and honor to serve the Most High God in any position high or low and under subjection to any other or all other servants appointed by God. Even Christ Jesus is subject to

---

4. In what ways does God show regard for their sex distinctions?

his heavenly Father and worships and serves him as God Most High. All through the Theocratic organization, from Jesus on down, the principle of subjection is in evidence. "I want you to know that the head of every man is the Christ; in turn, the head of a woman is the man; in turn, the head of the Christ is God."—1 Corinthians 11:3, *NW*.

⁵ God created a natural sign of subjection upon woman, that is, her long hair. "Does not nature itself teach you that if a man has long hair, it is a dishonor to him; but if a woman has long hair, it is a glory to her? Because her hair is given her instead of a headdress." (1 Corinthians 11:14, 15, *NW*) God did not create the first man and woman as twins at the same time, and equal in power and glory. He created the man first to work in the garden and gave him certain instructions on how to live forever and also had him name all the lower creatures. After this the woman was created as bone of his bone and flesh of his flesh and hence not independent of him, but to be a help suitable for him. She had things to learn from Adam, the first human created. It was not her business to change the names of the animals to suit her feminine taste. When she went contrary to what God told the man, and considered that the man had been deceived by God, she got into trouble and put trouble in the man's way. If there had been Theocratic subjection on her part with trustfulness, paradise happiness would have continued for her and her husband.

5. (a) What sign of subjection did God create upon woman? (b) How was woman created not independently of man, and safely so?

[6] The same apostle who wrote that there is, in union with Christ, neither male nor female and all members of Christ's body are a new creation did not ignore sex distinctions and arrange things in the congregation without regard for Theocratic subordination. For peace, good order and safe teaching in the congregation he wrote under inspiration: "Let a woman learn in silence with full submissiveness. I do not permit a woman to teach, or to exercise authority over a man, but to be in silence. For Adam was formed first, then Eve.

Also A d a m was not deceived, but the woman was thoroughly deceived and came to be in transgression. However, she will be kept safe through childbearing, provided they continue in faith and love and sanctification along with s o u n d n e s s of mind." (1 Timothy 2:11-15, NW) So at a congregational meeting woman is not to act as teacher and exercise authority over the consecrated men present. "For God is a God, not of disorder, but of peace. As in all the congregations of the holy ones,

6. What is woman's Theocratic place as to teaching and learning?

let the women keep silent in the congregations, for it is not permitted for them to speak, but let them be in subjection, even as the Law says. If, then, they want to learn something, let them question their husbands at home, for it is disgraceful for a woman to speak in a congregation. But let all things take place decently and by arrangement." —1 Corinthians 14:33-35, 40, *NW*.

[7] But was there to be absolute silence on the part of the women at a congregational meeting, not even joining in the singing of songs or asking or answering questions on which a person's faith and understanding are to be expressed? No! But woman was to learn in silence in the sense of not debating there with the men, challenging them and getting into a dispute and causing wrangling to break out, belittling man's appointed position. But if the holy spirit came upon a woman at the meeting in those apostolic days and it moved her to give a message in her own or a foreign language, then what man should resist or forbid the operating of God's spirit through the woman? No one rightfully could. However, the spirit operated Theocratically and the woman should express herself under inspiration of the spirit with fitting regard for Theocratic arrangements. Speaking of a congregational meeting of men and women the apostle goes on to say:

[8] "Every man that prays or prophesies having

---

7. In what way does woman "learn in silence"? When might she speak?
8. How was woman to pray or prophesy in the congregation? Why?

something on his head shames the one who is his head [Christ]; but every woman that prays or prophesies with her head unveiled shames the one who is her head [man], for it is one and the same as if she were a woman with a shaved head. For if a woman does not veil herself, let her also be shorn [if she wants to act the man that far, with no head covering, then let her go the whole way and have her hair shorn or shaved off to resemble a man of short hair]; but if it is disgraceful for a woman to be shorn or shaved, let her be veiled. For a man ought not to have his head veiled, as he is God's image and glory; but the woman is man's glory. For man is not out of woman, but woman out of man; and, what is more, man was not created for the sake of the woman, but woman for the sake of the man. That is why the woman ought to have a sign of authority upon her head because of the angels. Besides, in connection with the Lord neither is woman without man nor man without woman. For just as the woman is out of the man, so also the man is through the woman; but all things are out of God."—1 Corinthians 11:4-12, NW.

⁹ So women could pray and prophesy at a congregational meeting if they were moved by the holy spirit with an inspired message. That they were to do so the fulfillment of the prophecy required: "And it shall come to pass afterward, that I will pour out my spirit upon all flesh; and your

---

9. How and in fulfillment of what prophecy were women to prophesy?

sons and your daughters shall prophesy, your old men shall dream dreams, your young men shall see visions: and also upon the servants and upon the handmaids in those days will I pour out my spirit. . . . And it shall come to pass, that whosoever shall call on the name of Jehovah shall be delivered; for in mount Zion and in Jerusalem there shall be those that escape, as Jehovah hath said, and among the remnant those whom Jehovah doth call."—Joel 2:28-32, *ASV*.

¹⁰ The apostle Peter, under inspiration of that same spirit on the day of Pentecost A.D. 33, quoted this prophecy of Joel and declared it was beginning fulfillment that day. What "daughters" or what "handmaids" prophesied that day or later under inspiration of the spirit? Acts 21:8, 9 says concerning Philip the missionary: "This man had four daughters, virgins, that prophesied." (*NW*) We can be sure, however, that at assemblies of God's consecrated people these "daughters" and "handmaids" did so with Theocratic deportment, with heads veiled, with a sign of authority on their heads. They did this particularly out of regard for the heavenly angels who are "all spirits for public service, sent forth to minister for those who are going to inherit salvation".—Hebrews 1:14, *NW*.

¹¹ In the apostle's day, and especially there in the scandalously immoral city of ancient Corinth, it was the custom for respectable women to go

10. Did women thus prophesy? With what deportment? Why?
11. Need women everywhere go veiled in public today? Why?

veiled in public. For a woman to go otherwise to public assemblies was to brand her a woman of low moral standards and easy virtue. Women who were caught committing adultery or fornication were punished with shaving off all their hair; while slavegirls had their hair clipped short. So for consecrated women of the congregation to go unveiled in public and to meetings would bring a bad name and misunderstanding upon the faith and organization. In the public eye it would be all the same as if they had their hair shaved off as punishment for immoral conduct. In these modern times or in lands where custom does not require women of the community to go veiled as a sign of respectability, Christian decency does not require the woman to comply with that ancient custom for the sake of the faith and organization. If a woman is of a race whose females do not naturally grow long hair, then her short hair is no reproach to her.

[12] But regardless of popular custom, if a woman today should rise in a congregation and pray or prophesy to the believing men and women present, she should veil her head or have a "sign of authority upon her head because of the angels". Paul says of the congregation: "Judge for your own selves: Is it fitting for a woman to pray unveiled to God? . . . However, if any man seems to dispute for some other custom, we have no other, neither do the congregations of God."—1 Corinthians 11: 13-16, NW.

---

12. Still, how should woman pray or prophesy in a congregation of believers?

[13] In a certain community only women may be Christian believers. As is right, they meet together for prayer and study, as Lydia and other Jewish women used to do by the riverside in ancient Philippi of Macedonia. (Acts 16:13, 14) According to custom then, Lydia and her companion worshipers were veiled in that public place, but today women assembling together need not be. However, if any of them receives an appointment through the Theocratic organization to keep order and conduct the meetings for Bible study and for considering how to preach to others, it would appear proper for her to wear a sign of authority upon her head while so performing. This would symbolize that she recognizes the Theocratic headship of the man and that she is temporarily or circumstantially serving in the congregation in place of the man who should fill that position. In a home where a husband, the head of the house, calls upon his wife or other believing woman to offer prayer over the meal, the woman's recognition that the man presides over the woman should oblige her to wear a sign of authority on her head while so praying. In everything faithful women should show submission to the one whom God, the Head of the Christ, has placed in authority. This way she lovingly and beautifully portrays how the congregation, the bride of Christ, is subject to her Theocratic Head, the Bridegroom.—Ephesians 5:24-32.

---

13. What about her conducting meetings of women or praying at the mealtable, when so assigned?

CHAPTER XVI

OPERATIONS AND GIFTS OF THE SPIRIT

JUST before being betrayed into the hands of his murderous enemies Jesus Christ told his faithful apostles that he was about to leave them and go to his heavenly Father. He told them he would not leave them bereaved but would send a great comfort into their lives, to operate during his personal absence from them and guide them into all the needed truth. It would be God's holy spirit. Because of the comfort it would bring them, Jesus called it the "comforter" or "helper":

[2] "I will request the Father and he will give you another helper to be with you forever, the spirit of the truth, which the world cannot receive, because it neither beholds it nor knows it. You know it, because it remains with you and is in you. While remaining with you I have spoken these things to you. But the helper, the holy spirit which the Father will send in my name, that one will teach you all things and bring back to your minds all the things I told you. When the helper arrives that I will send you from the Father, the spirit of the truth which proceeds from the Father, that one will bear witness about me, and you, in turn, are to bear witness, because you have been with

1. How were the apostles not to be left bereaved by Jesus' leaving?
2. What did Jesus tell them about that "helper"?

me from when I began. . . . It is for your benefit I am going away. For if I do not go away, the helper will by no means come to you; but if I do go my way, I will send him to you. . . . However, when that one arrives, the spirit of the truth, he will guide you into all the truth, for he will not speak of his own impulse, but what things he hears he will speak, and he will declare to you the things coming. That one will glorify me, because he will receive from what is mine and will declare it to you."—John 14:16, 17, 25, 26 and 15:26, 27 and 16:7-14, NW.

[3] After his resurrection from the dead Jesus appeared and told them to remain in Jerusalem until they became "clothed with power from on high". "Because John, indeed, baptized with water, but you will be baptized in holy spirit not many days after this." (Luke 24:49 and Acts 1:4, 5, NW) Such language by Jesus gives us to understand that the spirit is a power, and not a person. It is God's holy active force of which he is the inexhaustible source. He gives it to Jesus and it is subject to Jesus' use and control. True to his promise, Jesus sent this helping force to his faithful disciples in Jerusalem on the feast day of Pentecost and they were baptized in it, just as a piece of steel can be immersed in a field of magnetism. Its coming upon them was accompanied by a rushing stiff breeze and by tongues as if of fire distributed to each of the company, about 120 in number. They were all filled with spirit,

---

3. What is that "helper", and how was it given at Pentecost?

and Peter said that, as Joel had prophesied, the holy spirit had been poured out on all flesh regardless of sex, age, and social, family or economic position.—Acts 2:1-33.

⁴ Jesus said: "A slave is not greater than his master, nor is one that is sent forth greater than the one that sent him." (John 13:16, *NW*) Jesus' sending the spirit and baptizing his disciples in it or pouring it out upon them proves it is an impersonal active force and is subject to Jesus. It is not a trinitarian person coequal with God and Jesus. Just as the radio waves act as carriers of the impulses from people speaking, singing, or performing in the studio and transmit the sound and the vision to the radio set and television screen in the distant home, so the holy spirit acts. As an active force it serves to carry the teaching, illumination, guidance or dynamic energy to Christ's followers on earth. It produces seeable, hearable and felt effects.

⁵ The Christian congregation under Christ the Head is the temple in which God dwells by means of his spirit or active force. (1 Corinthians 3:16, 17; Ephe-

4. How is it shown to be not a trinitarian co-equal person?
5. How does the spirit manifest itself in the congregation?

sians 2:20-22) It
manifests itself in
the congregation
by a great vari-
ety of operations
and gifts. It is all
one and the same
spirit of God
through Christ,
but this shows the endless variety of ways in
which it can be applied. "But the manifestation of the spirit is given to each one for a
beneficial purpose. For example, to one there is
given through the spirit speech of wisdom, to another speech of knowledge according to the same
spirit, to another faith by the same spirit, to another gifts of healings by that one spirit, to yet
another operations of powerful works, to another
prophesying, to another discernment of inspired
utterances, to another different tongues, and to
another interpretation of tongues. But all these
operations the one and the same spirit performs,
making a distribution to each one respectively just
as it wills. For just as the body is one thing but
has many members, and all the members of that
body, although being many, are one body, so also
is the Christ. For truly by one spirit we were all
baptized into one body, whether Jews or Greeks,
whether slaves or free, and we were all made to
drink one spirit."—1 Corinthians 12:4-13, *NW*.

⁶ On the day of Pentecost the spirit's manifes-

6, 7. In whose presence or through whom were its gifts
bestowed?

tation started with miraculous gifts of foreign languages and prophesying. Gifts of healing and other marvelous powers followed. We note that the miraculous gifts of the spirit were bestowed in the presence of the apostles of the Lamb or directly through them by the laying on of their hands. Philip the missionary went down to Samaria and preached and won believers there. Though baptized in water, they did not receive the holy spirit and any of its gifts. So the apostles sent down Peter and John. "These went down and prayed for them to get holy spirit. For it had not yet fallen upon any one of them, but they had only been baptized in the name of the Lord Jesus. Then they went to laying their hands upon them, and they began to receive holy spirit. . . . through the laying on of the hands of the apostles the spirit was given."—Acts 8:5-18, *NW*.

[7] At Ephesus Paul came upon men who had been baptized with John's baptism and had heard nothing of the holy spirit. So he preached Jesus to them. "On hearing this, they got baptized in the name of the Lord Jesus. And when Paul laid his hands upon them, the holy spirit came upon them, and they began speaking with tongues and prophesying." (Acts 19:1-6, *NW*) Paul wrote Timothy to "stir up like a fire the gift of God which is in you through the laying of my hands upon you". By letter he advised the congregation at Rome: "I am longing to see you, that I may impart some spiritual gift to you in order for you to be made firm." (2 Timothy 1:6 and Romans 1:11, *NW*)

So the twelve apostles of the Lamb were go-betweens for the bestowal of the spirit's gifts.

[8] Since this is so, it follows that when the apostles passed off the earthly stage, the imparting of miraculous gifts of the spirit passed away with them. Paul called attention to this. He showed that these miraculous gifts marked the infancy of the Christian congregation. They were necessary for its establishment, to prove that God's favor and power had turned away from the unfaithful house of natural Israel and now rested upon the Christian congregation as the "Israel of God". When the congregation of spiritual Israel had become firmly established on the twelve apostolic foundations and had grown to maturity, the miraculous gifts of its infancy would be needed no more and would be put away. "But whether there are gifts of prophesying, they will be done away with; whether there are tongues, they will cease; whether there is knowledge, it will be done away with. For we have partial knowledge and we prophesy partially; but when that which is complete arrives, that which is partial will be done away with. When I was a babe, I used to speak as a babe, to think as a babe, to reason as a babe; but now that I have become a man, I have done away with the traits of a babe." (1 Corinthians 13:8-11, *NW*) This accounts for it that miraculous gifts of the spirit are not bestowed upon the remnant today of members of Christ's body.

[9] This knowledge puts us on guard against any

---

8. Why are its miraculous gifts not bestowed now?
9. What deception does this knowledge put us on guard against?

deceptive operation of the power of Satan the Devil through his religious organization, "the man of lawlessness." We read: "But the lawless one's presence is according to the operation of Satan with every powerful work and lying signs and wonders and with every unrighteous deception for those who are perishing, as a retribution because they did not accept the love of the truth that they might be saved. So that is why God lets an operation of error go to them that they may get to believing the lie." (2 Thessalonians 2:3, 9-11, *NW*) The organization of religious error may claim to be exercising the miraculous gifts of the spirit, such as tongues, healings, etc., but we know that the operation of God's spirit does not work in support of error and worldliness. The spirit sanctifies a person away from this world and does so by means of Bible truth. It was not God's purpose that all members of Christ's body should have the miraculous gifts of the spirit, for we are told:

[10] "Now you are Christ's body, and members individually. And God has set the respective ones in the congregation, first, apostles; second, prophets; third, teachers; then powerful works; then gifts of healings; helpful services, abilities to direct, different tongues. Not all are apostles, are they? Not all are prophets, are they? Not all are teachers, are they? Not all perform powerful works, do they? Not all have gifts of healings, do they? Not all speak in tongues, do they? Not all are transla-

---

10. Why does lack of such gifts not prove us outside Christ's body?

tors, are they?" So the absence of prophets and inspired apostles today, and with that the absence of miraculous gifts of the spirit, does not prove that today's faithful remnant is not of Christ's body.—1 Corinthians 12:27-30, NW.

[11] The Christian congregation is not weaker today than in the first century because of not enjoying the miraculous gifts now. It does not need them now at this time of its coming to full growth. It is anointed with the same spirit to preach now as nineteen centuries ago, and it is just as full of the spirit. By this means it is performing a more powerful witness to God's kingdom now than ever before in its history. "Not by might, nor by power, but by my spirit, saith Jehovah of hosts." (Zechariah 4:6, ASV) By his "spirit of the truth" the meaning of the Scriptures and their prophe- ·cies is being opened up to our understanding as never before, making us strong in knowledge and understanding and in ability to preach the King- dom message. Moreover, being filled now with the spirit, we can bring forth just as abundantly the fruitage of the spirit. It is by this fruitage rather than by the miraculous gifts of the spirit that we prove we are the same Christian congregation as in the first century, members of the same "body of Christ". It is by cultivating and bringing forth this fruitage that we walk in the "surpassing way", that of love.

---

11. What proves us not weaker today because of lack- ing such gifts?

CHAPTER XVII

LOVE ESSENTIAL
TO ETERNAL LIFE

"DO NOT marvel, brothers, that the world hates you. We know we have passed over from death to life, because we love the brothers. He who does not love remains in death. Everyone who hates his brother is a manslayer, and you know that no manslayer has everlasting life remaining in him." From these words at 1 John 3:13-15 (*NW*) it is manifest that this world remains in death because it hates God's anointed children and if we want to enjoy everlasting life we must cultivate love. A test of our having love is our loving those who belong to God, for if we do not love those whom we can see on earth we cannot really love the God whom these represent and whom we cannot see.

² All the creation, visible and invisible, is the work of love, for God the Creator is love personified. By love this universal Sovereign rules all creation, and he holds and will forever hold all appreciative living creatures to him in the bonds of unbreakable love. He rules by love. That betokens eternal good and happiness for all creatures who gain everlasting life by their indestructible

1. What must we cultivate to gain life? What is a test of it?
2. How does love show itself predominantly in God?

172

devotion to him. It is his love toward us and our exercise of love to him and his creatures that makes life worth living. Since "God is love", he is the source of this wonderful quality, and he implanted it in his perfect, intelligent creatures, that they might be complete in his image and likeness. His own exercise of it toward us first warms up that quality in us in response. "We love, because he first loved us." He disclosed that wondrous love to us through his devoted Son Christ Jesus, while we were yet sinners. Because Jesus perfectly expressed that godlike love to his disciples, he said: "He that has seen me has seen the Father also."—1 John 4:19; John 14:9, *NW*.

[3] God is love in his unselfish devotion to righteousness and in his sincere interest in the lasting welfare of his creatures and in his active provision for their good and happiness. As for us, love is the quality he has implanted in us which expresses itself (1) in our complete, unbreakable attachment to him and to his Theocratic organization and (2) in our unselfish deeds to other creatures and our active concern for their eternal welfare. Love is a fruitage of God's spirit. "The fruitage of the spirit is love, joy, peace, longsuffering, kindness, goodness, faith, mildness, self-control. Against such things there is no law." So if we would exercise true love, we must have God's spirit. The world does not love us because it does not have his spirit. The world indulges in the works of the fallen flesh which are contrary to

---

3. What is love? To have it what must we have, and why?

the fruitage of the spirit, and all those who copy the world and have its spirit and practice the works of the flesh with it will never inherit God's kingdom.—Galatians 5:19-23, *NW*.

[4] On the Christian congregation during the first century the miraculous gifts of the spirit were instantaneously bestowed. But love is a fruitage of the spirit which it takes time, devotion and constant effort to cultivate to its perfection. In the infancy of the Christian congregation it was possible to have miraculous gifts of the spirit and yet fail of cultivating love and attaining to its perfection. That is why the possessing of miraculous gifts is not all-essential and will not gain for the possessor everlasting life. But the cultivating of love to perfection is essential to gaining it, for love is godlikeness. While the spirit's miraculous gifts are not to be despised, the bringing forth of its fruitage is a more vital thing for us; so Paul could say to the congregation of that apostolic period: "But keep striving after the greater gifts. And yet I show you a surpassing way." (1 Corinthians 12:31, *NW*) He then proceeds to show how in the good that it does to lover and loved one the way of love surpasses the way of operating by miraculous gifts.

[5] Did Paul speak in more foreign tongues than all those did to whom he wrote? Did he have an excess of revelations, even being caught up to the

---

4. How do love and miraculous gifts compare? Which is more needed?
5. How is love's way shown to surpass that of miraculous gifts?

third heaven and to paradise? Did he utter and record many important prophecies, writing more of the Christian Greek Scriptures than any other inspired writer? Yes! But listen: "If I speak in the tongues of men and of angels but do not have love, I have become a sounding piece of brass or a clashing cymbal. And if I have the gift of prophesying and understand all the sacred secrets and all knowledge, and if I have all the faith so as to transplant mountains, but do not have love, I am nothing. And if I give all my belongings to feed others, and if I hand over my body, that I may boast, but do not have love, I am not profited at all." (1 Corinthians 13:1-3, NW) Though he had all these things to his credit, yet if he did not have pure love in exercising these miraculous gifts and if his motive was not that of love in doing charitable and self-sacrificing works, it would not profit him at all toward gaining eternal life in God's favor. He would be nothing in God's estimation.

⁶ God can read the heart and the motive it has. He can discern whether the exercise of these gifts and the performing of charitable, self-sacrificing acts is really cultivating perfect love in the very fiber of the individual. If the individual is not doing so, but is acting for a selfish motive, he has his reward in this life, the reward he was after. He is not growing godlike but deepening his own selfishness. Such a self-seeking person with ulterior motives would be a danger to God's universe

---

6. Why would the user of gifts without love be nothing to God?

—it was selfishness that made Satan the Devil—
and God could not give him eternal life.

⁷ Love, such as God is, is so wonderful that it is
hard to define. It is simpler to tell how it acts.
After emphasizing how all-essential it is for a
Christian believer, the apostle next details how
it acts unselfishly:

⁸ "Love is long-suffering and obliging. Love is
not jealous, it does not brag, does not get puffed
up, does not behave indecently, does not look for
its own interests, does not become provoked. It
does not keep account of the injury. It does not
rejoice over unrighteousness, but rejoices with
the truth. It bears all things, believes all things,
hopes all things, endures all things."

⁹ Since love is of such a description, then even
in the midst of the permission of wickedness
throughout the universe, yes, in the midst of such
a world as this, love is unconquerable. Hate never
succeeds in overpowering it and driving it from
the field of action. Love comes off victorious,
overcoming evil with good. It is eternal. Certain
manifestations of the spirit of God may fail or
pass away because of no more being needed, but
this fruitage of the spirit, love, will never cease
manifesting itself and enriching itself. "Love
never fails. But whether there are gifts of prophesying, they will be done away with; whether
there are tongues, they will cease; whether there
is knowledge, it will be done away with. For we

_____
7, 8. How does godlike love act?
9. Why is this fruitage of the spirit unfailing amid
wickedness?

have partial knowledge and we prophesy partially; but when that which is complete arrives, that which is partial will be done away with. When I was a babe, I used to speak as a babe, to think as a babe, to reason as a babe; but now that I have become a man, I have done away with the traits of a babe. For at present we see in hazy outline by means of a metal mirror, but then it will be face to face. At present I know partially, but then I shall know accurately even as I am accurately known."

[10] When the congregation was in its infancy in the apostolic times it needed certain helps, like a babe, such as miraculous gifts of tongues, translations, knowledge, revelations of mysteries, and prophecies. But the knowledge that was thus given, the prophecies that were thus inspired, were all partial, being only for what was then needed and not being given in full detail. It was like seeing the hazy reflection in a polished metal mirror of those days. And with the death of the apostles through whom the miraculous gifts of the spirit were distributed to the believers, tongues, translations, healings, and such spiritual gifts failed and passed away. With the passing of the Christian congregation out of its infancy to fuller growth and strength it was proper for the things of its infancy to be set aside. The congregation must not be laying the foundation over again, but must advance toward maturity, to spiritual perfection. And as we near the day of accurate

10. Why have gifts been put away, but faith, hope and love grown?

knowledge and come face to face with the fulfill-
ments of the ancient prophecies, we see more
clearly. So our faith is strengthened and our hope
is made brighter and our love for God is deepened.
The three outstanding qualities are in evidence
today. They stamp the anointed remnant as being
of the same congregation that God established
nineteen centuries ago.

[11] Let fail and pass away what manifestations
of the spirit are not essential for the "body of
Christ" which has come to complete manhood.
"Now, however, there remain faith, hope, love,
these three, but the greatest of these is love."
(1 Corinthians 13:4-13, *NW*) Hope, which rests
on faith as its support, may pass away with our
realizing the things hoped for, but love will never
pass away or diminish. It will grow fuller and
broader throughout all eternity. It will always remain, because God is love and God is from everlasting to everlasting.

[12] Whoever does not know that God is love does
not know God. Whoever does not love could not
know God or claim to be his son, for love is his
dominant attribute and it is the fruitage of his
spirit. In not exercising love, a person is not copying God. He has not felt God's love and has not
been stirred to respond to God's love and to display that which most marks God. "He that does
not love has not come to know God, because God
is love. By this the love of God was made mani-

---

11. Why, among hope, faith and love, is love greatest?
12. Why has one that does not love not come to know
God?

fest in our case, because God sent forth his only-
begotten Son into the world that we might gain
life through him. The love is in this respect, not
that we have loved God, but that he loved us and
sent forth his Son as a propitiatory sacrifice for
our sins. Beloved ones, if this is how God loved us,
then we are ourselves under obligation to love one
another. . . . God is love, and he that remains in
love remains in union with God and God remains
in union with him."—1 John 4:8-11, 16, *NW*.

[13] There is no everlasting life without this godly
quality. We must have it to prove worthy of God's
gift of life through Jesus Christ, for our faith in
God and in his dear Son must operate through
love. This supreme requirement for gaining and
enjoying everlasting happiness and blessing is set
forth in an incident in Jesus' life: "A certain man
versed in the Law rose up, to test him out, and
said: 'Teacher, by doing what shall I inherit everlasting life?' He said to him: 'What is written in
the Law? How do you read?' In answer he said:
' "You must love Jehovah your God with your
whole heart and with your whole soul and with
your whole strength and with your whole mind,"
and, "your neighbor as yourself." ' He said to
him: 'You answered correctly; "keep on doing
this and you will get life." ' " (Luke 10:25-28,
NW) Jesus said that on these two great commandments the whole law of Moses and all the writings
of the prophets of God depend. This means that
the purpose of the Law and prophetic writings is

---

13. How did Jesus explain we must have love to gain
endless life?

to urge all of us to keep these two great commandments.—Matthew 22:37-40.

[14] If knowing God and Christ Jesus means everlasting life to us, then we must know their love and we must love them and our fellow creatures even as They loved both us and our neighbors. We must learn to know how their matchless love expressed itself toward us and we must appreciate what it means to be loved by them that way. We can love and copy a person whom we know. And so we respond by gratefully taking advantage of all the provisions for life that God has made for us through Christ Jesus. This brings us into relationship with God and we begin to increase in our feel of God's love and also to increase our own love for him. We must prove this love to God, not with mere words of lip-service, but with deeds in which we put our hearts. This we do by loving what God loves and hating what God hates and by keeping his commandments. (1 John 2:15; 5:3) This obligates us to love our fellow creatures for whom God gave his Son to die. If we do not love these, we cannot really know God, for we are not exercising his most outstanding quality; we show we are ignoring this quality and are lacking in the spirit of God. If we do not love our neighbor whom we have seen, how can we love God whom we have not seen? (1 John 4:20) We cannot do so. Hence we must love God and our neighbor. Since to know God means for us to copy him, we must love. This is essential to our eternal life.

---

14. So our knowing God and Christ in what respect means life?

CHAPTER XVIII

PUTTING UP A HARD FIGHT FOR THE FAITH

ACCEPTING the message of salvation and devoting ourselves to God through Christ and being baptized in water is only the beginning of our exercise of faith. It is only the beginning of our obedience to God. It sets us on the way to everlasting life, but it does not mean our final salvation. Both when sending forth his apostles on missionary work and when giving his prophecy on the end of the world Jesus said: "He that has endured to the finish is the one that will be saved." (Matthew 10:22 and 24:13, *NW*) To hold firm to the true faith in this opposing world means to put up a hard fight for it.

² The popular religious expression, "Once saved, always saved!" is false and dangerous. Jehovah God delivered the Israelites out of the land of Egypt, did he not? But did all those millions prove worthy of entering victoriously into the Promised Land of "milk and honey"? The angels who behold his face God created holy and perfect; but did even these heavenly creatures who originally had such a privileged position all keep in their proper dwelling-place where they could enjoy

---

1. What sets us on the way to everlasting life? What is required of us to make our final salvation certain?
2. How did the Israelites and angels furnish us warning examples?

God's favor and the right to everlasting life? Sounding a timely warning, the disciple Jude writes: "I desire to remind you, despite your knowing all things once for all time, that Jehovah, although he saved a people out of the land of Egypt, afterwards destroyed those not showing faith. And the angels that did not keep their original position but forsook their own proper dwelling-place he has reserved with eternal bonds under dense darkness for the judgment of the great day." The highly honored "covering cherub" in Eden gave way to ambitious selfishness and became the great Serpent, the deceiver. So Jehovah God sentenced him and his seed to destruction, to be crushed under the heel of the Seed of God's "woman". (Jude 5, 6, *NW;* Genesis 3:15) It behooves us to heed Jude's reminder to remain faithful.

³ That part of the world which is called "Christendom" is full of so many different religions called "Christian", some 256 being counted in the United States alone, that first of all we have to ascertain whether we have the true faith. We must have that faith, before we can heed Jude's exhortation "to put up a hard fight for the faith that was once for all time delivered to the holy ones".—Jude 3, *NW.*

⁴ We are nineteen centuries removed from the time when that faith was once for all delivered to the faithful followers of Jesus Christ. This has

---

3. To put up a hard fight for the faith, we ascertain what first?
4. Of what did Peter and Paul warn? Has this taken place?

allowed plenty of time for the prophecies which warn of the falling away from the pure, original faith to take place. The divided, confused, groping condition of Christendom proves it has taken place and has entrenched itself in this world. The apostle Peter warned: "Prophecy was at no time brought by man's will, but men spoke from God as they were borne along by holy spirit. However, there also came to be false prophets among the people, as there will also be false teachers among you. These very ones will quietly bring in destructive sects and will disown even the owner that bought them, bringing speedy destruction upon themselves. Furthermore, many will turn out of the way and follow their acts of loose conduct, and on account of these the way of the truth will be spoken of abusively." (2 Peter 1:21 to 2:2, *NW*) The apostle Paul warned in his day that "the mystery of this lawlessness is already at work". And not long before he died, about A.D. 65, he warned: "After my going away oppressive wolves will enter in among you and will not treat the flock with tenderness, and from among you yourselves men will rise and speak twisted things to draw away the disciples after themselves." —2 Thessalonians 2:7 and Acts 20:29, 30, *NW*.

⁵ How can we ascertain the true faith and prove we are in it? By going back to those prophets who Peter said were borne along by God's spirit. Yes, by going back to the writings also of the apostles and disciples themselves who were inspired to de-

---

5, 6. To ascertain the faith and prove we are in it what must we do? And why is that the right thing to do?

liver the genuine faith to the true congregation
of God. The apostolic command is, "Do not treat
prophesyings with contempt. Make sure of all
things; hold fast to what is right." And the apostle Paul himself submitted to having the message
he delivered subjected to proof by the already
written Hebrew Scriptures of the ancient prophets. His listeners at Beroea received Paul's word
with the greatest readiness of mind, but "carefully
examining the Scriptures daily as to whether
these things were so". In urging Christians in
later times to go back always to the original for
the pure, true faith Paul wrote: "There are certain ones who are disturbing you and wanting to
pervert the good news about the Christ. However,
even if we or an angel out of heaven were to declare to you as good news something beyond what
we declared to you as good news, let him be accursed."—1 Thessalonians 5:20, 21 and Acts 17:11
and Galatians 1:7, 8, *NW*.

6 The apostles fought hard to uphold the common faith of the congregation of the first century. Now for us to get away from the sectarian
creeds and religious confusion of this century we
must turn back to their common faith that was
delivered once for all time. It is contained unchanged in the inspired Scriptures of the Bible.
Both Moses, the writer of the first books of the
Bible, and the apostle John, the writer of the last
books of the Bible, wrote down God's warning
against adding uninspired religious traditions of
men to God's Word once delivered to his people.
—Deuteronomy 4:2; Revelation 22:18.

⁷ When once we have established by God's written Word what is the "common faith" originally delivered to the Christian congregation, what must we do? Well, if we are finally to make our salvation sure, we must now put up a hard fight for it, for the same reason that Jude stressed in his letter. Telling us his reason for not writing to describe the "salvation we hold in common", he said: "My reason is that certain men have slipped in who have long ago been appointed by the Scriptures to the judgment described below, ungodly men, turning the undeserved kindness of our God into an excuse for loose conduct and proving false to our only Owner and Lord, Jesus Christ. . . . these men, too, indulging in dreams, are defiling the flesh and disregarding lordship and speaking abusively of glorious ones. . . . all the things they do understand naturally like the unreasoning animals, in these things they go on corrupting themselves."—Jude 4-10, *NW*.

⁸ Putting up a hard fight for the faith means not only holding fast with our minds the things taught us from God's Word. It also means resisting corruption and sincerely applying God's teachings to our daily lives that the way of the truth may not be reproached and spoken of abusively. Our lives must harmonize with the things which our minds and hearts believe and accept and which our mouths confess. If we do not practice what we

---

7. After ascertaining the faith, what must we do? For what reason?

8. What does putting up a hard fight for this faith mean?

publicly declare from God's Word, then we belie
what we claim and we stumble those who look upon us as examples of what believers are and should
be. "Faith, if it does not have works, is dead in
itself."—James 2:17, *NW*.

⁹ Satan the Devil corrupted man and woman's
faith toward God in Eden. From the time that the
pure faith was originally delivered he has tried to
corrupt it and its practice. Not only does he twist
scripture, as he did to Jesus in the wilderness of
temptation, but he tries to corrupt the lives of
the believers with the faith-destroying "works of
the flesh". He tries to infiltrate a filthy, treacherous "fifth column" among the Theocratic organization of Jehovah's people, to debase the pure
living standards which they must uphold. These
agents of the Devil were foretold and forewarned
against, and the disastrous end which they and
all who yield to them must suffer was set down
with absolute certainty. These persons have not
at heart cleaned themselves up from the world.
Under hypocrisies they sneak into the congregation and try to use God's mercy and undeserved
kindness toward his people as an excuse for immoral conduct to gratify their sexual desires.
They persuade unstable believers that, to begin
with, God forgave us our sins through faith in
Christ's blood, including our former sins of fornication and adultery. 'Yes,' say they, 'God knows
we are weak and subject to passion, and so if we

---

9. (a) Whom does Satan try to infiltrate among the
congregation? (b) How do they try to turn God's mercy
into excuse for immorality?

indulge in loose relations with one another for the satisfying of our sexual desires, God will be merciful. It does not hurt to indulge once in a while, and God will forgive us if we confess this sin, just as when we first came to him through Christ. So come on! Let's!'

[10] Such defilers of the flesh are like brute beasts in being controlled by animal passions. Against them we need to put up a hard fight for the faith and the pure, clean living that it stands for and insists upon. If we yield to such enticers to willful uncleanness, it means working for our own destruction, at the same time bringing reproach upon God's congregation. God has delivered his people. He believes in a clean organization. So we should all fight hard to keep it that way for his honor and that we may recommend his truth and organization to others who seek life.

[11] Those who take up the practice of sin after God has once cleansed them from it through Jesus' blood are like a dog that licks up its own vomit or a sow that goes from its bath back to rolling in filthy mire. God will destroy all who willfully entangle themselves again in sin for the selfish pleasure it gives the depraved flesh. Their being associated with the Theocratic organization which is in the way of salvation will not save them or excuse them, but it means their greater responsibility. So in fighting hard for the faith that was delivered once for all time to the holy ones we

10. To resist them requires what? To yield to them results how?
11. Will association with us save those returning to sin? Why?

must resist those enticing defilers. We must keep strict self-control over ourselves. The apostle says:

[12] "I browbeat my body and lead it as a slave, that, after I have preached to others, I myself should not become disapproved somehow. Now I do not want you to be ignorant, brothers, that our forefathers were all under the cloud and all passed through the sea and all got baptized into Moses by means of the cloud and of the sea; and all ate the same spiritual food and all drank the same spiritual drink. For they used to drink from the spiritual rock-mass which followed them, and that rock-mass meant the Christ. Nevertheless, on most of them God did not express his approval, for they were laid low in the wilderness. Now these things became our examples, for us not to be persons desiring injurious things, even as they desired them. Neither become idolaters, as some of them did; just as it is written: 'The people sat down to eat and drink, and they rose up to revel boisterously.' Neither let us practice fornication, as some of them committed fornication, only to fall, twenty-three thousand of them in one day. Neither let us put Jehovah to the test, as some of them put him to the test, only to perish by the serpents. Neither be murmurers, just as some of them murmured, only to perish by the destroyer. Now these things went on befalling them as examples and they were written for a warning to us upon whom the accomplished ends of the systems of things have arrived. Consequently, let him that

---

12. In proof, to what warning examples does the apostle refer us?

thinks he has a firm position beware that he does not fall. No temptation has taken you except what is common to men."—1 Corinthians 9:27 to 10:13, NW.

[13] So let us not presume on God's mercy to the point of willfully trying to abuse it. But as we expect God's mercy, let us be merciful to others. "Happy are the merciful, since they will be shown mercy." (Matthew 5:7, NW) One way to display mercy and put up a good fight for the pure God-given faith is to build up one another on our most holy faith, praying in full harmony with the holy spirit that we may not enter into temptation through weakness of the flesh. We ourselves hate an inner garment or inner self that is stained up by sinful flesh. Yet we must mercifully endeavor to rescue anyone we see in the congregation yielding to enticement and staining his garment of Christian identification by fleshly passions. Since we have once died to sin through Christ, we can no more live to it and become its slave again. —Jude 20-23.

[14] If any member of the congregation sins in a personal way against us, we will seek to keep on brotherly terms with the sinner and keep the peace and unity of the congregation. To that end we will not advertise his sin against us by gossiping or by other publicity, but we will try to make it easier for him to recover from his sin, by keep-

---

13. How do we put up a good fight by mutual upbuilding, prayer, and showing mercy to endangered ones?
14. To restore one sinning against us, what will we not do?

ing it confidential between us and him. We will
not nurse hurt feelings and watch for a chance to
get even with him, but we will try to recover him
from the bad effects of his sin by our opening his
eyes to it and making a way for restoring peaceful relations. We will follow Jesus' instructions:

[15] "It is not a desirable thing with my Father
who is in heaven for one of these little ones to
perish. Moreover, if your brother commits a sin,
go lay bare his fault between you and him alone.
If he listens to you, you have gained your brother.
But if he does not listen, take along with you one
or two more, in order that at the mouth of two
or three witnesses every matter may be established. If he does not listen to them, speak to the
congregation. If he does not listen even to the
congregation, let him be to you just as a man of
the nations and as a tax collector."—Matthew
18:14-17, *NW*.

[16] Speaking at last to the congregation does not
mean calling for a so-called "church trial", in
which the whole congregation sits both as a jury
and as a body of judges to hear the matter and
to pass judgment, with likely the congregation becoming divided and indulging in a lot of wrangling
and internal disturbance. It means this: Let the
injured one approach the representative brothers
of the congregation, those who are appointed to
official service through the Theocratic organiza-

---

15. What were Jesus' instructions governing such a
case?
16. What does speaking at last to the congregation
mean?

tion. Take them along and let them hear the matter laid bare in the offender's presence. Then let these representative servants use their spiritual qualifications to restore the offender to his senses, to a recognition of his fault, that he may confess it and seek God's forgiveness through Christ and render proper amends to his injured brother.

[17] If the offender refuses to hear the congregation, that is, what its representatives have to say with meekness, Jesus did not say to drag the matter before the worldly law courts of the land. The apostle Paul said it would be better to suffer injustice than to do that, as this spares bringing the Christian congregation into a bad light before the worldly public. (1 Corinthians 6:1-8) Jesus said to let the stubborn offender alone to take his worldly course, like a worldly Gentile or an oppressive tax collector. In this way the one offended has suffered no real lasting hurt to his spiritual interests, but he has grown in love through the exercise of mercy to his brother. He has not been overcome by wrongdoing, but has put up a hard fight for the faith that was once for all time delivered to God's holy ones. He has kept himself in God's love and in the narrow path to eternal life.

---

17. If the offender refuses to hear the congregation, what does the offended one do without real lasting hurt to himself?

CHAPTER XIX

SUBJECTION TO
THE SUPERIOR AUTHORITIES

THE angel Gabriel told the Jewish virgin that her son was to be called Jesus: "This one will be great and will be called Son of the Most High, and Jehovah God will give him the throne of David his father, and he will be king over the house of Jacob forever, and there will be no end of his kingdom." This advice agreed with previous prophecies that the Supreme Authority, Jehovah God, had arranged for his Son to be the Permanent Heir of the Kingdom covenant made with David and to have a heavenly kingdom at God's own right hand. Satan the Devil tried to lure the Son of the Most High away from this heavenly prize. He took Jesus up into a high mountain and pointed to all the kingdoms of the inhabited earth in an instant of time. Proudly he said to Jesus: "I will give you all this authority and the glory of them, because it has been delivered to me and to whomever I wish I give it. You, therefore, if you do an act of worship before me, it will all be yours." Jesus refused this glamorous offer of the Devil. He chose to continue worshiping Jehovah and holding onto the divine offer,

1. How was it foretold at Jesus' conception that he would come into a kingdom? and against what offer did he hold fast to it?

the heavenly kingdom to which he has been anointed with Jehovah's spirit.—Luke 1:31-33 and 4:5-8, *NW*.

² For taking this course, it cost Jesus his earthly life, in a most disgraceful style. Yet it vindicated Jehovah's sovereignty over all the universe and it won for Jesus a place in the universe higher than he had before, second only to that of the Most High God himself. "When he found himself in fashion as a man, he humbled himself and became obedient as far as death, yes, death on a torture stake. For this very reason also God exalted him to a superior position and kindly gave him the name that is above every other name, so that in the name of Jesus every knee should bend of those in heaven and those on earth and those under the ground, and every tongue should openly confess that Jesus Christ is Lord to the glory of God the Father." To which Peter adds: "He is at God's right hand, for he went his way to heaven, and angels and authorities and powers were made subject to him." (Philippians 2:8-11 and 1 Peter 3:22, *NW*) By this divine arrangement the glorified Jesus stands in a position next to Jehovah, and so the Most High God and this highly exalted Jesus stand as the Superior Authorities over all the universe. This is so in spite of Satan the Devil and all the kingdoms of the inhabited earth.

³ Jesus refused the kingdoms of the earth be-

---

2. How did Jesus get to be exalted to be second-highest Authority?

3, 4. How did Jesus reveal symbolically the source from which the worldly kingdoms derived their power?

cause they were never ordained by God but are all man-made. When the aged apostle John was a prisoner exiled by the Roman government, the glorified Jesus disclosed to him the source from which all these kingdoms of this world derived their great power over the earth:

[4] "And I saw," says John, "a beast coming up out of the sea, having seven heads and ten horns, and upon his horns ten diadems, and upon his heads names of blasphemy. . . . And the dragon gave him his own strength, and great power. . . . And all the earth was in admiration after the beast. And they adored the dragon, which gave power to the beast: and they adored the beast, saying: Who is like to the beast? and who shall be able to fight with him?"—Apocalypse 13:1-4, *Douay*.

[5] Note this beast that came up out of the abyss of the sea. The Roman Catholic edition of the Bible (by John Murphy Company, Baltimore, Maryland, 1914) says in its footnote on it: "This first beast with seven heads and ten horns, is probably the whole company of infidels, enemies and persecutors of the people of God, from the beginning to the end of the world. The seven heads are seven kings, that is, seven principal kingdoms or empires, which have exercised, or shall exercise, tyrannical power over the people of God; of these, five were then fallen, viz.: the Egyptian, Assyrian, Chaldean, Persian, and Grecian monarchies: one was present, viz., the empire of

5. From whom do religious interpreters agree the visible world system received its power?

Rome: and the seventh and chiefest was to come, viz., the great Antichrist and his empire. The ten horns may be understood of ten lesser persecutors." At Apocalypse 12:9, 12 the Revelation says that the "dragon" is Satan the Devil.

⁶ Religious interpreters of Scripture thus agree that the visible ruling system in control of the earth received its power and strength from the great dragon, "that old serpent, who is called the devil and Satan, who seduceth the whole world." Revelation 17:12 says: "The ten horns which thou sawest are ten kings, which . . . receive power as kings one hour with the beast." Revelation, chapters 12, 13, 17, 19, also shows that the dragon and the beast from the sea and their allies all range themselves up against Jehovah God and his kingdom by Jesus Christ. This pushes into the place of chief dispute the issue of universal sovereignty, Who is the Most High and whose sovereignty must the universe acknowledge and obey?

⁷ Jesus Christ on earth set the right example for his followers to copy in deciding this issue. For his faithfulness to a martyr's death in favor of Jehovah's rightful sovereignty Jesus was exalted to the place of superior authority with only Jehovah God as Head over him. Just before his betrayal and death Jesus said to his faithful apostles: "The ruler of the world is coming. And yet he has no hold on me, . . . the ruler of this world has been judged." (John 14:30 and 16:11, *NW*)

6, 7. (a) Against whom do the world powers range themselves and force what issue? (b) In the clash to whom must we be subject?

The ruler of this world, the dragon, and the visible ruling system which he put in power range themselves up in opposition to God and his Kingdom Heir. So there is often a clash between the commands and laws of God and those of the visible ruling system of this world. Under such circumstances, to whom must the believing soul be subject in unwavering obedience? The answer is so simple: To the Authorities superior to men and devils. Subjection to them means eternal life.

[8] Rome was the dominant world power in Paul's day, and this apostle wrote a letter to the Christian believers there: "to all those who are in Rome as God's beloved ones, called to be holy ones." (Romans 1:1-7, NW) He did not address his letter to souls outside the Theocratic organization to discuss worldly politics with them. In chapter twelve of this letter he shows the Theocratic organization is like a human body with Jesus Christ as the God-appointed Head, and then he answers the question on universal sovereignty for us, saying:

[9] "Do not let yourself be conquered by the evil, but keep conquering the evil with the good. Let every soul be in subjection to the superior authorities, for there is no authority except by God; the existing authorities stand placed in their relative positions by God. Therefore he who ranges himself up against the authority has taken a stand

---

8. To whom did Paul address Romans, chapter 13? On what question?
9. What does he say, for us to benefit from existing authorities?

against the arrangement of God; those who have taken a stand against it will receive judgment to themselves. For those ruling are an object of fear, not to the good deed, but to the evil. Do you, then, want to have no fear of the authority? Keep doing good, and you will have praise from it; for it is God's minister to you for your good. But if you are doing evil, be in fear: for it is not without purpose that it bears the sword; for it is God's minister, an avenger to express wrath upon the one practicing evil."—Romans 12:21 to 13:4, *NW*.

[10] The Superior Authorities are the Most High God Jehovah and his exalted Son Jesus Christ. By Jehovah's own Theocratic arrangement these existing Authorities stand placed in their relative positions, first, God Supreme, and second, Jesus Christ his anointed King. God the great Lawgiver has committed to his royal Son the full power to judge, together with authority to execute judgment rendered. (John 5:22, 27-30) These existing Superior Authorities are the proper objects of fear above all others. Said Peter: "Be in fear of God, have honor for the king," and the King Jesus Christ said to Peter and other disciples: "I will indicate to you whom to fear: Fear him who after killing has authority to throw into Gehenna. Yes, I tell you, fear this One." (1 Peter 2:17 and Luke 12:4, 5, *NW*) And to set forth his own superiority over the worldly rulers of earth, Jesus gave the Revelation in which he pictured himself as gaining the final victory over them, because

10. Who are the "superior authorities"? So whom must we fear?

"he is Lord of lords, and King of kings".—Revelation 17:14; 19:16.

[11] As Supreme Authority, Jehovah God is the source of all delegated rightful authority. He is not the source of authority for totalitarian dictators, but these derive their unrighteous power from the one the Revelation pictures by the dragon. Jehovah has given rightful authority to his Son, by whom he made all other things. Jesus proved his integrity to God as Universal Sovereign under the most painful test, so that "angels and authorities and powers were made subject to him". (1 Peter 3:22, NW) The apostle Paul says that authority was also given to him as apostle in the visible Theocratic organization of God's people: "the authority which the Lord gave us to build you up and not to tear you down." In warning disorderly ones he said: "That is why I write these things while absent, that, when I am present, I may not act with severity according to the authority which the Lord gave me, to build up and not to tear down." (2 Corinthians 10:8 and 13:10, NW) So while they existed during the first century the twelve apostles of the Lamb were authorities appointed by God over their brethren for the proper conducting of the visible organization. Such apostolic authorities would especially be meant when the request is made to the brothers "to have regard for those who are working hard among you and presiding over you in the Lord and ad-

---

11. (a) Who is the source of delegated rightful authority? (b) To whom did he delegate authority in the first century?

monishing you, and to give them more than extraordinary consideration in love because of their work".—1 Thessalonians 5:12, 13, *NW*.

[12] We are to have a proper fear toward the Superior Authorities in the sense of not wanting to displease them. If we do good by carrying out the divine will we have no need to be afraid, because the Superior Authorities are against only the evildoers. Authority from God and through Christ is exercised for the good of Christians who pursue righteousness: "it is God's minister to you for your good." It praises those who do God's will. It does not persecute, ban, imprison and kill them. But if we do wrong by acting against the divine will, then we have reason to fear punishment, for the Superior Authorities have the power to execute judgment upon wrongdoers. This power of execution is symbolized by the "sword". The King of kings and Lord of lords is pictured with it: "And out of his mouth there protrudes a sharp long sword, that he may smite the nations with it, and he will shepherd them with a rod of iron." (Revelation 19:15, 16, *NW*) In that sense divine authority, being rightly exercised, "is God's minister, an avenger to express wrath upon the one practicing evil."—Romans 13:3, 4, *NW*.

[13] People of this world often conform outwardly

12. (a) In what way is the authority God's minister to us for our good? (b) What is the sword it bears? For use against whom?
13. (a) Besides wanting to escape wrath, on account of what else should we be in subjection to Authority? (b) So what do we pay?

to the laws of the land simply for the sake of escaping legal punishment. But a lover of righteousness does not subject himself to the Superior Authorities just to spare himself the divine wrath and execution of judgment. He does it because it is right and it gives him peace of heart. One's own conscience, says the apostle, should be a force stronger than fear to move Christians to do right. "There is therefore compelling reason for you to be in subjection, not only on account of that wrath but also on account of your conscience." This matter of conscience should also apply to the question of paying tribute or taxes to worldly rulers. The apostle was writing to God's holy ones living in Rome, and Rome was one of the great taxing powers of ancient times. (Daniel 11:20) The holy ones at Rome were paying taxes, and that with good conscience: "For that is why you are also paying tribute." (Romans 13:5, 6, NW) The apostle was also well acquainted with how at the time that Jesus was about to be born "a decree went forth from Caesar Augustus for all the inhabited earth to be registered; . . . and all people went traveling to be registered, each one to his own city". And Luke, Paul's close companion, records how Jesus' foster father Joseph and his human mother Mary complied with that decree of Caesar and were registered.—Luke 2:1-5, NW.

[14] To pay the taxes levied is Christlike and therefore can be done with good conscience toward

---

14. (a) What did Jesus say on payment of tax to Caesar? (b) What do we owe "Caesar" in payment, and what not?

God. Jesus resolved the question for us of whether it is lawful to God to do so: "Is it lawful to pay tribute to Caesar or not?" Shown a denarius with Caesar's image and inscription upon it, Jesus said to his questioners: "Pay back, therefore, Caesar's things to Caesar, but God's things to God." (Matthew 22:17-21, *NW*) Caesar coined his own money and did not accept Jewish coins as tax money; and so we must pay back Caesar or worldly political powers the coins made and which are required in tax payment. Through governmental operations "Caesar" renders us numerous services and we owe it therefore to pay our taxes. Thus we pay him back for the services he renders and from which we get earthly benefits, such as public service utilities and facilities, public schooling, postal service, fire prevention and protection, police service, roads and streets, etc. So pay him conscientiously for earthly services rendered. But none of such services require our worshiping Caesar and none are worthy of it. He cannot buy our worship with such things. None of such things buy or provide for us everlasting life, and none of such things are worth our lives, so that we should lay down our lives for "Caesar" in any cause. Our life now and in the future is from the great Life-giver: "With thee is the fountain of life." "Salvation belongeth unto Jehovah." (Psalms 36:9; 3:8, *ASV*) "For God loved the world so much that he gave his only-begotten Son, in order that everyone exercising faith in him might not be destroyed but have everlasting life."—John 3:16, *NW*.

[15] Jehovah God is the Supreme Authority. Jesus Christ is a Superior Authority and said his followers must pay God what belongs to God. This comes before paying back Caesar Caesar's things. So a believer dedicated to God through Christ conscientiously asks: "If I pay back Caesar more than belongs to him just because he demands it, and if I surrender my life in unquestioning obedience to Caesar and lay down my life for him, what life will I have left to pay to God, who bought me with the ransom price of his Son's blood? How, then, could I live my life in full devotion to God by following Christ's steps? The Scriptures tell me, 'That one surrendered his soul for us; and we are under obligation to surrender our souls for our brothers.' (1 John 3:16, *NW*) How could laying down my life for Christian brothers for whom Jesus died agree with my using carnal weapons for Caesar and hating and killing my brothers in lands against which Caesar wages untheocratic warfare?" This Scriptural position may not be understood or appreciated by modern worldly authorities, but neither was that of the Bible Christians of the first century, concerning whom we read:

Early Christianity was little understood and was regarded with little favor by those who ruled the pagan world. Pagan writers referred to it as "a new and vicious superstition," and to Christians as "misguided creatures" practicing "moral enormities," creatures guilty of "hatred of the human race," "criminals who deserved the most severe punishment." . . . Christians refused to share certain duties of Roman citizens. The

---

15. As to rendering our lives, who has rightful claim? Why?

Christians were regarded as anarchists hoping to destroy the state; as pacifists who felt it a violation of their faith to enter military service. They would not hold political office. They would not worship the emperor.—*On the Road to Civilization, A World History,* by Heckel and Sigman (1937), pages 237, 238. An American high-school textbook in Indiana, 1938-1943.

[16] The inspired Scriptures show our lives, our worship and our unquestioning obedience belong to the Supreme Authority, Jehovah God, and we must pay them back to Him because owing to him. When faced with the question of obeying the unrighteous commands of worldly rulers against the will and orders of the Supreme Authority, the apostles Peter and John said to the Jewish Sanhedrin: "Whether it is righteous in the sight of God to listen to you rather than to God, make your decision. But as for us, we cannot stop speaking about the things we have seen and heard. . . . We must obey God as ruler rather than men. . . . And we are witnesses of these matters, and so is the holy spirit which God has given to those obeying him as ruler."—Acts 4:19, 20 and 5:29-32, *NW.*

[17] As for the Theocratic organization, those in it who have divine authority serve God in a public way for the good of the organization. They are to be respected, and Theocratic submission is to be rendered in connection with them. "For they are God's public servants constantly serving this very purpose. Render to all their dues, to him who calls for tribute, the tribute; to him who calls

16. Faced with unrighteous human commands, whom must we obey?
17. (a) Who are God's public servants? (b) With what exception should we not be in debt to anybody?

for tax, the tax; to him who calls for fear, such fear; to him who calls for honor, such honor. Do not be owing anybody a single thing, except to love one another; for he that loves his fellow man has fulfilled the law."—Romans 13:6-8, *NW*.

[18] For obeying these Theocratic instructions Jehovah's witnesses cannot truthfully be called "anarchists" against the governments of this world. The Bible account shows that the apostle Paul, who wrote Romans, chapter 13, was respectful to earthly kings and considered their position, power and responsibility. And so were other servants of God who are reported on. Hence all the charges that they were seditionists, upsetters of the world, propagandists of unlawful customs, etc., were proved false. (Acts 16:19-21; 17:6-8; 24:10-13; 25:8, 10, 11; 26:1-3, 7, 19, 30-32) We conscientiously render to "Caesar" what belongs to such worldly ruling power. But we know, too, that Caesar is not first in his claims. We put first things first. We have come to know that Jehovah God is the Supreme Authority of heaven and earth and that he appointed Jesus Christ to be a Superior Authority; and faithful subjection to these Superior Authorities means everlasting life to us.

---

18. What proves we cannot truthfully be called "anarchists" for obeying such Theocratic instructions? What do we know on this?

CHAPTER XX

THE WORLD'S "TIME OF THE END"

BEGINNING with Nebuchadnezzar king of Babylon, who was first to destroy Jerusalem, the Gentile nations of this world were permitted to rule a long time without opposition or interference by God's kingdom, either earthly or heavenly. When Jerusalem was destroyed in 607 B.C., and her domain was completely desolated, the typical kingdom of God with that city as its capital was overturned. At that time Satan the Devil, the invisible power behind King Nebuchadnezzar, became in the broadest sense of the expression "the god of this system of things". (2 Corinthians 4:4, *NW*) He had now made a big step toward realizing his selfish ambition: "For thou hast said in thine heart, I will ascend into heaven, I will exalt my throne above the stars of God: I will sit also upon the mount of the congregation, in the sides of the north: I will ascend above the heights of the clouds; I will be like the most High." (Isaiah 14:4, 13, 14) So with the disappearance of the typical kingdom of God from the mount of the congregation at Jerusalem the "appointed times of the nations" began. God's kingdom was not to interfere with the Gentile

---

1. How far did Satan realize his ambition in 607 B.C.? Till when?

domination of the earth until the coming of Messiah the Prince in Kingdom power. Said Jehovah: "I will overturn, overturn, overturn, it: and it shall be no more, until he come whose right it is; and I will give it him."—Ezekiel 21:25-27.

² When Jesus Christ first came to establish his perpetual right as the Heir of the covenant for the Kingdom, it did not interfere with the course of the appointed times of the nations. The worldly powers executed him as a seditionist a g a i n s t Caesar. This disposed of Jesus' ruling as a man on earth. After running the full length of "seven times", or 2,520 years from 607 B.C., these "appointed times of the nations" expired in October, A.D. 1914. (See Chapter VI, pages 59-70.) Does that mean Satan's world ended in 1914? No; no more than Satan's world first began with the start of the times of the nations. But events of that year definitely marked the beginning of the end for Satan's world. Therefore what began in 1914 was the "time of the end". "To the time of the end: because it is yet for a time appointed," says Daniel's prophecy. So Jehovah God appointed unchangeably when the "time of the end" should begin, namely, at the close of the appointed times of the nations in 1914.—Daniel 11:35, 40; 12:4, 9.

³ The "time of the end" covers a period of time from 1914 until Satan's world is destroyed; and Jesus spoke of it as the "consummation of the system of things". In two parables Jesus spoke of

2. What ended A.D. 1914, and what also began that year?
3. What is the "time of the end"? What do Jesus' parables show?

this and showed it is a period of time marked by definite happenings. These reach their climax in the accomplished end of this system of things controlled by Satan the Devil. In explaining his parable of the wheat field which the Devil over-sowed with poisonous weeds (imitation wheat), Jesus said: "The harvest is a consummation of a system of things, and the reapers are angels. Therefore, just as the weeds are collected and burned with fire, so it will be in the consummation of the system of things. The Son of man will send forth his angels, and they will collect out from his kingdom all things that cause stumbling and persons who are doing lawlessness, and they will pitch them into the fiery furnace." In explaining his parable of the dragnet that scooped up fish of every kind, Jesus said: "That is how it will be in the consummation of the system of things: the angels will go out and separate the wicked from among the righteous and will cast them into the fiery furnace." (Matthew 13:39-42, 47-50, *NW*) All the operations which the parables describe as taking place required time. In the corresponding fulfillment such operations require time before the end is accomplished. This proves that the con-summation of this system of things is a time pe-riod with a definite beginning and a definite end.

[4] Jesus used the destruction of unfaithful Jeru-salem to picture the destruction of this system of things, beginning with its dominant part, "Chris-

---

4. What destruction did Jesus foretell? And so what questions did his disciples then ask and what do we now ask?

tendom." With vivid language he foretold the second destruction of the profaned city and its temple, this time by the Roman legions A.D. 70. (Luke 19:41-45; Matthew 23:37 to 24:2) Shortly after this prophecy four of his apostles privately asked him: "Tell us, When will these things be, and what will be the sign of your presence and of the consummation of the system of things?" (Matthew 24:3, NW) Inspired prophet that he was, Jesus proceeded to give them the sign. Has that sign put in appearance since 1914, proving that the consummation did begin in that year? Yes; and as we listen to Jesus' description of it we feel we are living again the epochal days which began with A.D. 1914.

[5] "You are going to hear of wars and reports of wars; see that you are not terrified. For these things must take place, but the accomplished end is not yet." No, the accomplished end of this political, commercial, religious system of things is not right then and there in 1914. That year marks only the beginning of the consummation, and lots must follow during the years of the consummation. What? "For nation will rise against nation and kingdom against kingdom, and there will be food shortages and earthquakes in one place after another. All these things are a beginning of pangs of distress." (Matthew 24:6-8, NW) Precisely on time, A.D. 1914, global war No. 1 broke out. All the distressing death-dealing things that Jesus foretold followed and accompanied it. The world

---

5. What did he say would mark the beginning of the consummation?

is no more the same. It has never recovered from those crippling initial pangs of distress, but the doomed condition of the whole world grows worse.

⁶ Who is responsible for all these pangs of distress from which the world writhes more and more in fear and agony? Do not let us be misled by religious clergymen who claim that God is responsible in that he is punishing the people for forsaking the religious systems of Christendom and turning to godless "isms". Just because he fixed the end of the times of the nations at 1914 and appointed the world's time of the end to start there, that does not make him responsible for the distress which Jesus foretold. God's revealed Word uncovers the guilty troublemaker and bares the reason for his outrageous treatment of human society. Wars, famines, pestilences and earthquakes have afflicted the earth before, but the times of the nations had not then ended. Nor were those disasters foretold in particular and neither were they accompanied by the overshadowing events in heaven that occurred from 1914 forward. So the meaning of world distress that began with A.D. 1914 is certain. We are in the "time of the end", the consummation of this system of things, and Satan the Devil is responsible for the mounting woes that pain the people.

⁷ The beginning of the "appointed times of the nations" in 607 B.C. was marked by the overturning of the typical kingdom of God, whose king sat

---

6. Whom do the clergy charge, but who is responsible for the woe?
7. As against what happened in 607 B.C., what does 1914 mark?

on the "throne of Jehovah" at Jerusalem. The end of those "times of the nations" A.D. 1914 must be marked by the setting up of the real, antitypical kingdom of God in the hands of his Permanent Heir of the Kingdom covenant. God said the Theocratic crown and diadem would be removed from human heads and that the acting government in the hands of a royal descendant of David would be no more until the Messiah comes whose right it is to rule. Then Jehovah God would give it to him. This coming of the rightful King and giving him the governmental rule is what puts an end to the times of the nations with their uninterrupted domination of this world. So 1914 marks not alone the end of the times of the nations but the beginning of Jehovah's kingdom by his Messiah. It marks the birth of the Theocratic government over this earth which belongs to Jehovah God. His holy universal organization in heaven is pictured as a woman with the combined lights of heaven focused upon her. She brought forth or gave birth to the Rightful Ruler. The Most High God at once enthroned him. So in 1914 the stage was all set for a war in heaven, with universal effects.

⁸ "And another sign was seen in heaven, and look! a great fiery-colored dragon, with seven heads and ten horns and upon its heads seven diadems; . . . And the dragon kept standing before the woman who was about to give birth, that, when she did give birth, it might devour her child.

---

8. By whom was the war in heaven fought? How did it result?

And she gave birth to a son, a male, who is destined to shepherd all the nations with an iron rod. [That fact writes *finis* to the 'times of the nations'.] And her child was caught away to God and to his throne. . . . And war broke out in heaven: Michael and his angels battled with the dragon, and the dragon and its angels battled but it did not prevail, neither was a place found for them any longer in heaven. So down the great dragon was hurled, the original serpent, the one called Devil and Satan, who is misleading the entire inhabited earth; he was hurled down to the earth, and his angels were hurled down with him. And I heard a loud voice in heaven say: 'Now have come to pass the salvation and the power and the kingdom of our God and the authority of his Christ, because the accuser of our brothers has been hurled down, who accuses them day and night before our God! . . . On this account be glad, you heavens and you who reside in them! Woe for the earth and for the sea, because the Devil has come down to you, having great anger, knowing he has a short period of time.' "—Revelation 12:1-12, *NW*.

⁹ There you are! It is Satan the Devil that is responsible for the woe that torments earth and sea! He opposed God's kingdom from its birth in 1914. But he was foiled in his efforts to overturn it and was hurled out of heaven down to earth. The endless succession of woe and distress since 1914 proves the Kingdom was born, the war in

9. So what does the world woe prove? Yet why should we rejoice?

heaven was fought, and the Devil and all his demons were cast out and are now raging about this
earth, faced with their dire end within a short
period of time. While it is a period of sore woe
and suffering for misled mankind, it is a time for
all men of good-will to rejoice with the holy heavens. The heavens are freed forever of Satan and
his demons, and within a short period of time our
earth will be also! God's kingdom has been born!
The universal Sovereign again reigns toward our
earth! And he has given authority to his King,
who is a Priest after the likeness of Melchizedek,
to rule with an iron rod in the midst of the nations
whose "seven times" of world domination have
run out, until he at last delivers all mankind from
their unsatisfactory, oppressive rule. God's kingdom by his Christ is in power to stay for all eternity. Rejoice with heaven above!

[10] Losing his fight in heaven, Satan and his demons keep up the fight on earth. Against whom?
Against the visible part of God's universal organization (God's "woman") and its members.
"Now when the dragon saw it was hurled down
to the earth, it persecuted the woman that gave
birth to the male child. . . . And the dragon grew
wrathful at the woman, and went off to wage war
with the remaining ones of her seed, who observe
the commandments of God and have the work of
bearing witness to Jesus." (Revelation 12:13-17,
NW) This prediction of persecution by the dragon
and his demons upon God's witnesses agrees with

---

10. How do we explain the persecution on Jehovah's
witnesses now?

Jesus' previous prophecy on the sign of the consummation of this system of things. After foretelling global war with famines, earth tremors, and pestilences, Jesus said: "Then people will deliver you up to tribulation and will kill you, and you will be hated by all the nations on account of my name. Then, also, many will be stumbled and will betray one another and will hate one another. . . . and because of the increasing of lawlessness the love of

the greater number will cool off. But he that has endured to the finish is the one that will be saved." (Matthew 24:9-13, *NW;* Luke 21:10-19) All this

persecution has come upon Jehovah's witnesses, who have taken no part in the global wars to date. It continues coming at the instigation of the Devil and his demons, because Jehovah's witnesses observe the commandments of God the Su-

preme Authority and they stick to the work of bearing witness to Jesus, God's enthroned King.

[11] The apocalyptic Revelation shows plainly that Satan and his demons are not bound or destroyed immediately after being hurled out of heaven. They are permitted to run loose like mad dogs at the earth until the consummation of this system of things hits its climax in destruction. With that destruction the consummation comes to its end. Before this comes, a work must be done by the faithful remnant of God's "woman" who keep his commandments by being witnesses to his kingdom by his enthroned Son Jesus Christ. This is part of the sign he foretold marking the consummation: "And this good news of the kingdom will be preached in all the inhabited earth for the purpose of a witness to all the nations, and then the accomplished end will come." (Matthew 24:14, *NW*) Since World War I this witness to the established Kingdom has been preached to all nations without letup. Despite the war the dragon and his demons wage against the remnant and their good-will companions, the witness to all nations increases in power and magnitude. For certain the accomplished end of this world draws near!

---

11. Before the end comes, what work must be done? Despite what?

CHAPTER XXI

SECOND PRESENCE
OF LIFE'S CHIEF AGENT

THE inquiring apostles linked up the consummation of this system of things with the second presence of Jesus Christ. Their question to him was: "When will these things be, and what will be the sign of your presence and of the consummation of the system of things?" (Matthew 24:3, *NW; Roth.; Yg.*) His second presence does need some visible evidence for us to discern it, because he must be present invisibly as a glorious immortal spirit. The purpose of his second presence requires it to be invisible, but by the sign given he appears to the eyes of understanding of "all those who have loved his manifestation". (2 Timothy 4:8, *NW*) If we love to have him manifest himself to us, we will study the sign indicating his longed-for second presence.

² His coming or return marks the beginning of his presence. When the disciples on the mount of Olives gazed into the sky, while he ascended heavenward and then disappeared in a cloud, two angels said to them: "This Jesus who was received up from you into heaven will come thus in the same manner as you have beheld him going

---

1. Why do we need a visible sign of Jesus' second presence?
2. How does the world see him no more? And yet, how will "every eye" see him?

into heaven." These angels did not say those very disciples would see Jesus come again nor that Jesus would come in the same form as when he ascended. The manner in which he returns is what is to be the same as when he went to heaven. Faithful disciples witnessed his ascension. None of this world did so. On the night of his betrayal to his enemies he said: "A little longer and the world will behold me no more, but you will behold me, because I live and you will live." (Acts 1:11 and John 14:19, *NW*) The manner of his going was quiet, without this world's perceiving it, and with his becoming invisible when a cloud caught him up from their vision. Moreover, it was as a spirit that he ascended to his Father's presence. All this requires him to come again quietly, without great display to awe the world, but in an invisible manner represented by clouds. Only his watching faithful followers now discern his presence in spirit with their eyes of understanding. But at the climax of the consummation of this system of things he makes an overpowering manifestation of his presence in spirit, so that all on earth, even his foes, become aware of his presence. "Look! he is coming with the clouds, and every eye will see him, and those who pierced him; and all the tribes of the earth will beat themselves in grief because of him."—Revelation 1:7, *NW*.

[3] At his first coming to earth he was present and showed himself before the public eye for the three and a half years of his ministry. It was then

---

3. For the sake of what lineage did Jesus come first in flesh?

necessary for him to come visibly in flesh, not by just materializing a human body and appearing the way a number of angels had done without giving up their spirit existence. He must become "the SON of man". He must be BORN as a man in human perfection. He must be born of a special line, to be born the promised Seed of Abraham and the Son of David, the Permanent Heir of the covenant made with David for the everlasting Kingdom. He was born such. This is proved by "the book of the history of Jesus Christ, son of David, son of Abraham", written for us by the apostle Matthew. (Matthew 1:1, NW) This inspired writer, in harmony with the other historians, Mark, Luke and John, shows how Jesus had his life, which he had formerly enjoyed in the spirit, transferred from heavenly glory to the womb of the virgin Jewess, Mary. Thus he did not inherit sin and condemnation from Adam, but was born a perfect man, the Son of God as well as son of Abraham and son of David. As such he could prove to be the Seed in whom all the nations of the earth are to be blessed and also prove to be the royal Seed of David in whom the Kingdom covenant finds its permanent heir. As such he vindicates Jehovah's promises.

[4] Jesus described also the secondary purpose of his coming to earth in human form: "The Son of man came, not to be ministered to, but to minister and to give his soul a ransom in exchange for many." (Matthew 20:28, NW) This required

---

4. What was the secondary purpose of Jesus' coming in flesh?

him to become a perfect man that he might be a corresponding ransom for the perfect human life that Adam forfeited for himself and lost for all mankind by his willful sin in Eden. But as long as Jesus enjoyed human life himself he could not be a corresponding ransom for dying mankind. He must sacrifice that perfect human life by dying in sinless innocence according to God's will. In that way he would release that perfect human life and the right to it and make it an asset which he could apply before God in heaven as a purchase price for mankind. He could apply the merit of his human righteousness as a means of canceling the sin and condemnation against believing men.

[5] Though condemned as a sinner by self-righteous religious Jews, he died holy and righteous as a ransom sacrifice. Peter said to them at the temple: "Yes, you disowned that holy and righteous one, and you asked for a man, a murderer, to be freely granted to you, whereas you killed the Chief Agent of life. But God raised him up from the dead, of which fact we are witnesses." (Acts 3:14, 15, NW) This same Peter tells us that God resurrected Jesus Christ a spirit: "Christ died once for all time concerning sins, a righteous person for unrighteous ones, that he might lead you to God, he being put to death in the flesh, but being made alive in the spirit." (1 Peter 3:18, NW) By not being made alive again in the flesh, he left his perfect human life as a sacrifice to ransom dying mankind. He said: "The bread that I

_____

5. Was Jesus resurrected a fleshly person? What is the reason?

shall give is my flesh in behalf of the life of the world."—John 6:51, *NW*.

⁶ To be born in flesh was a humiliation for the heavenly Son of God, since man is created a little lower than angels. (Psalm 8:5; Hebrews 2:9) But for Jesus' absolute faithfulness to the death on the torture stake God glorified Jesus by resurrecting him an immortal, incorruptible spirit. As such Jesus could ascend to God, whose face no man of flesh and blood could see with the possibility of remaining alive. But as a divine spirit Jesus the High Priest appeared in God's presence with the value or merit of his sacrifice of perfect blood and flesh. This he presented as a sin offering to God. "Christ entered, not into a holy place made with hands which is a copy of the reality, but into heaven itself, now to appear before the person of God for us."

⁷ On the following day of Pentecost his faithful disciples on earth began to receive the benefits of this surrender of his ransom sacrifice to God in heaven. So High Priest Jesus could never take that ransom sacrifice back again. Having given up his flesh for the life of the world he could never assume it again and become a man once more. For that basic reason his return and his second presence could never be in the flesh and blood which he sacrificed once for all time. Nor is his return in flesh necessary, for he does not return to die again for sins. So he returns without flesh

---

6. How was he thus glorified? How could he serve as High Priest?
7. Why could he not return in flesh? Why is that not necessary?

and blood for sacrifice: "And as it is reserved for men to die once for all time, but after this a judgment, so also the Christ was offered once for all time to bear the sins of many, and the second time that he appears it will be apart from sin [or, be without a sin offering] and to those earnestly looking for him for their salvation."—Hebrews 9:24, 27, 28, *NW*.

⁸ Why, then, does Jesus Christ return? It is to rule in his kingdom. His first coming, which was in perfect flesh and blood, was to vindicate Jehovah's universal sovereignty by his complete faithfulness to the interests of God's kingdom and also to ransom mankind. He did provide the ransom, but God did not then establish the Kingdom with him. And so the disciples were taught to pray: "Our Father in the heavens, let your name be sanctified. Let your kingdom come. Let your will come to pass, as in heaven, also upon earth." (Matthew 6:9, 10, *NW*) Christ's return being for him to rule in the Kingdom, then his second coming means his entering actively into the power of the Kingdom. When he ascended to heaven he sat down at God's right hand to wait for that time of entering into his authority and ruling like Melchizedek over his enemies as his footstool. Hebrews 10:12, 13 states: "This man offered one sacrifice for sins perpetually and sat down at the right hand of God, from then on awaiting until his enemies should be made a stool for his feet." (*NW*) The evidence already considered proves

---

8. Why does he return? So what does his second coming mean?

that A.D. 1914 God's kingdom was born and his Son was enthroned with authority to rule with an iron rod amid his foes. Eventually he will dash them to pieces and rid the universe of all fighters against God's rightful sovereignty.—Psalm 2:8, 9.

⁹ So A.D. 1914 marks the time of Christ's invisible return in spirit. Its invisibility is denoted by obscuring clouds, and Daniel 7:13, 14 describes it: "I saw in the night visions, and, behold, one like the Son of man came with the clouds of heaven, and came to the Ancient of days, and they brought him near before him. And there was given him dominion, and glory, and a kingdom, that all people, nations, and languages, should serve him: his dominion is an everlasting dominion, which shall not pass away, and his kingdom that which shall not be destroyed." This coming in clouds with Kingdom power and glory was the sign from heaven which the unbelieving Jews demanded of Jesus. But Jesus connected this event with his SECOND coming and the consummation of this system of things, saying: "And then the sign of the Son of man will appear in heaven, and then all the tribes of the earth will go to wailing and they will see the Son of man coming on the clouds of heaven with power and great glory." (Matthew 24:30, *NW*) His coming into the Kingdom in 1914 marks the beginning of his second presence or *par·ou·si'a*. This Greek word means *presence*.

¹⁰ His first presence, which was in flesh and

9. What sign did Jews ask of Jesus? When did he show it occurs?
10. What does the term *presence* denote? Why cannot it be hid?

blood, extended over a period of time. So does his second presence, which is in spirit. Although invisible in spirit, his second presence is of such importance to people over all the earth that it must not be kept secret, and it will not be. No, it cannot be, no more than a brilliant, crackling lightning flash from the clouds of heaven could be kept secret within a desert or a chamber of mystery. So Jesus warned: "Therefore, if people say to you, 'Look! he is in the wilderness,' do not go out; 'Look! he is in the inner chambers,' do not believe it. For just as the lightning comes out of eastern parts and shines over to western parts, so the presence [par·ou·si′a] of the Son of man will be." —Matthew 24:26, 27, NW.

[11] Since 1914 the present Christ has been making the evidences of his second presence or par·ou·si′a manifest and understandable to men everywhere. The remnant of Christ's faithful disciples and an increasing multitude of persons of good-will are discerning his illuminating second presence. They, in turn, are publishing it to still others that the eyes of their understanding may be opened to see. But many stubbornly refuse to believe the evidence before them and to see the truth and act with it, and these will be made to see his presence at the end of this world by the fiery destruction of this enemy of God's kingdom. That will be "at the revelation of the Lord Jesus from heaven with his powerful angels in a flaming fire, as he brings due punishment upon those who do not know God

11. How has his presence been made manifest? How will it yet be?

and those who do not obey the good news about our Lord Jesus. These very ones will pay the penalty of everlasting destruction from before the Lord and from the glory of his strength, at the time he comes to be glorified in connection with his holy ones".—2 Thessalonians 1:7-10, *NW*.

¹² It is in this capacity of Jehovah's Executioner to destroy his rebellious enemies that the King Jesus Christ comes like a thief. Wedging his warning in between a description of the preparations for the universal war of Armageddon which follow Satan's ousting from heaven, Jesus said: "They go forth to the kings of the entire inhabited earth, to gather them together to the war of the great day of God the Almighty. Look! I am coming as a thief. Happy is the one that stays awake . . . And they gathered them together to the place that is called in Hebrew Har-Ma·ged'on." (Revelation 16:14-16, *NW*) That destructive climax of the consummation of this system of things comes like a thief for its suddenness at an unknown, unexpected hour and in the night when the world is carousing wildly and self-reliantly in scoffing defiance of God. Jesus compared its coming with the unbelieved, sudden coming of the global flood in the time of Noah's presence.

¹³ For some years Noah and his three married sons had been building at God's command, and the ark was too big to escape public eyes. Noah explained its building by warning the ungodly world of the global flood. For their willful unbelief the

12. In what capacity and how does he come like a thief?
13. How is his presence to be just as the days of Noah?

flood of destruction gushed in on them with thief-like suddenness. So with the destructive climax of Jesus' invisible presence. "Concerning that day and hour nobody knows, neither the angels of the heavens nor the Son, but only the Father. For just as the days of Noah were, so the presence of the Son of man will be. For as people were in those days before the flood, eating and drinking, marrying and giving in marriage, until the day that Noah entered into the ark; and they took no note until the flood came and swept them all away, so the presence of the Son of man will be." (Matthew 24:36-39, *NW*) Christendom, professing to believe in a visible return of Christ in the flesh, refuses to believe the evidences of his parousia in spirit. Imitating the unbelief of the time of Noah's presence, Christendom scoffs and thus adds to the proof that we are in the consummation of this system of things.

¹⁴ "For you know this first, that in the last days there will come ridiculers with their ridicule, proceeding according to their own desires and saying: 'Where is this promised presence [*par·ou·si'a*] of his? Why, from the day our forefathers fell asleep in death, all things are continuing exactly as from creation's beginning.'" (2 Peter 3:3, 4, *NW*) This, too, adds to the proof that Christ's second presence would be invisible in spirit. To join those ridiculers leads to sudden destruction at Armageddon. To examine the evidence and then live and act as in the second presence of Jesus Christ the reigning King leads to everlasting life.

---

14. Of what does ridicule of his presence add proof?

CHAPTER XXII

THE REMNANT
OF KINGDOM HEIRS

DURING the second presence of Christ there must be a remnant of his faithful followers on earth, joint heirs with him of the heavenly kingdom. Nineteen centuries ago, after establishing the Memorial of Christ's death, he said to his loyal apostles: "You are the ones that have stuck with me in my trials; and I make a covenant with you, just as my Father has made a covenant with me, for a kingdom, that you may eat and drink at my table in my kingdom, and sit on thrones to judge the twelve tribes of Israel." (Luke 22:28-30, *NW*) With these words he notified them he was taking them into the Davidic covenant for the Kingdom with him. In his revelation to the apostle John he confirmed this covenant with his footstep followers by adding: "To him that conquers and observes my deeds down to the complete end I will give authority over the nations, and he shall shepherd the people with an iron rod so that they will be broken to pieces like clay vessels, the same as I have received from my Father, and I will give him the morning star." "To the one that conquers I will grant to sit down

---

1. (a) Who must be on earth during Christ's second presence? (b) With what words did Jesus speak of the covenant and confirm it to them?

with me in my throne, even as I conquered and
sat down with my Father in his throne."—Revelation 2:26-28 and 3:21, *NW*.

² During all the centuries since the giving of
those Kingdom promises, the calling and choos-
ing of the believers and the preparing and proving
of them worthy of the Kingdom has been going
on. Since the Kingdom class is finally only 144,000
with their Head Jesus Christ, then at the consummation of this system of things there must be
only the last members, a remnant of the ones
called and chosen for the Kingdom, yet on earth.

³ Describing the work that marks his second
presence, Jesus used a parable of the kingdom of
heaven and said: "As for the right kind of seed,
these are the sons of the kingdom; . . . The harvest is a consummation of a system of things, and
the reapers are angels. Therefore, just as the
weeds are collected and burned with fire, so it
will be in the consummation of the system of
things. The Son of man will send forth his angels,
and they will collect out from his kingdom all
things that cause stumbling and persons who are
doing lawlessness, and they will pitch them into
the fiery furnace. There is where their weeping
and the gnashing of their teeth will be. At that
time the righteous ones will shine as brightly as
the sun in the kingdom of their Father." (Matthew 13:38-43, *NW*) The harvesting of the King-

---

2. Why could there be only a remnant of such yet on
earth?
3. How did Jesus describe the harvest of the Kingdom
class?

dom class takes place during Christ's second presence, and he is the great Reaper as well as the one who first sowed the Kingdom seed.

⁴ The harvest work is part of the telltale sign of the parousia of the King Jesus Christ in spirit. By that work he separates the imitation Christians from the true Kingdom heirs, making the distinction between them very sharp and clear. He indicated that this harvest work would proceed after World War I and the casting of Satan and his demons out of heaven. Note his words to that effect in his prophecy on the sign of the consummation of this system of things: "Immediately after the tribulation of those days the sun will be darkened, and the moon will not give its light, and the stars will fall from heaven, and the powers of the heavens will be shaken. And then the sign of the Son of man will appear in heaven, . . . And he will send forth his angels with a great trumpet-sound and they will gather his chosen ones together from the four winds, from one extremity of the heavens to their other extremity." That would be a gathering of his faithful joint heirs from all the world under heaven, for "the field is the world". (Matthew 24:29-31, NW) Those alive on earth that are gathered make up the remnant. Revelation 12:17 speaks of them as the remnant of the seed of the woman. The dragon, wrathful because of being cast down to earth, makes war against them because they observe God's commands and carry forward the

4. When did Jesus show it must proceed? How do the remnant shine?

work of bearing witness to Jesus as King of kings. In this way they are already shining with the sun's brightness in their Father's kingdom by proclaiming the Kingdom message, so letting their light shine.

⁵ In perfect keeping with this visible gathering work on earth the resurrecting of the followers who conquered and died faithful takes place during the second presence of Jesus Christ. Revelation 12:1-13 does not picture them up in heaven at the time of the Kingdom's birth and the war in heaven which downed Satan. But a later chapter, immediately before describing the harvest of the earth, says: "And I heard a voice out of heaven say: 'Write: Happy are the dead who die in union with the Lord from this time onward. Yes, says the spirit, let them rest from their labors, for the things they did go right with them.'" (Revelation 14:13, NW) The expression "from this time onward" shows that this blessedness applies to the remnant at their death in faithfulness. But right before or when the harvesting of the remnant begins, the resurrection occurs for the victorious Kingdom heirs who had died faithful prior to Satan's ouster from heaven. This order of events is made certain for us at 1 Thessalonians 4:14-17 (NW):

⁶ "For if our faith is that Jesus died and rose again, so, too, those who have fallen asleep in

---

5. When does the resurrection of the sleeping conquerors occur?
6. How does 1 Thessalonians 4:14-17 make this certain for us?

death through Jesus God will bring with him. For this is what we tell you by Jehovah's word, that we the living who survive to the presence of the Lord shall in no way precede those who have fallen asleep in death, because the Lord himself will descend from heaven with a commanding call, with an archangel's voice and with God's trumpet, and those who are dead in union with Christ will rise first. Afterward we the living who are surviving will together with them be caught away in clouds to meet the Lord in the air; and thus we shall always be with the Lord."

⁷ Since the apostle is here addressing the congregation, his expression 'we the living who survive to the presence of the Lord' means the remnant on earth of those who are born from water and spirit and are called to the Kingdom. So the resurrection of suchlike ones who fell asleep in death before the harvest of the remnant begins takes place first. The Kingdom to which such are resurrected is heavenly. Since the second presence or parousia of the King Jesus Christ is in spirit and unseen to human eye, so, too, the resurrection of Kingdom heirs that slept in death is also unseen, it being to life in the spirit. They were buried with him in the likeness of his death, and the promise was that they would be in the likeness of his resurrection. How it is a spiritual resurrection is described in detail at 1 Corinthians, chapter 15:

---

7. How does the resurrection of those sleeping conquerors occur?

[8] "For just as in Adam all are dying, so also in the Christ all will be made alive. But each one in his own rank: Christ the firstfruits, afterward those who belong to the Christ during his presence. So also is the resurrection of the dead. It is sown in corruption, it is raised up in incorruption. It is sown in dishonor, it is raised up in glory. It is sown in weakness, it is raised up in power. It is sown a physical body, it is raised up a spiritual body. If there is a physical body, there is also a spiritual one. It is even so written: 'The first man Adam became a living soul.' The last Adam became a life-giving spirit. And just as we have borne the image of the one made of dust, we shall bear also the image of the heavenly one. However, this I say, brothers, that flesh and blood cannot inherit God's kingdom, neither does corruption inherit incorruption. Look! I tell you a sacred secret: We shall not all fall asleep in death, but we shall all be changed, in a moment, in the twinkling of an eye, during the last trumpet. For the trumpet will sound, and the dead will be raised up incorruptible, and we shall be changed. For this which is corruptible must put on incorruption, and this which is mortal must put on immortality. But when this which is corruptible puts on incorruption and this which is mortal puts on immortality, then the saying will take place that is written: 'Death is swallowed up forever.' "—1 Corinthians 15:22, 23, 42-45, 49-54, NW.

---

8. How does 1 Corinthians, chapter 15, describe it?

⁹ This definitely says that the Kingdom heirs who belong to the body of Christ are first resurrected from death "during his presence". It is when the Lord of lords himself descends from heaven, turning his attention downward to this earth at his second presence, that "those who are dead in union with Christ will rise first". A remnant of the 144,000 members of Christ's body are still left surviving on earth during his presence. It is that they might be witnesses to his kingdom in obedience to the commands of God. They must serve as witnesses of Jehovah God. (Isaiah 43:10-12; 44:8, *ASV*) So the members of this remnant are the "happy" ones who "die in union with the Lord from this time onward". Yes, they must die, being baptized into his death and sacrificing all right to perfect human life in the new world. They must fulfill the strict requirement for life with Christ Jesus in heaven: "Trustworthy is the saying: Certainly if we died together, we shall also live together; if we go on enduring, we shall also rule together as kings." (2 Timothy 2:11, 12, *NW*) The members of this remnant die, but they do not need to sleep in death as all those Kingdom heirs did who died prior to Christ's harvest work. They are the ones meant when the apostle says that "we shall not all fall asleep in death". The remnant do not die to sleep awaiting the beginning of Christ's parousia. Since he is then present, the moment of their death in the flesh becomes the moment of their resurrection change to life in the

---

9. Why must the remnant die? Why do they not sleep in death?

spirit, clothed upon with immortality and incorruption.

¹⁰ It is not first at the moment of death that this faithful remnant are "caught away in clouds to meet the Lord in the air". The Lord's being in the air shows he is not directly on or at the earth and that he is invisible, in the spirit, just as Satan has all along been in the spirit, "the ruler of the authority of the air, the spirit that now operates in the sons of disobedience." (Ephesians 2:2, NW) The existence of clouds then also denotes invisibility, as when the cloud received our ascending Lord out of the sight of the onlooking disciples. Their being caught away means first their being harvested, being separated from the power of the wicked world and brought into the free and delivered Theocratic organization under their invisible Lord.

¹¹ After warning his disciples against being misled by false Christs and false prophets with their deceptive signs and wonders at the consummation of this system of things, Jesus said: "Wherever the carcass is, there the eagles will flock together." (Matthew 24:28, NW) In a like prophecy describing the end of the world at Armageddon he also said: "I tell you, In that night two men will be in one bed; the one will be taken along, but the other will be abandoned. There will be two women grinding at the same mill; the one will be taken along, but the other will be abandoned." "So in

10. (a) How is the Lord now in the air, in clouds? (b) When or with what does the catching away of the remnant to meet him begin?

11, 12. How are some taken along, but others abandoned?

response they said to him: 'Where, Master?' He said to them: 'Where the body is, there also the eagles will be gathered together.' "—Luke 17:34-37, *NW*.

[12] Occurring in the time of the consummation, this applies to the remnant. It illustrates their being caught away from this wicked world which is doomed to become a carcass at the oncoming battle of Armageddon. Since the Kingdom has already been set up and the good news of it must be and is being preached to all nations, it is now the time of division over the issue of Jehovah's universal sovereignty by the kingdom of his Son. People may be members of the same family or human relationship, sleeping together in the same bed or grinding together at the household mill. But a separation can occur over this most important issue, whether among men or among women. People may be fellow workmen, laboring in the same field as family members or as employer and employee. They are able to get along peaceably on other matters, but when it comes to this chief

issue there is a division and those who belong to the remnant choose one destiny but the rest a different one. So one is taken along, but the other abandoned.

[13] One's being taken along corresponds with being received with Noah into the ark he built or the angels' taking Lot and his family out of Sodom to escape to the mountain. It means being taken to the place of safety in the Theocratic organization, safe from this world and its calamitous fate. It is because the remnant love Christ's appearing and kingdom and watch for the sign in evidence. Till the close of World War I in 1918 they were in forced bondage to this world, like the ancient Israelites when captive in Babylon. In 1919 their invisibly present Lord opened their eyes to the sign and made plain God's commanding call in his Word and brought them out of this prison condition. Rejoicing in his presence in the Kingdom which was shining like lightning that flashed light from east to west, they fearlessly took their stand on the side of the established Theocratic Government. They rejoiced that the battle of Armageddon was approaching and that there the King with iron rod would reduce the Devil's world organization to a carcass and so vindicate the universal sovereignty of the Most High God. The Lord, in view of the shortness of the time, quickly separated them or caught them away from the doomed organization and united them as a free people with himself in the Theo-

13. How have the remnant been gathered like eagles to a carcass?

cratic organization. Appreciating the situation and the issue involved, they hasten to that side like far-sighted, swift-flying eagles.

[14] Those who take the other side of the issue of universal sovereignty ignore and repel the light which reveals that God's Kingdom Heir and Theocratic Government are here. In willful ignorance and scoffing they go on in worldliness and are left or abandoned to their fate with Satan's world. When the day and hour, known only to God and his Executioner, come unexpectedly and surprise them like a thief, their carcasses will drop to the earth like carrion, along with that of their religious friend and ally, Christendom, the antitypical unfaithful Jerusalem. But the remnant of Kingdom heirs will rejoice over Jehovah's vindication and will feast like eagles upon the carcasses of his defeated foes. (Revelation 19:17-21) In God's appointed time and way their joy will be crowned with finishing their earthly course faithfully in death. But not to sleep in death. No, but they will be changed instantaneously to spirits immortal, incorruptible, to be personally in spirit with their Lord in the air, to be forever with him in his image, serving Jehovah God together. Happy are they in this special privilege, thus to "rest from their labors, for the things they did go right with them". This glorification of them completes the 144,000 in the heavenly Kingdom.

---

14. To what are the worldlings abandoned, but how is the catching away of the remnant to be with the Lord completed?

CHAPTER XXIII

THE "OTHER SHEEP" AND THE "GOATS"

JESUS Christ is the Right Shepherd of all those who gain life through him in the righteous new world. All others who pretend to be shepherds but who do not copy him as the Chief Shepherd are the wrong shepherds for us to gain life. These selfishly feed and clothe themselves at the expense of even the lives of their flocks. Jesus pointed up the qualifications that mark the proper shepherd, saying: "I have come that they might have life and might have it in abundance. I am the right shepherd; the right shepherd surrenders his soul in behalf of the sheep."—John 10:10, 11, *NW.*

[2] The Right Shepherd does not lay down his life for the wolves or beasts that prey upon the sheep, but does so for the sheep; and the sheep are the ones who benefit by the surrender of his soul as a human in their behalf. True, "Christ, while we were yet weak, died for ungodly men at the appointed time," and "God recommends his own love to us in that, while we were yet sinners, Christ died for us". But the apostle, in saying such things, was speaking for those weak, ungodly men and sinners who did not stay willfully in wicked-

---

1. What are the qualifications of the right shepherd? Who is he?
2. How did he die for *sheep,* if he died for weak, ungodly sinners?

ness. No, they were merely sheep going astray, and they heeded the Right Shepherd's call and responded to his voice and followed him.—Romans 5:6, 8, *NW;* 1 Peter 2:25.

[3] Those following him who become his spiritual brothers and joint heirs in the Kingdom are comparatively few, just 144,000 in number, and so he calls them a "little flock": "Have no fear, little flock, because your Father has approved of giving you the kingdom." (Luke 12:32, *NW*) These are the first to receive the life benefits of the surrender of his soul, from Pentecost forward. John the Baptist was the first man to introduce members of this little flock to Jesus, members taken from among the natural Jews whom John had baptized. Therefore Jesus likened him to the doorkeeper of a special sheepfold: "The doorkeeper opens to this one, and the sheep listen to his voice, and he calls his own sheep by name and leads them out." (John 10:3, *NW*) The sheep of this special Kingdom fold were not taken from only the natural Jews. No; but three and a half years after Pentecost A.D. 33 the Right Shepherd in heaven used the apostle Peter to take the key of knowledge and open the way for sheep from among the non-Jewish or Gentile nations to enter into the Kingdom fold.—Acts 10:1-48.

[4] But not all who eventually gain life through the Right Shepherd enter into the Kingdom sheep-

---

3. Who introduced him to the "little flock"? From among whom are such sheep taken?
4. Who are his "other sheep", and what do they attain to?

fold. Jesus called attention to this fact when he added: "And I have other sheep, which are not of this fold; those also I must bring, and they will listen to my voice, and they will become one flock, one shepherd. My sheep listen to my voice, and I know them, and they follow me. And I give them everlasting life, and they will by no means ever be destroyed, and no one will snatch them out of my hand." (John 10:16, 27, 28, *NW*) These "other sheep" are all others of humankind who acknowledge him as the one Right Shepherd who surrendered his soul for them to gain everlasting life. So they follow him as Shepherd and thus become members of his flock, though not of the Kingdom fold. They attain to eternal life on earth.

[5] Since the establishment of God's kingdom A.D. 1914 and the beginning of the harvest of the remnant of Kingdom sheep, a great number of these "other sheep" have begun to answer the Right Shepherd's call and to submit to his royal leadership. How many they will be before Armageddon's tribulation destroys Satan's organization we are not given to know. But, after stating the number of the Kingdom flock to be 144,000 and showing that they will be completely gathered, the apostle John under inspiration says: "After these things I saw, and, look! a great crowd, which no man was able to number, out of all nations and tribes and peoples and tongues, standing before the throne and before the Lamb, dressed in white robes, and there were palm branches in their

---

[5] Since when are they being gathered, and where and how is a great crowd of them pictured?

hands. And they keep on crying with a loud voice, saying: 'Salvation we owe to our God, who is seated on the throne, and to the Lamb.' . . . And he said to me: 'These are the ones that come out of the great tribulation, and they have washed their robes and made them white in the blood of the Lamb. That is why they are before the throne of God, and they are rendering him sacred service day and night in his temple, and the one seated on the throne will spread his tent over them. They will hunger no more nor thirst any more, neither will the sun beat down upon them nor any scorching heat, because the Lamb who is in the midst of the throne will shepherd them, and will guide them to fountains of waters of life.'" (Revelation 7:9-17, NW) The Lamb of God has begun shepherding these other sheep.

⁶ By being gathered now during the consummation of this system of things before the final conflict of Armageddon the "great crowd" of the Right Shepherd's "other sheep" are brought into earthly association with the remnant of Christ's spiritual brothers. Thus these other sheep can help these brothers of the King Jesus Christ and can prove that they uphold Jehovah's universal sovereignty and that they hope in his kingdom. This association of the other sheep with the remnant of Christ's royal brothers is now a fact. What it means for the other sheep to do good to these Jesus showed in a parable. Its fulfillment today

---

6. (a) With whom are they now associated, and with what opportunity? (b) How did Jesus introduce the parable about them?

adds to the sign that we are living in the consummation of this system of things and that he has come into his kingdom and is invisibly present. Jesus did not introduce it like other parables with the words, "The kingdom of the heavens is like (or, will become like)," but said: "When the Son of man arrives in his glory and all the angels with him, then he will sit down on his glorious throne. And all the nations will be gathered before him, and he will separate people one from another, just as a shepherd separates the sheep from the goats. And he will put the sheep on his right hand, but the goats on his left."—Matthew 25:31-33, *NW*.

⁷ In the preceding three parables Jesus described the judgment he holds with those who are in line for the heavenly kingdom. He separates them into the faithful, discreet slave class and the evil slave class, the discreet virgin class and the foolish virgin class, and the good, faithful servant class and the wicked sluggish slave class. Now in this final parable Jesus describes the judgment of the people of the nations which results in separating them, some like sheep to the King's right hand of favor and protection, and some like goats to his left hand of disfavor and condemnation. The angels share with him in the separating work.

⁸ "Then the king will say to those on his right: 'Come, you who have my Father's blessing, inherit the kingdom prepared for you from the

---

7. How are the people now separated? Who share in separating?

8, 9. How does the King address the sheep at his right hand?

world's foundation. For I became hungry and you gave me something to eat, I got thirsty and you gave me something to drink. I was a stranger and you received me hospitably; naked, and you clothed me. I fell sick and you looked after me. I was in prison and you came to me.' "—Matthew 25:34-36, *NW*.

⁹ The King does not address those on his right as "My brothers", no more than he addresses or speaks of the angels as his brothers, although the angels, too, are SONS of his heavenly Father. He calls these sheep "You who have my Father's blessing".

¹⁰ The kingdom which Jesus inherited was predestined BEFORE the new world's foundation. And so the Lamb of God was "foreknown before the world's foundation". His spiritual brothers who are heirs with him are blessed "with every spiritual blessing in the heavenly places in union with Christ, just as he chose us in union with him BEFORE the world's foundation". (1 Peter 1:18-20 and Ephesians 1:3, 4, *NW*) Theirs is a kingdom predestined for them BEFORE the foundation of the new world was laid at Christ's death and resurrection. It is a heavenly kingdom in common heirship with the King Jesus Christ, "the firstborn among many brothers." (Romans 8:28-30, *NW*) But the realm which the King invites the "other sheep" to inherit is the kingdom "prepared . . . FROM the world's foundation". This earthly realm

---

10. How is the kingdom which Christ's brothers inherit different from the kingdom which the King invites the "other sheep" to enter?

which they inherit is styled a "kingdom" because inheriting it means that the sheep become the King's children, his earthly children. This relationship to the King as "The Everlasting Father" will be something new and royal for earth's inhabitants, because back in Eden Adam and Eve were not the children of the "covering cherub" whom God appointed as their invisible guardian. The earth upon which the "other sheep" are to live forever is the visible realm of the kingdom of heaven, and it will have visible princely representatives on earth.

[11] The King extends this invitation to the "other sheep" at the time that the present judgment of the nations is finished, when the time for executing judgment is at hand at Armageddon. He speaks of these sheep as righteous. Not that they are at present justified by God for their faith to be acceptable for sacrifice with Christ in his death; but that they, in faith, have taken the right attitude toward Jehovah's King and have acted right toward the King's brothers and have joined with them in keeping God's righteous commandments. In the same way the Scriptures speak of men of faith before Christ as "righteous". "Then the righteous ones will answer him with the words: 'Lord, when did we see you hungry and feed you, or thirsty, and give you something to drink? When did we see you a stranger and receive you hospitably, or naked, and clothe you? When did we see

---

11. (a) Why does he speak of them as "righteous"? (b) What does their question and his reply indicate about his presence?

you sick or in prison and go to you?' " The King permits this question in order to show that he is not visibly present in flesh and blood on earth during this consummation of this system of things and so the "other sheep" cannot do these good deeds to him directly. "And in reply the king will say to them: 'Truly I say to you, To the extent that you did it to one of the least of these my brothers, you did it to me.' "—Matthew 25:37-40, *NW*.

[12] He did not mean that they did it to the angels, who are spirit sons of his heavenly Father. He meant they did it to the remnant of his spiritual brothers visibly upon the earth during the consummation of this system of things. While engaged in preaching the Kingdom good news to all nations for a witness, this remnant of his spiritual brothers are warred upon by the abased dragon and his demons, and get hungry, thirsty, naked, sick, in prison, in strange territory. The other sheep come to the help of these, not for just indiscriminate charitable, humanitarian reasons, but because these are the King's ambassadors and preach the good news of everlasting life by God's kingdom. In this way they do their good deeds indirectly to the King. This is the basis upon which the King's favorable judgment rests.

[13] "Then he will say, in turn, to those on his left: 'Be on your way from me, you who have been

---

12. How did they do such righteous deeds to the King? Why?
13. How does he address those on his left? How do they answer?

cursed, into the everlasting fire prepared for the Devil and his angels. For I became hungry, but you gave me nothing to eat, and I got thirsty, but you gave me nothing to drink. I was a stranger, but you did not receive me hospitably; naked, but you did not clothe me; sick and in prison, but you did not look after me.' Then they also will answer with the words: 'Lord, when did we see you hungry or thirsty or a stranger or naked or sick or in prison and did not minister to you?' " —Matthew 25:41-44, *NW*.

[14] Those placed on the King's left are the "goats", who do not belong to his flock. They are those people of the nations now under judgment who come in contact with the remnant in their preaching activities or who are affected by their Kingdom message. So they have a decision to make with respect to the remnant as the King's ambassadors. Selfishly they show no appreciation for the Kingdom message but keep on loving this world as they love themselves. They have no regard for what the King once said to his royal brothers: "He that receives you receives me also, and he that receives me receives him also that sent me forth. He that receives a prophet because he is a prophet will get a prophet's reward, and he that receives a righteous man because he is a righteous man will get a righteous man's reward. And whoever gives one of these little ones only a cup of cold water to drink because he is a disciple, I tell you truly, he will by no means lose his re-

---

14. Who are such "goats"? What sayings of Jesus do they ignore?

ward." "Whoever gives you a cup of water to drink on the grounds that you belong to Christ, I truly tell you, he will by no means lose his reward."—Matthew 10:40-42 and Mark 9:41, *NW*.

¹⁵ The refusal of the "goats" to render any help to the remnant of Christ's spiritual brothers is because these represent him enthroned in power as earth's Rightful Ruler. The "goats" love this world and its selfish rule. Hence they refuse to show any support to Jehovah's side of the great controversy over universal sovereignty. There are only two masters; and in this judgment day of the nations a person affected by the issue cannot be neutral. Jesus said: "He that is not on my side is against me." "He that listens to you listens to me too. And he that disregards you disregards me too. Moreover, he that disregards me disregards also him that sent me forth." (Matthew 12:30 and Luke 10:16, *NW*) A failure to do good to the King's brothers when the opportunity is presented in support of the Kingdom is sin, and of this the "goats" are guilty. With the question, "Lord, when did we see you?" they use as an excuse for their willful failure the fact that the King is now invisibly present and not directly reachable.

¹⁶ "Then he will answer them with the words: 'Truly I say to you, To the extent that you did not do it to one of these least ones, you did not do it to me.'" (Matthew 25:45, *NW*) Because by this faulty course they rejected Jehovah's universal

15. What is their sin? Why? What excuse do they offer?
16. Why does the King call them "cursed"? Where does he tell them to be on their way, and when?

sovereignty and his now enthroned King, he calls them "cursed". At the latest at the world's destruction at Armageddon he orders them to remove from him into the "everlasting fire prepared for the Devil and his angels". This means that there they are destroyed forever. "For our God is also a consuming fire," executing annihilation on the wicked.—Hebrews 12:29, NW.

[17] That such destruction together with the Devil and his angels is the fate of these goatish ones Jesus makes simple and certain by saying: "And these will depart into everlasting cutting-off, but the righteous ones into everlasting life." (Matthew 25:46, NW) The rewards of the righteous other sheep and the cursed goats are opposites; and the everlasting punishment upon the goats is the exact opposite of the everlasting life granted to the sheep. There is no eternal life destined for Satan and his angels, and there will be no eternal torment in literal fire and brimstone for goatish human souls with them. For them there is an everlasting cutting-off from all life and existence. They do not survive Armageddon.

[18] Be encouraged, then, by this parable in this time of vital decision. Actively take your position with the remnant of the King's brothers in support of the kingdom of God and inherit the earthly realm of the Kingdom with the boon of everlasting life.

---

17. How does Jesus make certain what their punishment is?
18. So to what action should persons be encouraged at this time?

CHAPTER XXIV

REARING CHILDREN IN DIVINE FAVOR

DIVINE wisdom says, at Proverbs 22:6 (*AAT*): "Train up a child in the way he should go; and even when he is old, he will not depart from it." This means that a human creature should be trained in the direction of his duty toward his Creator from his early childhood on. The ones to give the child such vital training are naturally his parents, particularly his father as head of the family, because the father and mother were the ones that gave existence to the child and they are responsible for its care, preservation and upbringing. God recognizes and emphasizes this parental responsibility, and in his law to the Theocratic nation of ancient Israel he commanded the parents to instruct their sons and daughters about the great Life-giver. This was important for that nation, for it guaranteed that the nation's future citizens would be lovers of God and the nation would thus continue to walk in his wholesome way.

² With his death a few days later in mind, the prophet Moses said in farewell to the Israelites as

1. From when on should humans be given vital instruction? Who properly give such instruction, according to God's law?
2. What did Moses in farewell say about such parental instruction?

they stood on the borders of the Promised Land: "What nation is there so great, that hath statutes and judgments so righteous as all this law, which I set before you this day? Only take heed to thyself, and keep thy soul diligently, lest thou forget the things which thine eyes have seen, and lest they depart from thy heart all the days of thy life: but teach them thy sons, and thy sons' sons; specially the day that thou stoodest before the LORD thy God in Horeb, when the LORD said unto me, Gather me the people together, and I will make them hear my words, that they may learn to fear me all the days that they shall live upon the earth, and that they may teach their children." Through teaching their children, the parents themselves would be kept from forgetting God's will and commandments.—Deuteronomy 4:8-10.

[3] The desire of all God-fearing parents or caretakers of children is that they may live forever in God's righteous new world. The foundation for such life everlasting is laid now during this system of things, now at the entrance of the child into his life-course. Our theme "rearing children in divine favor" does not refer to the rearing of the children of Armageddon survivors in that new world when all surrounding conditions and all forces in operation will be toward helping those who live to do righteousness. No; but it refers to rearing children who are born now before the battle of Armageddon. Not only is the life of all chil-

---

3. Why is proper rearing of children vital now before Armageddon?

dren endangered by the nearness of Armageddon, but their eternal destiny is involved. The prophetic foreview of the destruction of Christendom at Armageddon lays bare the alarming fact that the lives of ungodly children will not be spared by God's executional forces just because of their tender years. (Ezekiel 9:5, 6, 10) The parents will therefore be in large part responsible for what befalls their young offspring at Armageddon.

⁴ We are living in the world's "time of the end", and its last days are upon us. Widespread child delinquency was foretold to prevail now, together with parental neglect because of lack of natural affection and care for children's eternal interests: "Know this, that in the last days critical times hard to deal with will be here. For men will be lovers of themselves, lovers of money, self-assuming, haughty, blasphemers, disobedient to parents, without gratitude, with no loving-kindness, having no natural affection, . . . lovers of pleasures rather than lovers of God, having a form of godly devotion but proving false to its power." (2 Timothy 3:1-5, NW) Hence parents need to be specially mindful of God's commandments that concern the lasting good of their offspring. They need to fight the worldly tendency and put up a hard fight for the faith once for all time delivered to the holy ones by doing their utmost to rear their children aright.

⁵ For the Christian congregation it is a qualifi-

---

4. As respects children, what was foretold to prevail in the last days? And so what do parents need to do?
5. What is a qualification for an appointed servant with children?

cation required of men who are made overseers and ministerial servants that each rear his natural children in God's way: "Having believing children that were not under a charge of debauchery nor unruly"; "having children in subjection with all seriousness; (if indeed any man does not know how to preside over his own household, how will he take care of God's congregation?) . . . presiding in a right manner over children and their own households." (Titus 1:6 and 1 Timothy 3:4, 5, 12, *NW*) Such appointed servants were to be examples to other parents in the congregation.

⁶ Today, as long ago foretold, political regimes both totalitarian and so-called "democratic" have arisen, which deprive children of instruction by parents who fear Jehovah God and follow Jesus Christ. It is time for the parents to copy the apostle's decision: "We must obey God as ruler rather than men." And the Supreme Ruler commands parents who are devoted to him to rear their children in the way of life. (Acts 5:29, *NW*) Such parents will obediently teach their children that obeying God's laws and commands is a person's highest obligation and that it is always right to obey these when man-made laws are to the contrary. If worldly governments do not believe we are living in the "time of the end" and hence provide no true refuge and security against the world disaster ahead, then parents cannot afford to depend upon the politicians and their worldly allies. Par-

6. What course must faithful parents take when political regimes would debar them from teaching the children God's way?

ents obedient to God must themselves take steps looking to the security and preservation of their children during the world-destroying war of Armageddon.

⁷ Combined with the greatest of all commandments is the order to godly parents to cultivate love of Jehovah God in their children: "Hear, O Israel: Jehovah our God is one Jehovah: and thou shalt love Jehovah thy God with all thy heart, and with all thy soul, and with all thy might. And these words, which I command thee this day, shall be upon thy heart; and thou shalt teach them diligently unto thy children, and shalt talk of them when thou sittest in thy house, and when thou walkest by the way, and when thou liest down, and when thou risest up." (Matthew 22:37, 38; Deuteronomy 6:4-7, *ASV*) Parents must teach and demonstrate to their children this first and greatest commandment. From waking up till lying down to rest, and in all the relations of family life, they were to think of the lasting good of their offspring and strive to increase their knowledge and love of the Creator, whom to know means everlasting life. The duty was not to be left to a rabbi or Sabbath-school teacher or a religious school, but parents themselves must be every-day teachers and day-long instructors of their offspring in the things of God.

⁸ Those who believe in Jesus Christ as Messiah

---

7. Who must be the children's instructors? How long? How often?

8. (a) In connection with the Fifth Commandment what does Paul say both to children and to parents? (b) What inheritance is best?

and Ransomer are not under the old law of Moses. However, the apostle Paul shows that the Law foreshadowed what believers should do. Quoting the fifth of the Ten Commandments, he says: "Children, be obedient to your parents in union with the Lord, for this is righteous: 'Honor your father and mother'; which is the first command with a promise; 'That it may go well with you and you may endure a long time on the earth.' And you, fathers, do not be irritating your children, but go on bringing them up in the discipline and authoritative advice of Jehovah." (Ephesians 6:1-4, *NW;* Colossians 3:20, 21) Natural or foster fathers will not irritate or exasperate their children and make them downhearted by overlooking and neglecting them in a spiritual way. Spiritual things work in the opposite direction from irritation, exasperation, wrath and downheartedness. Parents must be not merely material breadwinners and physical caretakers over their own, but must also be spiritual providers. By this provision they lay up a better future for their children, a future that has the prospect of everlasting life in the new world. By giving offspring simply material comforts, conveniences and worldly education, a parent may be giving something harmful. So give both the material and the spiritual inheritance: "Wisdom is good with an inheritance: and by it there is profit to them that see the sun. For wisdom is a defence, and money is a defence: but the excellency of knowledge is, that wisdom giveth life to them that have it." (Ecclesiastes 7:11, 12) Wisdom preserves life.

⁹ In this time of the end the world tends to turn the impressionable mind of children in the wrong direction. So the proverb bears repeating: "Foolishness is bound in the heart of a child; but the rod of correction shall drive it far from him." (Proverbs 22:15) Unless properly taught and guided by its guardians, the heart or mind of a child will go in the way of worldly foolishness or deadly folly. The child is not well acquainted with this world and its selfish, wicked way. Also through its parents the child has inherited sinfulness from Adam. Satan and the demons, though cast out of heaven, are yet alive and on the loose, and are bent on mischief against everything related to God and his Theocratic organization. Consequently now, more than ever before, the minds and hearts of children need Scriptural guidance and protective knowledge to help them to right thinking and acting. If parents are delinquent and let a child run a foolish, evil course uncorrected, the child mind or heart in its formative state will become habituated in such folly. So do not let that occur.

¹⁰ If parents unwisely fail to correct the foolishly inclining heart or mind of children while young and manageable, then in the certain outworkings of God's purposes a correction will catch up with those children. They will not fare well, and parents will have grief. "Withhold not correction

---

9. How can a child make foolishness a habit? What corrects it?

10. What is the "rod of correction"? Why must it be applied?

from the child: for if thou beatest him with the rod, he shall not die. Thou shalt beat him with the rod, and shalt deliver his soul from hell [*Sheol,* mankind's common grave]." (Proverbs 23:13, 14) The rod of correction that is used to turn the children from the way of death in disobedience to God does not need to be a literal stick. The *rod* symbolizes parental authority and power, and applying the "rod of correction" means for parents to exercise the power and authority entrusted to them in whatever way may seem Scripturally wise and suitable to correct the child. The parents' grip on the rod of power, authority and responsibility should never be relaxed. Respect for it should be impressed upon the young mind and heart.

[11] Such use of the rod for their lasting good does not spell brutality or oppression, but spells a parental love combined with wisdom and with godly strength. In the benefits resulting later the corrected child will open its eyes to the wisdom and loving-kindness of its earthly caretakers and will respect them for the faithful correction. During correction it has the opportunity to show obedience and so learn in a most impressional manner the proper respect for God-given authority. Thus it will learn to fear God and his supreme authority also.—Hebrews 12:9-11.

[12] Merely instructing the child by word of mouth will not teach and train it to take an active part

---

11. What does use of it spell? Under it what does a child learn?
12. How do parents give a child training in actively serving God?

in serving God as its parents do. Besides hearing the Bible truths at the parents' mouth and at the congregational meetings to which the parents take it, the child must be instructed, disciplined and trained to take part in actively serving God, to appreciate that faith without works is dead. The parents must help the child to get a practical view of the truth and of the way that God's visible organization works on earth. The parents must give the child a practical demonstration of how the work is actually done in the field and how both rough and pleasant experiences are met with, by taking it along to the witness work in the field. Deuteronomy 11:19 says in regard to teaching God's words to children: "Ye shall teach them your children, speaking of them when thou sittest in thine house, and when thou walkest by the way, when thou liest down, and when thou risest up." When the parent is on the road, walking by the way from house to house in publishing the Kingdom message, then with his child by his side he can teach it God's words. How? Both by talking to it and by letting it listen in on the witnessing that the parent gives to persons at the doors. In this way the parent fulfills God's will and gives parental training in the direct service of the Creator, whom the child should remember in the days of its youth.—Ecclesiastes 12:1.

[13] A child can be trained for no greater career than that of being God's minister. A child can never be too young in intelligence to begin ministering to its Creator. Samuel's mother dedicated

---

13. How early may one begin ministering to God?

him before birth to the special ministry of God, and right after weaning him she turned him over to Israel's high priest for service. While Samuel thus served, Jehovah made him his prophet, so recognizing his boyhood ministry. (1 Samuel 1:11 to 3:21) When he chose Jeremiah to be his prophet, God told him: "Say not, I am a child." (Jeremiah 1:4-7) Say the same thing to your offspring, when directing it early into the ministry of our God.

14 Parents, in the above ways fortify your loved young ones against the subtle, mighty tests of faith and devotion that lie ahead as we near the accomplished end of this system of things. Bring them up in the discipline and authoritative advice of Jehovah. Be yourselves a demonstration to them, that they may take note of your faithful ways. Show them in a practical manner the true fear of the Supreme Authority, Jehovah God. For doing this your rewards of comfort, joy and heavenly approval will be great, to yourselves and to your obedient children. Treat them as something "holy" to God. (1 Corinthians 7:14) Remember: "In the fear of Jehovah is strong confidence; and his children shall have a place of refuge. The fear of Jehovah is a fountain of life, that one may depart from the snares of death." (Proverbs 14:26, 27, ASV) In your flight now to the secure refuge during Armageddon, take your children with you by rearing them in divine favor.

---

14. Against what must parents fortify children? How and why?

CHAPTER XXV

SURVIVING
THIS WORLD'S END

WITH the armaments race on between nations and with all the scientific inventions for mass destruction, such as germ warfare, long-range guided missiles, atomic bombs and the latest hydrogen or "hell" bomb which might blow a chunk out of the earth the size of the moon, some men of insight fear it will be easier in the next global war to destroy all human life on earth than to save a part of it. If that is true of a world war waged by mere man in this electronic age, what can be said of that yet unequaled catastrophe which God's Word foretells, the complete end of this world! The great Creator has promised to bring about this end, and he has at his disposal great cosmic forces besides mighty invisible angels under the command of his powerful Executioner, the King Jesus Christ. The nations are but as the drop of a bucket to God, and more easily than any nations at war can destroy he could snuff out all human life and reduce this earth to a desolate waste at Armageddon. The prospect would be terrifying were it not for one thing: Almighty God has given his written promise over his own irreproachable name

1. Prospect of the world's end would terrify us in this electronic age except for what promise?

that he will miraculously preserve his faithful people through the world's end.

² God will not undo his own good work of creation by destroying this earthly planet. What he will righteously destroy is the wicked organization which Satan the Devil has built up since the days of Noah's flood and with which that great adversary has surrounded the earth in defiance of Jehovah's universal sovereignty. Without destroying this globe He will "bring to ruin those ruining the earth". (Revelation 11:18, *NW*) How he will do this he illustrated by flooding the entire globe in Noah's day. That any animal and human life survived that world-destroying deluge was only a miracle of God Omnipotent. Four human pairs and also pairs of the basic types of animals and birds were preserved through that global flood of more than nine months, to refill the cleansed earth with creature life.

³ Not only that destruction of the ungodly antediluvian world was illustrative, but also the preservation of some humans and beasts was. This illustrated how some will be preserved when this present evil world is destroyed. On the authority of God's greatest Prophet, Jesus, "just as it occurred in the days of Noah, so it will be also in the days of the Son of man: they were eating, they were drinking, men were marrying, women were being given in marriage, until that day when Noah en-

---

2. What will God destroy? How did he illustrate this long ago?
3. What besides the destruction was illustrative? Why so?

tered into the ark, and the flood arrived and destroyed them all. Likewise, just as it occurred in
the days of Lot: they were eating, they were
drinking, they were buying, they were selling,
they were planting, they were building. But on the
day that Lot came out of Sodom it rained fire and
sulphur from heaven and destroyed them all. The
same way it will be on that day when the Son of
man is to be revealed."—Luke 17:26-30, *NW*.

⁴ The normal eating, drinking, marrying and
building by the people in Noah's day was indicative of their lack of interest in his message and
their not taking note of the great sign of the
times. There was another kind of building going
on, too, and that was Noah's building. But this
was indicative of his faith in God's warning of a
flood, for it was the building of a huge boat at
God's command and according to his specifica-
tions. By this act of faith Noah condemned that
old world and acted for the preserving of himself
and his household. (Hebrews 11:7) "Certainly if
God . . . did not hold back from punishing an
ancient world, but kept Noah, a preacher of righteousness, safe with seven others when he brought
a deluge upon a world of ungodly people; . . .
Jehovah knows how to deliver people of godly
devotion out of trial, but to reserve unrighteous
people for the day of judgment to be cut off, especially, however, those who go on after flesh with
the desire to defile it and who look down on lord-

4. (a) How did Noah condemn that preflood world?
(b) What deliverance did God then show himself able
to bring about?

ship." (2 Peter 2:4-10, *NW*) Yes, God knows how to deliver people from the destruction of this wicked world at Armageddon. His promise stands that he will do so. The survivors were pictured by faithful Noah and his household in the ark.

⁵ By his private prophecy to his apostles Jesus foretold the many-featured sign by which believers of this generation can know we are in the "consummation of the system of things" and that the world's end is near, though we cannot know the definite day and hour. But if we are watching and doing God's will, the day and hour will not be upon us unawares like a thief. Nineteen centuries ago Jesus said: "Heaven and earth will pass away, . . . Concerning that day and hour nobody knows, neither the angels of the heavens nor the Son, but only the Father. For just as the days of Noah were, so the presence of the Son of man will be." And then Jesus described how the preflood world took no note of the sign of impending calamity, and so the majority of the people were abandoned to destruction whereas those taken into the ark were spared alive to the subsequent world. (Matthew 24:35-42, *NW;* 1 Thessalonians 5:4, 5) But how can such a miracle as that take place at Armageddon, if both heaven and earth are now to pass away?

⁶ The heavens and earth which Jesus predicted

---

5. Who on earth knows the day and hour of the end? Why, then, does it not come on all like a thief?
6. What prayer and promise concerning God's kingdom assure us our literal heavens and earth will not pass away at the end?

will pass away are not our literal earth and the
solar system or the great milky way of which our
planet is a part. For Jesus taught his disciples on
this earth to pray: "Our Father in the heavens,
let your name be sanctified. Let your kingdom
come. Let your will come to pass, as in heaven,
also upon earth." (Matthew 6:9, 10, *NW*) In regard to God's kingdom by Christ Jesus, the Seed
of David, the heavenly Father said with an oath:
"My covenant will I not break, nor alter the thing
that is gone out of my lips. Once have I sworn by
my holiness: I will not lie unto David: His seed
shall endure for ever, and his throne as the sun
before me. It shall be established for ever as the
moon, and as the faithful witness in the sky."
(Psalm 89:34-37, *ASV*) The glorious sun, moon
and earth of God's creation are as sure to exist
forever as God's kingdom by his King Jesus Christ
will endure forever.

⁷ The heaven and earth doomed to destruction
at Armageddon are symbolic ones, the creation
of Satan the Devil. Just as the literal heavens are
higher than the earth, so the doomed symbolic
heaven is the higher part of Satan's organization,
the invisible spirit part. It is composed of the demons for whom Jesus said the "everlasting fire"
of destruction is prepared. The doomed symbolic
earth is Satan's visible human organization. It is
composed of his earthly seed, the seed of the
Serpent, sons of the wicked one, who are sentenced to destruction under the heel of the Seed
of God's "woman". Together, the wicked heaven
and earth make up Satan's world or complete or-

---

7. What are the heaven and earth that will be destroyed? What shows a world can be destroyed without
destroying our planet?

ganization, and it is this which is to be brought to an eternal end. That such a world can suffer destruction without our planet earth, the apostle Peter proves, despite the certainty of ridicule by religious ridiculers: "For, according to their wish, this fact escapes their notice, that there were heavens in ancient times and an earth standing compactly out of water and in the midst of water by the word of God, and by those means the world of that time suffered destruction when it was deluged with water." (2 Peter 3:3-6, *NW*) The apostle holds that act of God forth as an example of how God can and will wipe out Satan's present world organization without destroying our earth or entirely depopulating it.

⁸ The present heavens and earth of Satan's world have stood now for over four thousand three hundred years, and people of this world imagine that they are as permanent as the literal heavens and earth which God created. Satan the Devil, "the god of this system of things," would like to make them endure as long as the sun, moon and earth, but God has given his unchangeable word that they will end in an unparalleled catastrophe by a deliberate act of Jehovah God. For that reason it is called "Jehovah's day". Contrasting the end of the preflood world with the end of this world, Peter writes: "But by the same word the heavens and the earth that are now are stored up for fire and are being reserved to the day of judgment and of destruction of the ungodly men. Yet Jehovah's day will come as a thief, in which the heavens will pass away with a hissing noise, but the elements being intensely hot will be dis-

---

8. Why are Satan's heaven and earth not permanent? On what day will they be destroyed?

solved, and earth and the works in it will be discovered."—2 Peter 3:7, 10, *NW*.

[9] Many religionists argue that because the waters with which the old world suffered destruction were literal, the fire with which this world will be destroyed is likewise literal. But a careful examination of the prophecies shows the fire is symbolic just as the heavens and earth doomed to be burnt up are symbolic. Various prophecies indicate that Jehovah God by his Warrior King Jesus Christ will strike the enemy with confusion and the various elements of Satan's visible organization will fight and annihilate one another. If they use their "hell" bombs and atomic bombs and other explosive weapons of wholesale destruction there will doubtless be a great deal of literal fire over great areas of the earth. Besides this, Jehovah's Executioner Jesus Christ will use supernatural means to destroy completely as by fire all the enemies of Jehovah's universal sovereignty and all their organization invisible and visible. But no matter how furiously that fiery destruction may rage, enveloping all the globe and the invisible neighborhood of the earth where Satan and his demons have been cast down from heaven, God can preserve his people alive through it into the glorious new world.

[10] When God rained down fire and brimstone upon Sodom and Gomorrah and nearby cities he brought Lot and his daughters safely out of it; and Jesus used that as an illustration of what is to happen at this end of the world. When enraged

_____

9. Will the fire of that day be literal? What assurance have we?

10. What do Lot's and the three Hebrews' experiences illustrate?

King Nebuchadnezzar had the burning fiery furnace heated seven times more than it was usual for it to be heated, he had Daniel's three Hebrew companions thrown in for refusing to renounce Jehovah's universal sovereignty by worshiping the king's golden image. But Almighty God preserved his faithful servants in the very heart of the fire without letting their hair be singed or their cloaks be damaged or even smell of smoke settle on them. Those illustrations of God's care and preservation of his devoted people prove he can and will carry them safely alive through all the violent destruction at the end of this world. —Luke 17:28-30; 2 Peter 2:6-9; Daniel 3:1-28.

[11] Neither gold nor silver, neither national armies nor systems of electronic defense, neither political institutions nor religious buildings, images or relics will then be able to save any people from destruction with Satan's world. Our being in the favor of Jehovah God and his Executioner Jesus Christ and being hid under their protection is the only place of security. But how may we locate and hide ourselves in that sure place of survival, as in Noah's ark? Out of the far past before Jerusalem's first destruction, in 607 B.C., the prophecy says: "Their blood shall be poured out as dust, and their flesh as dung. Neither their silver nor their gold shall be able to deliver them in the day of Jehovah's wrath; but the whole land shall be devoured by the fire of his jealousy: for he will make an end, yea, a terrible end, of all them that dwell in the land. Gather yourselves together, yea, gather together, O nation that hath no shame; before the decree bring forth, before the day pass as the

---

11. What things will not provide security? Where is security?

chaff, before the fierce anger of Jehovah come
upon you, before the day of Jehovah's anger come
upon you. Seek ye Jehovah, all ye meek of the
earth, that have kept his ordinances; seek righteousness, seek meekness: it may be ye will be hid
in the day of Jehovah's anger."—Zephaniah 1:17
to 2:3, ASV; Isaiah 26:20, 21.

[12] "Hid in the day of Jehovah's anger!" The apostle Peter gives advice like Zephaniah's on the only
way anyone could survive the firelike destruction
of this world. His words offer hope that a remnant of those having true faith in Jehovah God
and Jesus Christ will be spared alive into the new
world of righteousness. Peter says: "Since all these
things are thus to be dissolved, what sort of persons ought you to be in holy acts of conduct and
deeds of godly devotion, awaiting and keeping
close in mind the presence of the day of Jehovah,
through which the heavens being on fire will be
dissolved and the elements being intensely hot will
melt. But there are new heavens and a new earth
that we are awaiting according to his promise, and
in these righteousness is to dwell. Hence, beloved
ones, since you are awaiting these things, do your
utmost to be found finally by him spotless and unblemished and in peace."—2 Peter 3:11-14, NW.

[13] The remnant of the "little flock" of Kingdom
heirs are the "chosen ones" whom Jesus meant
when he said of our day: "Then there will be
great tribulation such as has not occurred since
the world's beginning until now, no, nor will occur again. In fact, unless those days were cut

12. What advice like Zephaniah's does Peter give for
surviving?
13. Who are now associated together in the only safe
place?

short, no flesh would be saved; but on account of the chosen ones those days will be cut short." (Matthew 24:21, 22, *NW*) This remnant have now associated with them a "great crowd" of the Right Shepherd's "other sheep" of good-will. He has brought them all together into the condition of 'one fold, one Shepherd', just as Noah brought all his household into the ark immediately before the deluge began. In fact, the three sons and three daughters-in-law of Noah prefigured the "great crowd" of other sheep whom the Right Shepherd gathers before Armageddon. The "one fold" is the only safe place in which to be "hid" during the rapidly approaching day of the blazing expression of Jehovah's anger against the wicked world.

[14] Though that day comes as a thief on all worldlings who scoff and are to be destroyed, it will not come so upon the sheep in the "one fold", in the antitypical "ark" condition. They are conducting themselves in holy acts of conduct and deeds of godly devotion and are awaiting the wicked world's end. They are ever keeping it close in mind. So when Jehovah's executional forces begin the destruction of Satan's heavens and earth, the sheep will be found finally by him spotless, unblemished and in peaceable relations with him. He will perform a stupendous miracle in preserving them through the terrifying destruction. When it is done, their eyes will behold the new heavens and new earth which we have been awaiting so long with faith in God's unfailing promise. Blessed survivors of this world's end!

---

14. On those in that fold of safety why will not that day come as a thief and with destruction?

CHAPTER XXVI

THE KINGDOM
OF A NEW WORLD

THE kingdom of Jehovah God with sovereignty over this misruled earth was born in the heavens A.D. 1914. That was a year of universal importance. In it Jehovah's *woman,* his holy universal organization of the heavens, brought forth the anointed King by whom Jehovah exercises his universal sovereignty henceforth, Jesus Christ. After a royal trumpetlike announcement voice after voice in the holy heavens caught up the joyous cry: "The kingdom of the world has become the kingdom of our Lord and of his Christ, and he will rule as king for ever and ever." Grateful worshipers of God prostrated themselves and said: "We thank you, Jehovah God, the Almighty, the one who is and who was, because you have taken your great power and begun ruling as king. But the nations became wrathful, and your own wrath came, and the appointed time for the dead to be judged, and to give their reward to your slaves the prophets and to the holy ones and to those fearing your name, the small and the great, and to bring to ruin those ruining the earth."—Revelation 11:15-18, *NW.*

² The Revelation makes very clear that there is

---

1. Why was A.D. 1914 a year of universal importance? How did the holy heavens greet the great event of that year?
2. Does Satan's world disappear at his ousting from heaven, or when?

a period of time between the Kingdom's birth by
Jehovah's assumption of power and the kingdom
for the first thousand years of the new world.
That period in between is the world's "time of the
end", "the consummation of the system of things."
Note: In 1914, the year of the Kingdom's birth,
the ungrateful, faithless nations of the earth with
the blessings of their religious clergy went to
war for world domination. Also war in heaven
broke out against the newborn heavenly Government. In the fight this Government proved itself
the rightful sovereign power of the universe, and
Satan and his demons were hurled down to the
earth. This humiliating defeat of Satan and his
demons did not destroy Satan's world and consume his wicked heavens and earth. But they
must depart forever at the day and hour fixed by
Jehovah God on his throne. With a symbolic por-
trayal of that coming world-disappearance, the
apostle John writes: "And I saw a great white
throne and the one seated on it. From before him
the earth and the heaven fled away, and no place
was found for them." (Revelation 20:11, NW)
Too pure of eyes than to look upon wickedness
with approval, God cannot countenance Satan's
heavens and earth. They must be obliterated.
First after that the righteous world of a new heavens and a new earth will begin.

[3] Cast down to earth, the great dragon Satan
and his demons bring all the postwar woes upon
sea and land. They persecute all representatives
of God's "woman" (universal organization) and
make war against the remnant of her spiritual
seed. Knowing he has but a short time before the

3. In what main activities are Satan and his demons
engaged now?

final fight, he and his demons inspire many war-mongering messages against Jehovah and the Kingdom and send these forth through the mouth-pieces of Satan's invisible and visible organiza-tion. By these they madden the "kings of the en-tire inhabited earth, to gather them together to the war of the great day of God the Almighty. . . . And they gathered them together to the place that is called in Hebrew Har-Ma·ged'on". Sanguinary battles of ancient times at Armaged-don in Palestine foreshadowed the universal war of Armageddon. Leading the holy hosts of heaven for the vindication of Jehovah's universal sover-eignty is Jesus Christ, the Word of God, as on a white horse.

[4] Reporting long in advance the final line-up of sides, John writes: "And I saw the wild beast and the kings of the earth and their armies gathered together to wage the war with the one seated on the horse and with his army." Not a single ruler of this earth, no matter of what political ideology or religious belief, is missing from that battle array against Jehovah's King of kings and Lord of lords. Though at odds among themselves, they are unit-ed to a man in their unyielding opposition to Je-hovah's rule of the earth by Christ. The day and hour known to God arrive. Signal! His Warrior King catches it. By a move that surprises and dis-concerts all who fight for this old world he begins the "war of the great day of God the Almighty". The symbolic earth flees into destruction as all enemies of Jehovah and his Christ are annihilated and all the visible systems of this world are

4. (a) What is the final line-up of sides? (b) Who leads off in the fight and what results to the earth and its works?

plunged into the "fiery lake that burns with sulphur", the Gehenna of everlasting destruction.
—Revelation 12:13 to 19:21, *NW*.

⁵ The destruction of this wicked world mounts higher, up into the invisible realms. Satan and his demons have witnessed the utter consumption of their mobilized earthly organization, and now their own "short period of time" is up! The Seed of God's "woman" now has his day. The moment has now arrived to crush the head of the heel-bruiser, the Serpent, and trample to death his demon seed! And so Christ Jesus the Seed is Jehovah's mighty "angel" or Deputy now empowered to do this. He is the archangel Michael, whose name means "Who is like God?", the one who cast Satan and his demons out of heaven by a successful war up there. Now he must render that wicked one and his demons totally inactive. With symbolic description John writes: "And I saw an angel coming down out of heaven with the key of the abyss and a great chain in his hand. And he seized the dragon, the original serpent, who is the Devil and Satan, and bound him for a thousand years. And he hurled him into the abyss and shut it and sealed it over him, that he might not mislead the nations any more until the thousand years were ended."—Revelation 20:1-3, *NW*.

⁶ When the Serpent bruised the heel of the Seed of God's "woman", Jesus went into the abyss of death; but on the third day "God resurrected him by loosing the pangs of death, because it was not

---

5. (a) Where does the destruction finally extend? (b) How does John picture this and those mainly involved in it?
6. What is that abyss into which Satan and his demons are cast?

possible for him to continue to be held fast by it".
(Romans 10:7 and Acts 2:24, *NW*) Now Satan
and his demons are hurled into the abyss of total
deathlike inactivity, for a thousand years. "After
these things he must be let loose for a little while."
—Revelation 20:3, *NW*.

⁷ By motivating the king of Babylon to crush
Jerusalem in 607 B.C. Satan the Devil had become
like the "shining one, son of the dawn", in his organization heavenly and earthly. He had exalted
his throne above the royal stars of the ruling line
of King David, and he was sitting on the mount
of congregational assembly where the Israelites
worshiped Jehovah. He had brought reproach on
Jehovah's name and appeared then like a rival of
the Most High God. But A.D. 1914 Satan, the king
of Greater Babylon, tried to complete his climb
to a rival position by overwhelming the Permanent Heir of the Kingdom covenant, the starry
Seed of David, and by swallowing up God's kingdom. (Numbers 24:17) He failed and was cast
down to earth. Insanely mad and desperate, he
tries to hold the earth as his last stronghold
against the "bright morning star", the King Jesus Christ. But without first killing Satan the
Devil, this mighty King binds him and his demons
to powerlessness and hurls them into the abyss of
deathlike inaction under a seal no other creature
can break to loose him. Then is when the taunt-
song against Satan the Devil, the wicked king of
Greater Babylon, reaches the height of its cre-
scendo:

⁸ "How hast thou fallen from heaven, O Shining

---

7. From what height of his ambitious climb does Satan
then fall? To what depth is he brought, and by what act?
8. What is the taunt-song that then reaches its cre-
scendo?

One—Son of the Dawn! Hewn down to the earth, O crusher of nations! Yet thou didst say in thy heart—The heavens will I ascend, above the stars of GOD will I lift up my throne, that I may sit in the Mount of Assembly in the Recesses of the North: I will mount on the hills of the clouds, I will match the Most High! Howbeit to Hades shalt thou be brought down, to the Recesses of the Pit! . . . thou art flung out from thy grave like a scion detested, beshrouded with slain, the pierced of the sword, like a carcase trod underfoot: as for them who go down to the stones of the Pit thou shalt not be united with them in burial." (Isaiah 14:12-20, *Roth.*) The dead condition of the king of Babylon, flung out from the grave, from Hades, like an execution stake that is loathsome, corresponds with the abyss into which Satan the Devil is cast.

[9] With the wicked heaven and earth destroyed at Armageddon, the new world of righteousness begins under the Kingdom which will occupy the first thousand years in a special work for mankind. The binding of Satan and his demons for a thousand years allows for this work to proceed without invisible demon interference. Before they are loosed for a little while, the Kingdom will employ the thousand years in giving mankind a perfect government and the opportunity for everlasting salvation. The revelation makes this point certain: "And I saw thrones, and there were those who sat down on them, and power of judging was given them. Yes, I saw the souls of those executed with the ax for the witness they bore to Jesus and for speaking about God, and those who had

---

9. When does the new world begin? Under what government?

worshiped neither the wild beast nor its image and who had not received the mark upon their forehead and upon their hand. And they came to life and ruled as kings with the Christ for a thousand years. (The rest of the dead did not come to life until the thousand years were ended.) This is the first resurrection. Happy and holy is anyone having part in the first resurrection; over these the second death has no authority, but they will be priests of God and of the Christ, and will rule as kings with him for the thousand years."—Revelation 20:4-6, *NW*.

[10] The one with whom they reign is the glorified Son of David, the Permanent Heir of the covenant for the everlasting Kingdom. In ancient time King David ruled on the literal Mount Zion, one of the hills of Jerusalem; but the great Son of David, whom David called "my Lord", reigns on the far loftier royal height, the heavenly Mount Zion. Those who reign with him are the 144,000 called, chosen and faithful followers, his spiritual brothers and joint heirs. At Revelation 14:1-3 they are pictured as standing with him on the heavenly Mount Zion and singing as if a new song. They refuse to be identified in hand or forehead, that is, in action or mind, with any part of the Devil's beastly organization. They have been willing to go to the death, even at the headsman's ax, for bearing witness to Jesus the King and for speaking the truth about Jehovah God. Baptized into Christ's death, they submit to his kind of death and are buried with him in the likeness of his death. After he comes into his kingdom and casts

---

10. (a) Who are those that reign then with Christ? (b) Their kind of resurrection enables them to reign with him how long?

Satan out of heaven they are raised in the likeness of his resurrection. Because he is the "firstborn from the dead" and his resurrection is not only first in time but also first in importance, his kind is the first resurrection, and the 144,000 take part in it. They are resurrected immortal, incorruptible spirits. That is why the "second death has no authority" over them. Hence they do not need to be succeeded to office by others on account of dying and leaving the royal office vacant; but their immortality permits them to continue ruling individually with Christ Jesus for the full thousand years or millennium.—Romans 6:3-5; Philippians 3:10, 11; Colossians 1:18.

[11] However, Christ Jesus is to be a "priest for ever after the likeness of Melchizedek". Like Melchizedek, he will be a priest upon his throne, a royal priest of the Most High God. (Zechariah 6:12, 13) During the nineteen centuries from Pentecost A.D. 33 down to the time of the glorification of the last member of the royal priesthood, Christ Jesus in the presence of God has applied the ransoming, cleansing value of his human sacrifice in favor of his followers who are accepted in sacrifice with him. For this purpose they need the help of his righteousness in order for them to be declared righteous by God. On earth they offered up spiritual sacrifices to God through their High Priest Christ Jesus, the sacrifices of praise and godly works. Now that they have been consecrated by the first resurrection to be priests of God forever with Christ Jesus, they join with him in dispensing the benefits of Christ's ransom sacri-

---

11. How did they serve on earth as priests, but how do they now?

fice to the believers of mankind during the thousand years of the Kingdom rule.

[12] Thus their rule as kings with Christ makes sure for mankind not only a perfect, superhuman government of righteousness but also the life-giving blessings resulting from the human sacrifice of the Son of God. It is from heaven that Christ and his 144,000 associate kings rule, for Christ Jesus sits at God's right hand and God says: "The heaven is my throne, and the earth is my footstool." (Isaiah 66:1; Acts 7:49; Matthew 5:34) The throne, heaven, is the place for kings to rule from, and not the footstool, the earth. Moreover, it is the Most Holy of all, the heaven itself of God's presence, where the High Priest of God applies the merit of his sacrifice for the sake of humankind. And so it is there in God's heavenly presence that the royal priests must officiate for the everlasting good of mankind, even to bringing back all the dead who are in the graves. All the "other sheep" of mankind are

their subjects, and these inhabit God's footstool, the earth which he preserves all through the battle of Armageddon.

---

12. So what does their rule as kings with Christ make sure for mankind? Where is it that they rule, and why there?

¹³ Because he carries a "great crowd" of these other sheep safely through that battle with which this world ends, the earth will never be depopulated, from the beginning of the thousand years' rule to its successful end. The Kingdom will have subjects with which to begin its rule, and the organization of the new earth will begin at once. The spiritual Kingdom of Christ Jesus and his 144,000 will make up the righteous new heavens, and the visible organization of mankind according to the divine will then makes up the new earth. "And I," says John, "saw a new heaven and a new earth, for the former heaven and the former earth had passed away, and the sea is no more."—Revelation 21:1, NW.

¹⁴ Concerning those who sit on the heavenly throne with him it is written: "And power of judging was given them." This further proves that this kingdom of judgment is to be a millennium in length. The apostle Peter states that to be the length of the world's great judgment day: "By the same word the heavens and the earth that are now are stored up for fire and are being reserved to the day of judgment and of destruction of the ungodly men. However, let this one fact not be escaping your notice, beloved ones, that one day is with Jehovah as a thousand years and a thousand years as one day." (2 Peter 3:7, 8, NW) By the Kingdom of the Son whom he first raised from the dead Jehovah God will judge the world in righteousness and will teach truth, justice and righteousness.—Acts 17:31.

13. Why will our earth never be depopulated? What is the new earth?
14. (a) What power is given to those on the throne with Christ? (b) How does this fact prove the length of the Kingdom rule?

CHAPTER XXVII

THE PARADISE
OF LIFE RENEWED

ONE of the proper works of any righteous kingdom is the providing of adequate housing or spacious, comfortable, happy living quarters for its subjects. This the Kingdom of the new world will do for mankind by renewing Paradise. It was the original purpose of Jehovah God the Creator that all the earth should be a paradise. With this in view he produced a section of the earth called Eden, meaning "pleasure", and there he planted a paradise. The name means "garden", a spacious one with many and varied beautiful features. "And the Lord God had planted a paradise of pleasure from the beginning: wherein he placed man whom he had formed. And the Lord God brought forth of the ground all manner of trees, fair to behold, and pleasant to eat of: the tree of life also in the midst of paradise: and the tree of knowledge of good and evil. And a river went out of the place of pleasure to water paradise, which from thence is divided into four heads. And the Lord God took man, and put him into the paradise of pleasure, to dress it, and to keep it." (Genesis 2:8-10, 15, *Douay*) Outside the paradise of pleasure all the land was left uncultivated. Not to remain that way forever, but within seven

---

1. What proper provision will the Kingdom make for the comfort of its subjects? What original feature of earth will this renew?

thousand years of time it was to be brought everywhere to the perfect state of cultivation that obtained in the paradise of Eden, and to be fully enjoyed by perfect human inhabitants.

[2] God revealed this to be his purpose to perfect man. He informed man that he was to have a part in it. Toward the end of the sixth creative day God completed the human couple by creating a wife for Adam, to be his perfect helpmate, bone of his bones and flesh of his flesh. "And God created man to his own image: to the image of God he created him: male and female he created them. And God blessed them, saying: Increase and multiply, and fill the earth, and subdue it, and rule over the fishes of the sea, and the fowls of the air, and all living creatures that move upon the earth." (Genesis 2:18-25; 1:27, 28, *Douay*) Preliminary to filling the earth with their perfect human kind, they must subdue the earth outside of Eden. Subduing it for comfortable human living meant extending the boundaries of Paradise to the extremities of the land surface of the earth. A Paradise of life!

[3] Cain, Abel, and Seth, the named sons of Adam and Eve, never had a chance to join with them in enlarging the paradise. Before ever they were born their perfect parents sinned and the great Lawgiver and Life-giver judged them and sentenced them to death and drove them out of the paradise of pleasure. Paradise was a home for sinless perfect humans to live in forever, and that

---

2. How did God reveal to man that this was his purpose?
3. For what creatures was paradise the place? So what proper symbolism did God place in its midst?

was why God placed in the midst of it the tree of life as a symbol of the right to everlasting life. —Genesis 2:9; 3:22-24; 4:1, 2, 25.

⁴ The person behind this loss of paradise for man was the invisible caretaker whom God placed over man. But he became ambitious, turned treacherous, and led humankind into sin and rebellion with him. To begin with, he was a protecting cherub, perfect in the day of his creation by Jehovah God. In a lamentation God's prophet indirectly addresses him: "Thus saith the Lord God: Thou wast the seal of resemblance, full of wisdom, and perfect in beauty. Thou wast in the pleasures of the paradise of God: . . . Thou a cherub stretched out, and protecting, and I set thee in the holy mountain of God, thou hast walked in the midst of the stones of fire. Thou wast perfect in thy ways from the day of thy creation, until iniquity was found in thee. By the multitude of thy merchandise, thy inner parts were filled with iniquity, and thou hast sinned." (Ezechiel 28:11-16, *Douay*) As the earthly paradise was lost to mankind by the treachery of this cherub who turned devil, so God's promise in Eden, that his seed by his "woman" would bruise the serpent's head, carried with it the restoration of paradise. It would be for mankind to enjoy in perfection forever under God's kingdom by his Seed.

⁵ The Paradise of Eden in its original dimensions continued on earth until the global flood

---

4. (a) By whose treachery was paradise lost for mankind? (b) Hence what assurance did God's Edenic promise carry with it?
5. Why have men's efforts with the soil failed to convert earth into a paradise? Why was Canaan's paradise-like state lost?

wiped it out; but neither Abel nor Enoch nor Noah, whom Hebrews 11:4-7 names as godly men of faith, were permitted to enter it. They were descendants of Adam and were conceived by Eve and her daughters in sin. And so they were born sinners and imperfect and hence undeserving to enter the Paradise and partake of the tree of life in its midst and live forever. But they offered animal sacrifices to God and looked forward to the coming of the Seed of God's "woman", to be bruised at the heel in the conflict with the Serpent and to triumph and bruise the Serpent's head and reopen the way to everlasting life for man. God's curse on the earth outside Eden lasted till the flood, but all of men's efforts since then at cultivating the soil have failed to convert the now widely populated earth into a paradise. Men cannot restore paradise without God's kingdom. In the day of faithful Abraham the land of Canaan was like paradise: "the country about the Jordan, which was watered throughout, before the Lord destroyed Sodom and Gomorrha, as the paradise of the Lord." But that was because Jehovah God had promised to give it to Abraham, and his eyes were over this promised land to reserve it as a 'land of milk and honey' for Abraham's descendants, the Israelites. (Genesis 8:21; 13:10, *Douay;* Deuteronomy 11:8-15) But because of rebellious unfaithfulness of the Israelites the paradiselike condition of the Promised Land was lost.

⁶ Four thousand years after Adam's loss of Paradise for his descendants the Seed of God's "woman" was being bruised at the heel by the

6. (a) What did Jesus preach during his three-and-a-half-year ministry, and to whom? (b) On the stake what hope did he offer? To whom?

Serpent. He was hanging on the torture stake at Calvary. During the three and a half years of his public activity in Israel prior to this cruel death, he had preached, not paradise, but the kingdom of heaven. To the lost sheep of the house of Israel he sounded the theme on which his disciples would preach after his death, in order to gather out the 144,000 joint heirs of the heavenly kingdom. But now, when dying, he held forth an earthly hope, too. But to whom? To a man then dying with him and who would never survive till the outpouring of the holy spirit at Pentecost fifty-one days later and never be born of water and spirit to enter the spiritual kingdom. This man was one of two evildoers hung on stakes on each side of Jesus. Over Jesus' head was posted the charge for which he was impaled: "This is the king of the Jews," and the taunt of his being a king was loudly being hurled into his teeth by his enemies below.

[7] "But one of the hung evildoers began to say abusively to him: 'You are the Christ, are you not? Save yourself and us.' In reply the other rebuked him and said: 'Do you not fear God at all, now that you are in the same judgment? And we, indeed, justly so, for we are receiving in full what we deserve for things we did; but this man did nothing out of the way.' And he went on to say: 'Jesus, remember me when you get into your kingdom.' And he said to him: 'Truly I tell you today, You will be with me in Paradise.' "—Luke 23:35-43, *NW;* see also Reinhardt's German Version.

[8] The English translation by Dr. Wm. Cureton

7, 8. What did this man say? and what did Jesus reply?

of an old Syriac Version of the gospels* agrees with that and renders Luke 23:42, 43: "And he said to Jesus, My Lord, remember me when thou comest in thy kingdom. Jesus said to him, Verily I say to thee to-day that with me thou shalt be in the Eden's garden." *The Emphasised Bible* by J. B. Rotherham (1902) renders the verses: "And he went on to say—Jesus! remember me whensoever thou shalt come into thy kingdom. And he said unto him—Verily I say unto thee this day: With me shalt thou be in Paradise." *The Modern New Testament* from Aramaic by G. M. Lamsa (1940) says: "Jesus said to him, Truly I say to you today, You will be with me in Paradise."

* *Remains of a Very Antient Recension of the Four Gospels in Syriac* by William Cureton, D.D., F.R.S., published in London, England, in 1858 and dedicated to "His Royal Highness The Prince Consort, K.G.," Prince Albert, husband of Queen Victoria of Great Britain.

⁹ By these comforting words of Jesus the dying evildoer had an earthly hope raised in him, of Paradise restored to earth and of himself in it by a resurrection from the dead under the kingdom of this innocent Jesus who was dying under the misapplied charge of being the Messiah, the Christ of God. He had not asked Jesus to take him to heaven, and Jesus knew that by the unalterable requirements of the heavenly kingdom the dying evildoer could not get there. Jesus knew from Psalm 16:10 that his life as a perfect soul would go that day to Sheol, Hades, or mankind's common grave, but would not be left there. He was faithful as the Christ, the Seed of God's "woman"; and on the third day God would repair his heel-wound, by resurrecting him from the grave. Forty days later he would ascend to heaven, sit down at his Father's right hand, and in due time receive the promised kingdom. Then he would crush the Serpent's head, deliver mankind, and restore paradise to the earth. Also as King and Ransomer he would resurrect that sympathetic evildoer from the grave to which he went with Jesus that Passover day. So Jesus raised no false hope in him but truthfully said: "You will be with me in Paradise."

¹⁰ When the "great crowd" of other sheep, who survive the end of this world with the remnant of Kingdom heirs, come forth from their hidden condition under God's protection after Armageddon, what a hope they will have! The hope of seeing the earth, then scarred with the marks of that universal war, transformed under the Kingdom's

9. How and when would he be with Jesus in Paradise?
10, 11. (a) What hope as to earth will the great crowd surviving Armageddon have? (b) On this what does Isaiah 11:1-10 show?

blessing into a global paradise! And they will have a part from the beginning in caring for the cleansed earth and cultivating it to the beauty and productiveness of Eden. Christ Jesus their King is Abraham's Seed through King David, the son of Jesse of Bethlehem. Hence their King is the royal "branch" or "shoot" of Jesse, and thus in Jesus the "root of Jesse" never fails to have a royal offspring. Plainly foretelling that a peaceful paradise will be renewed on earth the Kingdom prophecy says of the thousand-year rule of the royal "shoot" of Jesse:

[11] "And there shall come forth a shoot out of the stock of Jesse, and a branch out of his roots shall be fruitful; and the spirit of Jehovah shall rest upon him, . . . and he shall not judge after the sight of his eyes, neither reprove after the hearing of his ears; but with righteousness shall he judge the poor, and reprove with equity the meek of the earth: and he shall smite the earth with the rod of his mouth, and with the breath of his lips shall he slay the wicked. And righteousness shall be the girdle of his reins, and faithfulness the girdle of his loins. The wolf also shall dwell with the lamb, and the leopard shall lie down with the kid, and the calf and the young lion and the fatted beast together, and a little child shall lead them. And the cow and the she-bear shall feed; their young ones shall lie down together; and the lion shall eat straw like the ox. And the sucking child shall play on the hole of the adder, and the weaned child shall put forth its hand to the viper's den. They shall not hurt nor destroy in all my holy mountain; for the earth shall be full of the knowledge of Jehovah, as the waters cover the sea. And in that day there shall

be a root of Jesse, standing as a [signal] of the peoples: the nations shall seek it; and his resting-place shall be glory."—Isaiah 11:1-10, *Dar.; AAT.*

[12] So powerful is the King's word sentencing the wicked world to destruction that the smiting of the earth with the rod of his mouth and the slaying of the wicked with the breath of his lips means the destruction of Satan's earthly organization and the binding and abyssing of him and his demons.

[13] The remnant of Kingdom heirs who survive the destruction of this world do not set their hope on inheriting the earthly paradise with the great crowd of "other sheep" who also survive. These heirs belong to Christ's congregation of conquerors, to whom he says by inspired utterance: "To him that conquers I will grant to eat of the tree of life, which is in the paradise of God." (Revelation 2:7, *NW*) Not that there is a paradise up in heaven with literal trees, rivers, animals, birds and fishes; but that this statement is made in symbolic language as part of the book of Revelation. Just as the literal paradise of Eden on the sixth day of earth's creation had a tree or grove of life in its midst which meant the right to everlasting life to the eater of its fruit, so, too, the symbolic "tree of life, which is in the paradise of God". It means life to the eater of its fruit, but immortal heavenly life. When the surviving remnant finish their earthly course after their temporary service on earth after Armageddon and die, they will be rewarded as conquerors. By a

12. How powerful is the rod of the King's mouth and his breath?
13. Of what "tree of life" does the conquering remnant eat? How?

spiritual resurrection they will be instantaneously changed and be clothed upon with immortality and incorruption in heaven. It is in this way they will be granted the prize of eating of the symbolic tree of life. (1 Corinthians 15:44, 51-54) At that time, too, God's heavenly universal organization is in a glorious condition like a paradise.

14 This paradise condition of God's universal organization is what the apostle Paul miraculously saw in vision. He describes it in these words: "I know a man in union with Christ who, fourteen years ago—whether in the body I do not know, or out of the body I do not know; God knows— was caught away as such to the third heaven. Yes, I know such a man—whether in the body or apart from the body, I do not know, God knows—that he was caught away into paradise and heard un- utterable words which it is not lawful for a man to speak." (2 Corinthians 12:2-4, NW) When Je- sus Christ was resurrected and ascended to heav- en as the full-born Seed of God's "woman", God's heavenly universal organization which had been like a barren woman, desolate without royal chil- dren till then, took on a flourishing appearance like a paradise. This was added to at the following day of Pentecost, when Jesus Christ poured out the holy spirit upon the waiting congregation on earth. There his faithful disciples were born of water and spirit to be children of God's universal organization, free Jerusalem above. His "woman" now abounded with royal children and spiritual prosperity. (Galatians 4:26-28, 31) This flour- ishing, paradiselike condition of God's "woman"

---

14. (a) What was the paradise to which the apostle Paul was caught away? (b) Why does it flourish more so since A.D. 1914?

and of her realm became more marked when she gave birth to the Kingdom A.D. 1914. Shortly afterward her faithful children sleeping in death were resurrected in heavenly glory and her faithful remnant still alive in the flesh were delivered from bondage to this world.

15 The prophet Isaiah describes this with paradisaic terms and tells of the great comfort it brings to God's faithful spiritual remnant: "Look unto Abraham your father, and unto Sarah that bore you; for I called him when he was alone, and blessed him, and multiplied him. For Jehovah shall comfort Zion, he shall comfort all her waste places; and he will make her wilderness like Eden, and her desert like the garden of Jehovah [as the paradise of Jehovah, LXX]: gladness and joy shall be found therein, thanksgiving, and the voice of song." (Isaiah 51:2, 3, Dar.) The apostle Paul, caught up to a high state of prophetic ecstasy as if to the "third heaven", was greatly comforted with the vision of the prosperity of God's "woman" or universal organization. Today we are comforted at the fulfillment of prophecy which shows that the paradisaic prosperity of God's universal organization is at its peak. This provides sure proof that the renewing of earth's paradise for delivered mankind is near, because God's universal organization must flourish with its royal children in Kingdom power and prosperity before paradise is restored to men on earth.

_____

15. (a) How did Isaiah describe this paradisaic state? (b) Of what does its fulfillment now provide sure proof, and why?

CHAPTER XXVIII

THE ABOLITION OF DEATH

THE original paradise of Eden was meant to be a place, not of human death, but of everlasting life in human perfection. Consequently when Adam and Eve were sentenced to death in punishment for their sinful rebellion, they were driven out of paradise to die. When the paradise of pleasure is renewed on earth by God's kingdom, death which arose with sinful Adam will be forever abolished from the earth. Death itself will die in the "new earth". This was made absolutely certain nineteen centuries ago at the manifestation of God's Son in the flesh.

² On this basis the apostle says gratefully: "This was given us in connection with Christ Jesus before times long lasting, but now it has been made clearly evident through the manifestation of our Savior, Christ Jesus, who has abolished death but has shed light upon life and incorruption through the good news." (2 Timothy 1:9, 10, *NW*) It was the death which mankind inherited from Adam that Jesus died to counteract, and it is this death traceable to Adam that he abolishes forever from paradise. This earth which the paradise of the new world is to cover with living beauty now holds the graves of many who died

---

1. When paradise is renewed on earth what will be abolished? Why?
2. (a) What is the death which Jesus abolishes? (b) What must therefore be removed from the paradise premises, and how?

from Adam's sin and who do not inherit heavenly Kingdom glory. If all the deadly effects of Adam's sin are to be wiped out, those graves must be completely removed, and this they will be by the resurrection of their dead inmates, by the power of God's Son who once died as a perfect man. "For since death is through a man, resurrection of the dead is also through a man."—1 Corinthians 15:21, NW.

[3] The symbolic vision which the apostle John saw of the new world depicts the destruction of the particular death which it was reserved for mankind to taste once for all time due to Adam's sin. "And I saw a great white throne and the one seated on it. From before him the earth and the heaven fled away, and no place was found for them. And I saw the dead, the great and the small, standing before the throne, and scrolls were opened. But another scroll was opened; it is the scroll of life. And the dead were judged out of those things written in the scrolls according to their deeds. And the sea gave up those dead in it, and death and Hades gave up those dead in them, and they were judged individually according to their deeds. And death and Hades were hurled into the lake of fire. This means the second death, the lake of fire. Furthermore, whoever was not found written in the book of life was hurled into the lake of fire. And I saw a new heaven and a new earth, for the former heaven and the former earth had passed away, and the sea is no more. I saw also the holy city, New Jerusalem, coming down out of heaven from God and prepared as a bride adorned for her husband. With that I heard

---

3. How did John's vision depict the wiping out of that death?

a loud voice from the throne say: 'Look! the tent of God is with humankind, and he will reside with them, and they will be his peoples. And God himself will be with them. And he will wipe out every tear from their eyes, and death will be no more, neither will mourning nor outcry nor pain be any more. The former things have passed away.' And the one seated on the throne said: 'Look! I am making all things new.' "—Revelation 20:11 to 21:5, NW.

⁴ The "great crowd" of other sheep who come out of the great tribulation and survive the fleeing away of the present heavens and earth at Armageddon will be alive on the cleansed earth when this marvelous vision takes on reality. Without needing to be raised from the grave they are in the path to perfect human life which the rule of the heavenly New Jerusalem then opens up for mankind. However, they need to be relieved of all the disabilities which they inherited as Adam's descendants. They will not be made instantaneously perfect immediately after Armageddon. But as they travel the way of obedience during the thousand years of the Kingdom they will be healed of every trace of sin and its deadly effects. Continuing in this course of unbreakable obedience even through the "little while" that Satan and his demons are loosed at the end of the millennium, they may live forever with full divine approval, being declared actually righteous in every sense. In them Jesus' words at the time of raising Lazarus from the tomb will be literally realized: "I am the resurrection and the life. He that exercises

---

4, 5. (a) What will the great crowd of survivors need to be relieved of? (b) How will many such now living "never die at all"?

faith in me, even though he dies, will come to life, and everyone that is living and exercises faith in me will never die at all."—John 11:25, 26, *NW*.

⁵ This makes it perfectly possible that members of the "great crowd" of his other sheep now living will never die at all. But even if any members of this "great crowd" do die before the new heavens and new earth are fully ushered in after Armageddon, they have the King's promise of coming to life by resurrection under the Kingdom, if they died exercising faith in him. Reasonably, an early resurrection in their case!

⁶ Death, not the battle of Armageddon, dissolves the marriage tie. (Romans 7:1-3) Human marriage relationships and new marriages will not cease among that great crowd of survivors of Armageddon, just as marriage ties between Noah's household survived the global deluge. After they took up life again outside the ark, God authorized them to bring forth a multitudinous offspring, giving them his blessing with this mandate: "Be fruitful and multiply and fill the earth; . . . Ye therefore be fruitful and multiply, swarm in the earth and multiply therein." Noah and his wife did not themselves bring forth any more children, but they did so indirectly through their three sons and three daughters-in-law.—Genesis 9:1-7, *Roth*.

⁷ As the "great crowd" of other sheep surviving Armageddon are destined for life in the paradise earth, Jesus' statement that things during his presence would be like those of Noah's day includes doubtless this postflood mandate to be fruitful, multiply and fill the earth. There is noth-

6. Does Armageddon dissolve marriage ties and stop new marriages? What furnishes an illustration?
7. Will there be childbearing after Armageddon? Under what arrangement? For how long?

ing in the Bible to show that married couples must dissolve their marriage ties and companionship and that the surviving single men and women must not marry. Jehovah's mandate to the deluge survivors gives the Armageddon survivors reason for the expectation that Jehovah by his King, the Greater Noah, will issue a like mandate to them. This in no way nullifies His purpose and promise of the general resurrection of the dead. The King can adjust the carrying out of the marriage mandate of Armageddon survivors with the resurrection. When the King judges that the earth has been adequately filled, human childbearing will cease; it will have served its purpose.

⁸ The children born to such post-Armageddon parents will not be born perfect, for their parents will not be perfect, and hence they will feel the effects of their parents' being descendants from Adam. For this reason they, too, will need the benefits of Christ's ransom sacrifice and the help of God's kingdom just as much as their parents do. They will have the blessing, though, of being born under the Righteous Government and being engendered and reared by righteously disposed parents of integrity toward God. But they must yet stand the final trial with all mankind.

⁹ However, before Jesus' death and resurrection and the Pentecostal outpouring of God's holy spirit there was a long line of faithful men and women. They exercised faith in the coming Seed of God's "woman", the promised Seed of Abraham for mankind's blessing, and the Messianic Seed or

---

8. Will children then born need Christ's ransom and kingdom? Why?
9. What long line of faithful men and women preceded Christ's death? How did they live and die?

Son of David for mankind's perfect government. The eleventh chapter of Hebrews runs the line back for four thousand years to the first shepherd, Abel, who offered animal sacrifice from his own flock to Jehovah God. Even though those preceding John the Baptist did not know exactly who the promised Seed was to be, they had faith that God would produce him. So they lived their lives in harmony with that faith and refused to be a part of the world about them. They were witnesses of Jehovah, and he, in turn, bore witness to them that they pleased him and would see the day when his promised Seed would be in power over earth. After telling of Abraham, Sarah, Isaac and Jacob, the apostle says: "In faith all these died, although they did not get the fulfillment of the promises, but they saw them afar off and hailed them and publicly declared that they were strangers and t e m p o r a r y residents in the land."—Hebrews 11:13, NW.

¹⁰ Wondrous acts of God were performed through and for them because of their indestructible faith. Many of them were cruelly tortured for holding fast to their integrity to Jehovah and for refusing to compromise with the faithless worldlings about them. Though they were put to death for not sinfully bargaining with the e n e m y, they hoped to come to life again by a resurrection in a better world, never to die again for Adam's sin or at enemy hands. The apostle's brief record of their exploits of faith says to his fellow heirs of the Kingdom: "Women received their dead by resurrection; but other men were tortured because they would not accept release by some ransom, in

---

10. For faithfulness what kind of resurrection did they expect?

order that they might attain a better resurrection. Yes, others received their trial by mockings and scourgings, . . . in tribulation, under ill-treatment; and the world was not worthy of them. They wandered about in deserts and mountains and dens and caves of the earth. And yet all these, although they had witness borne to them through their faith, did not get the fulfillment of the promise, as God foresaw something better for us, in order that they might not be made perfect apart from us."—Hebrews 11:35-40, *NW*.

[11] That "something better" for the apostle Paul and his spiritual brothers is the heavenly kingdom, with glory, honor and incorruptibleness. Confirmatory of this Jesus said: "Among those born of women there has not been raised up a greater than John the Baptist; but a person that is a lesser one in the kingdom of the heavens is greater than him. From the days of John the Baptist until now the kingdom of the heavens is the goal toward which men press, and those pressing forward are seizing it." (Matthew 11:11, 12, *NW*) From John the Baptist, who died more than a year before the Pentecostal outpouring of spirit, back to the first martyr Abel, none of the faithful ancients received the fulfillment of the promise of being blessed by the Seed with Kingdom opportunities. So they had no opportunity to press toward the Kingdom at Jesus' invitation and to seize it by their faithfulness. Their blessings will all be of an earthly kind in Paradise under the kingdom of heaven; and naturally, then, the least member of the heavenly Kingdom will be greater

---

11. Why or how is what the Kingdom heirs get "something better"?

than John the Baptist and all other faithful persons that preceded him.

¹² By the faith of God's prophets of old a number of persons were resurrected from the dead, but because they were inheritors of death from Adam and the Kingdom was not yet established, they returned to death. All those faithful ones of old, down to John the Baptist, died in faithfulness to Jehovah God, and for this they will have a resurrection better than what those had who were resurrected to a life still under the regime of sin and death. It will be a "better resurrection" because it will be performed by Jehovah's greatest Prophet, the King Jesus Christ, and it will be performed under God's kingdom in his hands. It will be without the unavoidable need to die again, because it will be under the rulership of the Son of God, whose ransom secures their release forever from death. The opportunity to gain life on earth eternally will then be set before them; and with Satan and his demons abyssed and his wicked world gone there will be no forces to hinder their efforts to gain the latest knowledge on God's kingdom and to walk the paths of enlightened righteousness toward everlasting life in this Paradise. And since they exercised faith as far as they had knowledge and they died in their unbreakable integrity toward God, they have inclined toward righteousness, and this will be to their advantage at the resurrection under His kingdom by Christ.

¹³ They will not immediately be made perfect at their resurrection, for they will have much to learn of God's works and his revelations of

12. How will those faithful ancients have a better resurrection?
13. Will they be made perfect immediately? For what reason?

knowledge since their death long ago, and they will have to accept such knowledge and instruction and take their stand for God's established kingdom and its requirements. But, promptly obeying, they will advance to human perfection with the rest of the "other sheep".

¹⁴ As the kingdom of God's 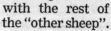 dear Son is now in operation, a number of those faithful ancients will be made "princes" throughout the earth. Their office of prince denotes that they are children of a king, not children of any king of ancient time, but children of the reigning King Jesus Christ, who gave his perfect human life for them and who raises them from the dead. As he becomes the royal channel through whom God bestows everlasting life, the King is directly their regal father. He will be an "Everlasting Father". (Isaiah 9:6, *ASV*) A number of them, like Enoch, Noah, Shem, A b r a h a m, Isaac, Jacob, and D a v i d, were the earthly fathers of "the man Christ Jesus".

---

14. Whose children will they become? What official servants will a number of them be made in all the earth?

And to show that princely office and service will be open to such persons as these, the psalm in praise of the Messianic King plainly says: "Instead of thy fathers shall be thy children, whom thou shalt make princes in all the earth."—Psalm 45:16, *ASV*.

¹⁵ Daniel the prophet was a faithful upholder of Jehovah's universal sovereignty, a man for whom Jehovah "stopped the mouths of lions". Giving Daniel a direct resurrection hope, Jehovah's angel said to him in the close of his prophecy: "So go your way, and rest till the end comes; then you shall rise to enjoy your portion at the end of the days." (Daniel 12:13, *AAT*) Since the record God gives us of these men proves their righteous and faithful lives, then the King's putting men of such type in princely offices in all the earth guarantees that the visible organization of the "new earth" will be carried on with godly integrity for the highest good of all obedient men and women. Because they will be "princes in all the earth", it argues they will have an early resurrection.

¹⁶ Since the first resurrection of the Kingdom heirs that slept in death began after the Kingdom was born, the war in heaven was fought and Satan and his demons were abased to the earth, well over thirty years have elapsed without the resurrection of any of those faithful persons of ancient time. This has been, as the apostle Paul says to his fellow heirs, "in order that they might not be made perfect apart from us."–Hebrews 11:40, *NW*.

15. How was Daniel given a direct resurrection hope? What is guaranteed by making princes of resurrected men like him?
16. How have Paul's words actually proved true, "that they might not be made perfect apart from us"?

CHAPTER XXIX

WRITING THE NAMES
IN THE BOOK OF LIFE

IN DUE time, when the paradise conditions are developing and the Armageddon survivors and their lovely children are engaging in constructive activities over all the earth and the princes of the King are supervising and taking a right and exemplary lead in the new earth, the resurrection of the rest of the human dead will take place. When on earth as a man Jesus not only healed those with faith in him but also raised the dead. At the appointed hour he will exercise his resurrection power toward the evildoer who he said would be with him in paradise and toward all the other entombed dead. "For just as the Father has in himself the gift of life, so he has granted to the Son to have also in himself the gift of life. And he has given him authority to do judging, because Son of man he is. Do not marvel at this, because the hour is coming in which all those in the memorial tombs will hear his voice and come out, those who did good things to a resurrection of life, those who practiced vile things to a resurrection of judgment." (John 5:26-29, *NW*) So it is that John in vision "saw the dead, the great and the small, standing before the throne, and scrolls were opened. But another scroll was opened; it is the scroll of life. And the dead were judged out

1. When will resurrection power be exercised toward the others in the memorial tombs? By whom?

298

of those things written in the scrolls according to their deeds".

² At John 5:28 Jesus mentioned only the memorial tombs. But many persons have lost their lives in the sea, and thoughtfully Revelation 20:13 tells us that the sea also is to give up those dead in it. Hades, which is there said to give up its dead, is equivalent to the memorial tombs Jesus mentioned, for Hades means, not just one individual's grave, but the common grave of all mankind who lie dead within God's memorial provision. Contrary to Hades' being a fiery place of excruciating torment for conscious immortal human souls, Hades gives up all the DEAD in it. The "great crowd" of Armageddon survivors and the children they bring forth do not need to return from Hades. All the same, they are still imperfect in their flesh and subject to the death-inducing effects inherited from Adam. The men and women of old who died faithful in hope of a "better resurrection" will not be raised instantaneously perfect in the flesh, not even those made "princes in all the earth". So with respect to these the power of death due to Adam's fatherhood of our race must give up those whom it has held in its grip. But the King, the resurrected Jesus Christ, has the power to release all from the power of death and of Hades: "Do not be fearful. I am the First and the Last, and the living one; and I became dead, but, look! I am living for ever and ever, and I have the keys of death and of Hades." (Revelation 1:17, 18, NW) He uses the keys toward hu-

---

2. (a) What is Hades that gives up its dead, and what besides it gives up the dead? (b) How and why must death give up its dead?

mankind during the judgment day of a thousand years.—2 Peter 3:7, 8.

[3] The fact that "scrolls were opened" in the vision shows that the judgment day is to be a time of much education in the righteous will of God and his requirements for everlasting life. Now that God's kingdom has been set up it is already proving true: "When thy judgments are in the earth, the inhabitants of the world will learn righteousness," if they seek God as Teacher and obey him.—Isaiah 26:9.

[4] That another scroll, "the scroll of life," is opened in the vision proves that the judgment day affords an opportunity for life. All those restored from the grave and all those alive on earth, from the least of them to the greatest of them (the princes), all may win the prize of everlasting life in perfection on the paradise earth. This wondrous opportunity is further made possible in that they are all then judged, not according to their past works before the establishment of God's kingdom in 1914, but according to their works under God's Righteous Ruler, Jesus Christ. He, as God's High Priest who was himself once a man amid Satan's world, can sympathize with them. He can use his sacrifice and priestly powers to cleanse them, forgive them and lift them out of sin to a perfectly pure condition mentally and physically, able to meet God's perfect approval. But before God justifies them or declares them righteous in themselves and writes their names in the scroll of life, they

3. What does the opening of scrolls in the vision indicate?

4. (a) What does "opening the scroll of life" afford for all those on earth? (b) To be written in it what must they first do?

must pass the one final test over the supreme issue, that of Jehovah's universal sovereignty. This comes as a result of loosing Satan.

⁵ "Now as soon as the thousand years have been ended, Satan will be let loose out of his prison, and he will go out to mislead those nations in the four quarters of the earth, Gog and Magog, to gather them together for the war. The number of these is as the sand of the sea. And they advanced over the breadth of the earth and encircled the camp of the holy ones and the beloved city. But fire came down out of heaven and devoured them. And the Devil who was misleading them was hurled into the lake of fire and sulphur, where both the wild beast and the false prophet already were; and they will be tormented day and night for ever and ever."—Revelation 20:7-10, *NW*.

⁶ There will be those who side with the released Satan and his demons on the issue of universal sovereignty, rebelling as the perfect Adam and Eve did in the original paradise. These are pictured as removing themselves far from Jehovah's universal organization, and so are spoken of as "Gog and Magog", attackers of Jehovah's recovered people. (Ezekiel 38:1 to 39:6) This assault by these rebels deceived by Satan imposes a great test on all mankind then fully uplifted to human perfection and complete ability to resist all temptation. Princes, Armageddon survivors and their children born during the thousand years, and all the remainder of humankind recovered from the

---

5. When and why is Satan released? With what developments?

6. Who will then be tested? Who will stand the test, who fall?

graves and sea, will feel the test. All will have to take a faithful stand in the "camp of the holy ones". All are then deciding their destiny for eternity. Their decision in support of Jehovah's universal sovereignty, if faithfully held to, will give them a part in vindicating him against his nefarious reproacher Satan the Devil. Standing the final test loyally, they will rejoice to witness the divine fire descend from heaven and consume the rebellious hosts of Gog and Magog, whose number is not disclosed to us but is left as indeterminate as the sand by the sea. (Isaiah 66:24) The names of these rebels are not written in the scroll of life. "The name of the wicked shall rot." —Proverbs 10:7.

7 Although the devoted survivors of the test cannot see it with the natural eye, the Devil and his demons, who mislead the rebellious human hosts, are cast into the "lake of fire and sulphur". That is the same place where the symbolic beast and false prophet were cast a thousand years previous, while still living, going concerns, able to feel the torment of going down into disgraceful destruction. This betokens the unending destruction of Satan and his demons, for that symbolic lake "means the second death". (Revelation 19:20 and 21:8, NW) The statement that the wild beast and the false prophet and Satan are to be tormented day and night forever and ever in that "lake" proves that Satan and his demons are never released from destruction as once they were from the abyss. At last in a complete sense for all time Jesus Christ finishes his mission to "destroy the

7. Where is the Devil then cast? How is he tormented forever?

one having the means to cause death, that is, the Devil".—Hebrews 2:14, *NW*.

⁸ Now comes total abolition of the death due to Adam: "And death and Hades were hurled into the lake of fire. This means the second death, the lake of fire. Furthermore, whoever was not found written in the book of life was hurled into the lake of fire." (Revelation 20:14, 15, *NW*) Those acting rebellious during the thousand years prove unfit to be enrolled in the book of life and they would be plunged into the lake of fire, the second death, without waiting for the final general test at the close of the millennium. Their submerging in the lake of everlasting destruction would not mean the continuance forever of death due to Adam. No; for the fiery, sulphurous lake symbolizes the "second death", a death not suffered for our natural inheritance from Adam but inflicted for the rebellious sinner who sins out of his own willful choice against God's requirements for life. Second death could at any time throughout eternity be inflicted upon any who might choose to sin. That always remains within God's power.

⁹ Death and Hades are hurled into the lake of fire to experience everlasting destruction. Hades, mankind's common grave, is destroyed by emptying it of all the dead and by never returning the rebellious sinners to Hades but pitching them into the symbolic lake of fire. Death is destroyed by the sin-removing sacrifice of Jesus Christ which cancels all the disabilities the believers

8. (a) Who of mankind are hurled into the lake of fire? (b) Does that mean the continuance forever of death due to Adam? Or what?
9. How are death and Hades cast into the lake of fire? Of what prophecy does this mark the climax for Christ's reign?

have inherited from Adam and by raising the dead from the graves and then by removing every trace of imperfection and sinfulness in mind, body and heart transmitted by him. Mankind must willingly and obediently cooperate with the King toward that desirable end during the thousand years of uplift. This marks the climax of fulfilling the prophecy: "For he must rule as king until God has put all enemies under his feet. As the last enemy, death is to be destroyed."—1 Corinthians 15:25, 26, *NW*.

[10] The willing and obedient subjects of the King will take full advantage of his priestly and governmental services and will be cured of all sin and its effects. They will be taught absolute righteousness in the love of it. So when in this perfection of body, mind and heart they have proved their integrity to God by standing immovably for his universal sovereignty during the brief loosing of Satan and his demons and the assault of "Gog and Magog", then their justification to eternal life on the paradise earth will come. This means God will declare them righteous, for he is the final Judge and to him Christ Jesus turns over the Kingdom at the end of the thousand years. On this it is written:

[11] "Next, the accomplished end, when he hands over the kingdom to his God and Father, when he has destroyed all government and all authority and power. For he must rule as king until God has put all enemies under his feet. As the last

---

10. When will the justification of mankind to life occur? By whom?
11, 12. (a) How does Christ Jesus then show his subjection to his God and Father? (b) What issue is then completely settled forever?

enemy, death is to be destroyed. For God 'subjected all things under his feet'. But when he says that 'all things have been subjected', it is evident that it is with the exception of the one who subjected all things to him. But when all things will have been subjected to him, then the Son himself will also subject himself to the one who subjected all things to him, that God may be all things to everyone."—1 Corinthians 15:24-28, *NW*.

[12] Christ Jesus shows his subjection to the Most High God by completely exterminating the rebellious hosts in this their final uprising against Jehovah's universal sway. Thus the seven-thousand-year-old issue of universal sovereignty will at last be settled for all eternity.

[13] When Jehovah God declares his loyal subjects righteous in view of their unwavering faithfulness

to him under the final determining test, this corresponds with writing their names in the "book of life". This signifies that they have the God-given right to everlasting life as the perfect inhabitants of the earthly paradise. No other creature in the

---

13. (a) What does this justification correspond with? (b) In what sense can those attaining this on earth not die any more?

universe, therefore, can cause their death. It is in this sense that these loyal ones gain the endless world to come and can never die any more. Jesus said: "The children of this system of things marry and are given in marriage, but those who have been counted worthy of gaining that system of things and the resurrection from the dead neither marry nor are given in marriage. In fact, neither can they die any more, for they are like the angels, and they are God's children by being children of the resurrection." (Luke 20:34-36, *NW*) Of course, Almighty God can at any time exercise the power of the "second death" to annihilate creatures. But he will not use this against these perfect human creatures, because they have proved that they will continue in their absolute devotion to him as universal Sovereign.

[14] Since their full entrance into everlasting life occurs at the close of the millennium when God declares them righteous and registers their names permanently in the "book of life", the statement of Revelation 20:5 (*NW*) proves truthful: "The rest of the dead did not come to life until the thousand years were ended." The death which spread from Adam to all mankind will then have been abolished forever. Praise to Jehovah by Christ!

---

14. How is it that the rest of the dead do "not come to life until the thousand years were ended"?

CHAPTER XXX

HOW LONG DO YOU CHOOSE TO LIVE?

EVERY intelligent creature on earth must determine his own destiny. Now at the consummation of this system of things when the judgment of the nations is under way and the separating of the sheep and the goats with opposite destinies is nearing a conclusion, yes, now is the urgent time to make your determination. The question becomes quite pertinent, How long do you choose to live? You can choose to live forever in a perfect new world of righteousness, by virtue of God's gift of everlasting life through Jesus Christ our Lord, and not by virtue of any inborn immortality of the human soul. Before you heard of this gracious gift which he offers, you could not accept it. But now that you have heard of it and the terms on which it is offered, you can gratefully arrange and strive to meet the terms and so make the gift your own. By doing this you help to prove that such undeserved kindness of God was not spent in vain, and you have a precious part in vindicating his universal sovereignty.

[2] Do not be anxious about your life in this world and make it your chief concern. Do not be driven

---

1. (a) Why is it now a pertinent question, How long do you choose to live? (b) For how long can you choose to live, and on what basis?
2. Why not make this life our chief concern? What parable of Jesus should we take to heart?

to pursue the fleeting things which the doomed world pursues and which can never give everlasting life. Do not be lured into piling up material wealth with its supposed security, for neither it nor the commercial system which encourages accumulating it can guarantee your life for one night. Take Jesus' illustration to heart: "The land of a certain rich man produced well. Consequently, he began reasoning within himself, saying: 'What shall I do, now that I have nowhere to gather my crops?' So he said: 'I will do this: I will tear down my storehouses and build bigger ones, and there I will gather all my grain and all my good things, and I will say to my soul: "Soul, you have many good things laid up for many years; take your ease, eat, drink, enjoy yourself."' But God said to him: 'Unreasonable one, this night they are demanding your soul from you. Who, then, is to have the things you stored up?' So it goes with the man that lays up treasure for himself but is not rich toward God."—Luke 12:16-21, *NW*.

[3] It is not the greedy acquiring of any of the wealth which this world has to offer that brings real happiness, contentment and profit in this life. Nor can you buy life in the future by such riches. Only our unselfish devotion to God through Jesus Christ proves healthful and profitable in every way in this world and only it gives sure hope of life in the world to come. How true it is: "Those who are determined to be rich fall into temptation and a snare and many senseless and hurtful desires which plunge men into destruction and ruin. For the love of money is a root of all sorts

---

3. Why does the acquiring of worldly wealth not bring real profit? But what does give hope of life in the world to come?

of injurious things, and by reaching out for this love some have been led astray from the faith and have stabbed themselves all over with many pains"! There is good reason, then, for the charge to be given overseers of God's devoted people: "Give orders to those who are rich in the present system of things not to be arrogant, and to rest their hope, not on uncertain riches, but on God, who furnishes us all things richly for our enjoyment; to work at good, to be rich in right works, to be liberal, ready to share, safely treasuring up for themselves a right foundation for the future, in order that they may get a firm hold on the real life."—1 Timothy 6:9, 10, 17-19, *NW*.

⁴ The political governments of this world, which favor and depend upon the commercial system, claim to be the protectors of the people, and they appropriate great sums of money for the national defense. In the attempt to hold the world organization together in a mutual tolerance and to stave off further world war with its possible destruction of civilization, they build up a form of international union. The political promoters, the commercial systems, and the religious clergy who are allied with these and who court these for favor, support and protection, plead with the people to support and trust in the loosely jointed international union. Many are the people of all nations who are persuaded or frightened into placing their trust in such man-made political devices. They do this contrary to God's warning: "Put not your trust in princes, nor in the son of man, in whom there is no help. His breath goeth forth, he

---

4. In what worldly devices are people being induced to trust for peace and security? Against what divine command?

returneth to his earth; in that very day his thoughts perish. Happy is he that hath the God of Jacob for his help, whose hope is in Jehovah his God." (Psalm 146:3-5, *ASV*) Even rulers are helpless mortals!

⁵ This world's rulers are not moved by divine wisdom, despite all the prayers and nicely worded blessings of their clergy allies. At the present-day climax of the controversy over the paramount issue of universal sovereignty the rulers of all nations are making the mistake their political prototypes made nineteen centuries ago. They side with the "god of this system of things" and are opposing Jehovah God and his Christ, our Lord Jesus. They match worldly wisdom against divine wisdom: "This wisdom not one of the rulers of this system of things came to know, for if they had known it they would not have impaled the glorious Lord." (1 Corinthians 2:8, *NW*) In effect, the world rulers of today impale the faithful witnesses who preach the good news of the kingdom of our glorious Lord Jesus Christ, whom God enthroned A.D. 1914 at the end of the "appointed times of the nations".

⁶ The world rulers cannot bind and abyss Satan and his demons. The rulers and the clergy can offer no protection to the people against Satan and his demons who, in their rage at being ousted from heaven, are bringing appalling woes upon land and sea, threatening them now with such a thing as a "hell" bomb. While making frantic efforts to hold off another global war and while

5. By what wisdom are world rulers not moved? What shows it?
6. Why is the battle of Armageddon now unavoidable? Where, then, should we flee now, and why?

trusting to a so-called "better self" of the people to save civilization, the rulers are being irresistibly gathered by the demon-inspired mouthings of worldly systems. The march is on! Where? To the field of Armageddon for the "war of the great day of God the Almighty"! God will not hear the unscriptural prayers of all the religious clergy combined on "world prayer" days for the sparing of this old world from Armageddon. It is unavoidable, for Jehovah's time has come to settle definitely the issue of universal sovereignty. It is old-world rule versus New World rule! The forces of two worlds are about to crash against each other. The new world is all-powerfully irresistible. It will scatter its foes, grind them to powder, and take its rightful place in an eternal triumph over all mobilized opposition. The old world will vanish in the superintense heat of this decisive universal war. So then our only trust and protection and means of survival are in Jehovah's Messianic Kingdom. Flee now to it!

[7] In the new world lovers of life who follow divine wisdom can live forever. Now is the time to determine our destiny and to work toward it. This is the course of practical wisdom. "Happy is the man that findeth wisdom, and the man that getteth understanding. For the gaining of it is better than the gaining of silver, and the profit thereof than fine gold. She is more precious than rubies: and none of the things thou canst desire are to be compared unto her. Length of days is in her right hand; in her left hand are riches and honor. Her ways are ways of pleasantness, and all her paths are peace. She is a tree of life to them that lay

---

7. What is the course of practical wisdom that tends toward life?

hold upon her: and happy is every one that retaineth her. Jehovah by wisdom founded the earth; by understanding he established the heavens." (Proverbs 3:13-19, *ASV*) By the same superlative wisdom Jehovah establishes the new heavens and earth.

[8] Remember Jesus' farewell words, that our taking in knowledge of Jehovah the only true God and of Jesus Christ whom he sent means everlasting life. (John 17:3, *NW*) In the remaining days before the war at Armageddon do your utmost to take in such vital knowledge and to increase it. Prayerfully study your Bible at home with faithful Bible helps. Go to meetings where you can study it with others or hear it preached. Let the knowledge you gain be your guide, for it means your everlasting life. And in your love of your neighbor share that knowledge with others, with your parents, your marriage mate, your children, your brothers and sisters, with those of your acquaintance or your congregation, with all those with whom you come in touch in this critical time.

[9] In his certain knowledge of what is immediately ahead Jehovah God is causing the means of knowledge to flow forth like an ever-widening, ever-deepening river of crystal-clear water. It is a river of Kingdom truth. It flows, not from a spring that may fail with a disastrous water shortage for the people, but forth from the established kingdom of God and of his Christ. Prefiguring

---

8. What knowledge should we take in? With whom must we share it?

9. Like what is divine knowledge now flowing forth? Accordingly, what invitation is being extended, and to whom?

the faithful remnant who live in these days of the fulfillment of the revelation, the apostle John says: "And he showed me a river of water of life, clear as crystal, flowing out from the throne of God and of the Lamb down the middle of its broad way. And on this side of the river and on that side there were trees of life producing twelve crops of fruit, yielding their fruits each month. And the leaves of the trees were for the curing of the nations." Now, with the spirit of God upon them, the remnant of Christ's bride extend the divine invitation to people of good-will in all the nations to come to the life-giving river. "And the spirit and the bride keep on saying, 'Come!' And let anyone hearing say, 'Come!' And let anyone thirsting come; let anyone that wishes take life's water free."—Revelation 22:1, 2, 17, NW.

[10] The King, the Right Shepherd, guides his flock of "other sheep" to this water of life-giving truth. His flock is ever increasing because every faithful, appreciative one of those who hear the divine invitation does not selfishly keep it to self but passes it on to others by preaching the Kingdom good news.

[11] How precious is life! Without it nothing exists for your enjoyment. It is your privilege now to choose it in preference to destruction. As when Moses stood before the chosen people of God long ago on the plains of Moab, across the Jordan river from the Promised Land of milk and honey, so now Jesus Christ, God's Prophet greater than Moses, stands before his devoted sheep and says: "See, I have set before thee this day life and good,

---

10. Where does the Right Shepherd lead his other sheep? Why is his flock constantly increasing?
11. What choice is now set before the sheep? By whom?

and death and evil; in that I command thee this day to love Jehovah thy God, to walk in his ways, . . . I call heaven and earth to witness against you this day, that I have set before thee life and death, the blessing and the curse: therefore choose life, that thou mayest live, thou and thy seed; to love Jehovah thy God, to obey his voice, and to cleave unto him; for he is thy life, and the length of thy days."—Deuteronomy 29:1; 30:15-20, *ASV*.

¹² Heed the Greater Moses! Choose now to live forever in the blessedness of the new world under God's kingdom by Jesus Christ.

---

12. What choice should we make?

INDEX TO SCRIPTURES CITED

New World Translation
of the
Christian Greek Scriptures

Now you may possess a new and highly accurate translation of the Greek Scriptures based on the widely accepted Westcott and Hort text of 1881. It possesses the advantages of a modern English translation, since all archaic expressions have been eliminated in favor of expressions currently in use; yet it retains the dependability of more literal translations. Accuracy has been at all times the goal of the translators, the New World Bible Translation Committee. Preconceived ideas, and religious traditions and creeds, have been carefully avoided. The result is a superb translation, understandable to all and worthy of the scrutiny of the most critical Bible students.

STUDY HELPS INCLUDED

Besides the new translation, this book provides copious marginal references, chain references on outstanding Bible subjects and proper Bible names, footnotes and an appendix. It is bound in attractive green leatherette and measures $7\frac{1}{4}$" x $4\frac{1}{2}$" x 1". It will be mailed anywhere, postpaid, on a contribution of $1.50.

Send your order and remittance to the Branch office nearest you. See list on page 320.

"Let God Be True"

is a basic textbook for Bible study. It makes Bible understanding easy by following the topical arrangement for considering Bible teachings. Prayer, images, the Devil, resurrection, end of the world, judgment day, Jehovah—these are but a few of the many subjects discussed. Erroneous conceptions are exposed, and seemingly contradictory Scripture texts are shown to be harmonious.

More than eleven million copies of *"Let God Be True"* have been printed since its first edition in 1946, demonstrating its wide acceptance as a Bible study help. It has 320 pages, with scripture and subject indexes. Send for your copy today, 50c postpaid.

What Has Religion Done for Mankind?

is unique in presenting the history of religion. It shows how man's original true worship was corrupted; how many of the basic current religions came into existence and what their teachings are; and how the one true religion established by God himself will ultimately triumph over all false religion.

Seventeen different Bible versions are quoted from in this book. Even the so-called "pagan" religions are discussed, not omitting the "red religion" of communism. It has 352 pages, with scripture and subject indexes. Sent postpaid anywhere for 50c.

See addresses on last page for ordering the above.

Chief Office and Official Address of

WATCH TOWER BIBLE & TRACT SOCIETY
WATCHTOWER BIBLE AND TRACT SOCIETY, INC.
INTERNATIONAL BIBLE STUDENTS ASSOCIATION

is

124 Columbia Heights, Brooklyn 2, New York, U. S. A.

Addresses of Branch offices:

America (U. S.), 117 Adams St., Brooklyn 1, N. Y. **Argentina**, Calle Honduras 5646-48, Buenos Aires. **Australia**, 11 Beresford Road, Strathfield, N.S.W. **Austria**, Liechtensteinstr. 24, Vienna IX. **Belgium**, 28 Ave. Gen. Eisenhower, Schaerbeek-Brussels. **Bolivia**, Casilla No. 1440, La Paz. **Brazil**, Rua Licínio Cardoso 330, Rio de Janeiro. **British Guiana**, 5 Croal Street, Georgetown, Demerara. **British Honduras**, Box 257, Belize. **British West Indies**, 21 Taylor St., Woodbrook, Port of Spain, Trinidad. **Burma**, 39 Signal Pagoda Road, Rangoon. **Canada**, 40 Irwin Ave., Toronto 5, Ontario. **Chile**, Moneda 2390, Santiago. **China**, P. O. Box 1903, Shanghai. **Colombia**, Calle 21, No. 16A-43, Bogotá. **Costa Rica**, Apartado 2043, San José. **Cuba**, Calle D No. 206, Almendares, Marianao, Havana. **Cyprus**, Box 400, Nicosia. **Denmark**, Sondre Fasanvej 54, Copenhagen - Valby. **Dominican Republic**, Calle Estrelleta No. 37, Ciudad Trujillo. **Ecuador**, Casilla 4512, Guayaquil. **Egypt**, Post Box 387, Cairo. **El Salvador**, Apartado 401, San Salvador. **England**, 34 Craven Terrace, London, W. 2. **Finland**, Vainamoisenkatu 27, Helsinki. **France**, 3 Villa Guibert, Paris 16e. **Germany (Soviet Zone)**, Wachtturmstrasse 17/19, Magdeburg. **Germany (U.S. Zone)**, Am Kohlheck, (16) Wiesbaden-Dotzheim, Hesse. **Gold Coast**, B.W.A., Box 760, Accra. **Greece**, 16 Tenedou St., Athens. **Guatemala**, 11 Avenida Norte No. 8, Guatemala. **Haiti**, Post Box B-185, Port-au-Prince. **Hashemite Jordan Kingdom**, c/o K. A. Kobrossi, Beit-Jala, Via Beirut, Amman. **T. Hawaii**, 1228 Pensacola St., Honolulu 14. **Honduras**, Apartado 147, Tegucigalpa. **Hungary**, Gvadányi-u 8, Budapest XIV. **India**, 167 Love Lane, Bombay 27. **Israel**, P.O. Box 994, 10 Hechalutz St., Haifa. **Italy**, Via Monte Maloia 10, Monte Sacro, Rome 742. **Jamaica**, 151 King St., Kingston. **Japan**, 1 Toyooka-Cho, Shiba-Mita, Minato-Ku, Tokyo. **Lebanon**, P.O. Box 1122, Beirut. **Liberia**, c/o G. Watkins, Camp Johnson Rd., Monrovia. **Luxembourg**, 95 Rue Eugene Welter, Luxembourg-Howald. **México**, Calzada Melchor Ocampo 71, México 4, D.F. **Netherlands**, Koningslaan 1, Amsterdam-Z. **Netherlands West Indies**, Breedestraat 12, Otrabanda, Curaçao. **Newfoundland**, Canada, Post Box 521, St. John's. **New Zealand**, G.P.O. Box 30, Wellington, C. 1. **Nicaragua**, Apartado 183, Managua, D.N. **Nigeria, West Africa**, P. O. Box 695, Lagos. **Northern Rhodesia**, Box 5, Lusaka. **Norway**, Inkognitogaten 28 B., Oslo. **Nyasaland**, Box 83, Blantyre. **Panama**, Box 274, Ancon, C. Z. **Paraguay**, Río de Janeiro y Esq. Mary Lyons, Asunción. **Peru**, Ramón Danino 256, Lima. **Philippine Republic**, Box 274, Roosevelt Rd., San Francisco del Monte, Quezon City. **Puerto Rico**, 704 Calle Lafayette, Pda. 21, Urb. Hip., Santurce 34. **Sierra Leone**, Box 136, Freetown. **Singapore**, 33 Poole Road. **South Africa**, 623 Boston House, Cape Town. **Southern Rhodesia**, P.O. Box 1462, Salisbury. **Surinam**, 141A Rust en Vredestraat, Paramaribo. **Sweden**, Luntmakaregatan 94, Stockholm Va. **Switzerland**, Allmendstrasse 39, Berne 22. **Thailand**, Box 67, Bangkok. **Uruguay**, Joaquín de Salterain 1264, Montevideo. **Venezuela**, Ave. Prin. del Paraíso 27, Quinta Savtepaul, Paraíso, Caracas.